THE BOOK ®

Peugeot Diesel Engine
Service and Repair Manual

A K Legg LAE MIMI and Finn Deacon

Models covered

(0950 - 184 - 6Y5)

This manual covers the Peugeot 1769 cc and 1905 cc (1.7 & 1.9 litre) Turbo and non-Turbo diesel engines. As fitted to Peugeot 205 (inc. Van), 305 (inc. Van), 309, 405 and in Talbot Horizons

Does not cover specific application to Peugeot 306 models, or the 1548 cc diesel engine (used on early 305 models)

ABCD

2

Printed in the USA

© Haynes Publishing 1996

A book in the **Haynes Service and Repair Manual Series**

ISBN **1 85960 225 8**

British Library Cataloguing in Publication Data
A catalogue record for this book is available from the British Library

Haynes Publishing
Sparkford, Nr Yeovil, Somerset BA22 7JJ, England

Haynes North America, Inc
861 Lawrence Drive, Newbury Park, California 91320, USA

Editions Haynes S.A.
Tour Aurore - IBC, 18 Place des Reflets,
92975 Paris La Défense 2, Cedex, France

Haynes Publishing Nordiska AB
Box 1504, 751 45 Uppsala, Sverige

Contents

LIVING WITH YOUR PEUGEOT DIESEL

Introduction

MAINTENANCE

Routine maintenance and servicing

Contents

About this manual

The aim of this manual is to help you get the best value from your vehicle. It can do so in several ways. It can help you decide what work must be done (even should you choose to get it done by a garage), provide information on routine maintenance and servicing, and give a logical course of action and diagnosis when random faults occur. However, it is hoped that you will use the manual by tackling the work

Peugeot 205 GRD Van

yourself. On simpler jobs it may even be quicker than booking the car into a garage and going there twice, to leave and collect it. Perhaps most important, a lot of money can be saved by avoiding the costs a garage must charge to cover its labour and overheads.

The manual has drawings and descriptions to show the function of the various components so that their layout can be understood. Then the tasks are described and photographed in a step-by-step sequence so that even a novice can do the work.

Unlike most Haynes manuals, which cover a particular vehicle in different trim levels and engine sizes, this book covers one engine and its associated equipment as fitted to a range of vehicles. Items which are common to diesel and petrol models - e.g. bodywork, transmission and running gear - are not covered in this book.

The vehicles used in the preparation of this manual and which appear in many of the photographs, were a 205 GRD, a Horizon, a 309 GRD Turbo, a 405 GLD and a 405 GRD Turbo.

Acknowledgements

Thanks are due to Champion, who supplied replacement component information. Certain illustrations are the copyright of Peugeot Motor Company Limited, and are used with their permission. Illustrations denoted by the line '© Robert Bosch Limited' are used by kind permission of that company. Thanks are also due to Sykes-Pickavant Limited, who provided some of the workshop tools, and to all those people at Sparkford who helped in the production of this manual.

We take great pride in the accuracy of information given in this manual, but vehicle manufacturers make alterations and design changes during the production run of a particular vehicle of which they do not inform us. No liability can be accepted by the authors or publishers for loss, damage or injury caused by any errors in, or omissions from, the information given.

Peugeot 309 GRD

Peugeot 405 GLXD Saloon

Working on your car can be dangerous. This page shows just some of the potential risks and hazards, with the aim of creating a safety-conscious attitude.

General hazards

Scalding

• Don't remove the radiator or expansion tank cap while the engine is hot.
• Engine oil, automatic transmission fluid or power steering fluid may also be dangerously hot if the engine has recently been running.

Burning

• Beware of burns from the exhaust system and from any part of the engine. Brake discs and drums can also be extremely hot immediately after use.

Crushing

• When working under or near a raised vehicle, always supplement the jack with axle stands, or use drive-on ramps. *Never venture under a car which is only supported by a jack.*

• Take care if loosening or tightening high-torque nuts when the vehicle is on stands. Initial loosening and final tightening should be done with the wheels on the ground.

Fire

• Fuel is highly flammable; fuel vapour is explosive.
• Don't let fuel spill onto a hot engine.
• Do not smoke or allow naked lights (including pilot lights) anywhere near a vehicle being worked on. Also beware of creating sparks (electrically or by use of tools).
• Fuel vapour is heavier than air, so don't work on the fuel system with the vehicle over an inspection pit.
• Another cause of fire is an electrical overload or short-circuit. Take care when repairing or modifying the vehicle wiring.
• Keep a fire extinguisher handy, of a type suitable for use on fuel and electrical fires.

Electric shock

• Ignition HT voltage can be dangerous, especially to people with heart problems or a pacemaker. Don't work on or near the ignition system with the engine running or the ignition switched on.

• Mains voltage is also dangerous. Make sure that any mains-operated equipment is correctly earthed. Mains power points should be protected by a residual current device (RCD) circuit breaker.

Fume or gas intoxication

• Exhaust fumes are poisonous; they often contain carbon monoxide, which is rapidly fatal if inhaled. Never run the engine in a confined space such as a garage with the doors shut.
• Fuel vapour is also poisonous, as are the vapours from some cleaning solvents and paint thinners.

Poisonous or irritant substances

• Avoid skin contact with battery acid and with any fuel, fluid or lubricant, especially antifreeze, brake hydraulic fluid and Diesel fuel. Don't syphon them by mouth. If such a substance is swallowed or gets into the eyes, seek medical advice.
• Prolonged contact with used engine oil can cause skin cancer. Wear gloves or use a barrier cream if necessary. Change out of oil-soaked clothes and do not keep oily rags in your pocket.
• Air conditioning refrigerant forms a poisonous gas if exposed to a naked flame (including a cigarette). It can also cause skin burns on contact.

Asbestos

• Asbestos dust can cause cancer if inhaled or swallowed. Asbestos may be found in gaskets and in brake and clutch linings. When dealing with such components it is safest to assume that they contain asbestos.

Special hazards

Hydrofluoric acid

• This extremely corrosive acid is formed when certain types of synthetic rubber, found in some O-rings, oil seals, fuel hoses etc, are exposed to temperatures above 400°C. The rubber changes into a charred or sticky substance containing the acid. *Once formed, the acid remains dangerous for years. If it gets onto the skin, it may be necessary to amputate the limb concerned.*
• When dealing with a vehicle which has suffered a fire, or with components salvaged from such a vehicle, wear protective gloves and discard them after use.

The battery

• Batteries contain sulphuric acid, which attacks clothing, eyes and skin. Take care when topping-up or carrying the battery.
• The hydrogen gas given off by the battery is highly explosive. Never cause a spark or allow a naked light nearby. Be careful when connecting and disconnecting battery chargers or jump leads.

Air bags

• Air bags can cause injury if they go off accidentally. Take care when removing the steering wheel and/or facia. Special storage instructions may apply.

Diesel injection equipment

• Diesel injection pumps supply fuel at very high pressure. Take care when working on the fuel injectors and fuel pipes.

⚠ *Warning: Never expose the hands, face or any other part of the body to injector spray; the fuel can penetrate the skin with potentially fatal results.*

Remember...

DO

• Do use eye protection when using power tools, and when working under the vehicle.

• Do wear gloves or use barrier cream to protect your hands when necessary.

• Do get someone to check periodically that all is well when working alone on the vehicle.

• Do keep loose clothing and long hair well out of the way of moving mechanical parts.

• Do remove rings, wristwatch etc, before working on the vehicle – especially the electrical system.

• Do ensure that any lifting or jacking equipment has a safe working load rating adequate for the job.

DON'T

• Don't attempt to lift a heavy component which may be beyond your capability – get assistance.

• Don't rush to finish a job, or take unverified short cuts.

• Don't use ill-fitting tools which may slip and cause injury.

• Don't leave tools or parts lying around where someone can trip over them. Mop up oil and fuel spills at once.

• Don't allow children or pets to play in or near a vehicle being worked on.

History of the diesel engine

Rudolf Diesel invented the first commercially successful compression ignition engine at the end of the 19th century. Compared with the spark ignition engine, the diesel had the advantages of lower fuel consumption, the ability to use cheaper fuel, and the potential for much higher power outputs. Over the following two or three decades such engines were widely adopted for stationary and marine applications, but the fuel injection systems used were not capable of high-speed operation. This speed limitation, and the considerable weight of the air compressor needed to operate the injection equipment, made the first diesel engines unsuitable for use in road-going vehicles.

In the 1920s the German engineer Robert Bosch developed the in-line injection pump, a device which is still in extensive use today. The use of hydraulic systems to pressurise and inject the fuel did away with the need for a separate air compressor and made possible much higher operating speeds. The so-called high-speed diesel engine became increasingly popular as a power source for goods and public transport vehicles, but for a number of reasons (including specific power output, flexibility and cheapness of manufacture) the spark ignition engine continued to dominate the passenger car and light commercial market.

In the 1950s and 60s, diesel engines became increasingly popular for use in taxis and vans, but it was not until the sharp rises in oil prices in the 1970s that serious attention was paid to the small passenger car market.

Subsequent years have seen the growing popularity of the small diesel engine in cars and light commercial vehicles, not only for reasons of fuel economy and longevity but also for environmental reasons. Every major European car manufacturer now offers at least one diesel-engined model. The diesel's penetration of the UK market has been relatively slow, due in part to the lack of the considerable fuel price differential in favour of diesel which exists in other parts of Europe, but it has now gained widespread acceptance and this trend looks set to continue.

Future developments

Development of the diesel engine, and particularly the fuel injection system, has been relatively slow compared with the advances which have been made in petrol engine fuel injection and management systems. However, new systems such as 'EPIC' (Electronically Programmed Injection Control) by Lucas and EDC (Electronic Diesel Control) by Bosch are already in production or in an advanced stage of development. These systems will provide further improvements in smoothness, economy and reduced exhaust emissions.

Principles of operation

All the diesel engines covered in this book operate on the familiar four-stroke cycle of induction, compression, power and exhaust. Two-stroke diesels do exist, and may in future become important, but they are not used in light vehicles at present. Most have four cylinders, some larger engines have six, and five- and three-cylinder engines also exist.

Induction and ignition

The main difference between diesel and petrol engines is in the means by which the fuel/air mixture is introduced into the cylinder and then ignited. In the petrol engine the fuel is mixed with the incoming air before it enters the cylinder, and the mixture is then ignited at the appropriate moment by a spark plug. At all conditions except full throttle, the throttle butterfly restricts the airflow and cylinder filling is incomplete.

In the diesel engine, air alone is drawn into the cylinder and then compressed. Because of the diesel's high compression ratio (typically 20:1) the air gets very hot when compressed - up to 750°C. As the piston approaches the end of the compression stroke, fuel is injected into the combustion chamber under very high pressure in the form of a finely atomised spray. The temperature of the air is high enough to ignite the injected fuel as it mixes with the air. The mixture then burns and provides the energy which drives the piston downwards on the power stroke.

When starting the engine from cold, the temperature of the compressed air in the cylinders may not be high enough to ignite the fuel. The preheating system overcomes this problem. The engines in this book have automatically-controlled preheating systems, using electric heater plugs (glow plugs) which heat the air in the combustion chamber just before and during start-up.

On most diesel engines there is no throttle valve in the inlet tract. Exceptions to this are those few engines which use a pneumatic governor, which depends on a manifold depression being created. Even more rarely a throttle valve may be used to create manifold depression for the operation of a brake servo, though it is more usual for a separate vacuum pump to be fitted for this purpose.

Direct and indirect injection

In practice, it is difficult to achieve smooth combustion in a small-displacement engine by injecting the fuel directly into the combustion chamber. To get around this problem the technique of indirect injection is widely used. With indirect injection, the fuel is injected into a pre-combustion or swirl chamber in the cylinder head, alongside the main combustion chamber.

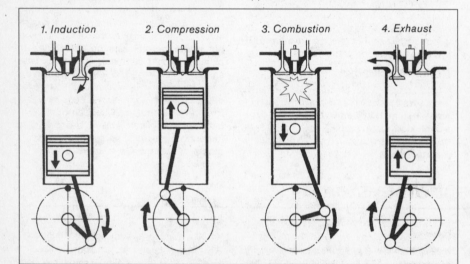

1. Induction 2. Compression 3. Combustion 4. Exhaust

Four-stroke diesel cycle
© Robert Bosch Limited

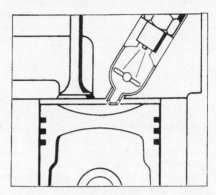

Injection into pre-chamber.

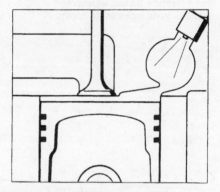

Injection into turbulence chamber.

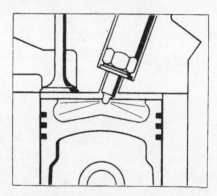

Direct injection.

Direct and indirect injection
© Robert Bosch Limited

Indirect injection engines are less efficient than direct injection ones and also require more preheating when starting from cold, but these disadvantages are offset by smoother and quieter operation.

Mechanical construction

The pistons, crankshaft and bearings of a diesel engine are generally of more robust construction than in a petrol engine of comparable size, because of the greater loads imposed by the higher compression ratio and the nature of the combustion process. This is one reason for the diesel engine's longer life. Other reasons include the lubricating qualities of diesel fuel on the cylinder bores, and the fact that the diesel engine is generally lower-revving than its petrol counterpart, having much better low-speed torque characteristics and a lower maximum speed.

Turbocharging

Turbochargers have long been used on large diesel engines and are becoming common on small ones. The turbocharger uses the energy of the escaping exhaust gas to drive a turbine which pressurises the air in the inlet manifold. The air is forced into the cylinders instead of being simply sucked in. If more air is present, more fuel can be burnt and more power developed from the same size engine.

Greater benefit can be gained from turbocharging if the pressurised air is cooled before it enters the engine. This is done using an air-to-air heat exchanger called an intercooler. The cooled air is denser and contains more oxygen in a given volume than warm air straight from the turbocharger.

Exhaust emissions

Because combustion in the correctly functioning diesel engine nearly always occurs in conditions of excess oxygen, there is little or no carbon monoxide (CO) in the exhaust gas. A further environmental benefit is that there is no added lead in diesel fuel.

At the time of writing there is no need for complicated emission control systems on the diesel engine, though simple catalytic converters are beginning to appear on production vehicles. Increasingly stringent emission regulations may result in the adoption of exhaust gas recirculation (EGR) systems and carbon particle traps.

Knock and smoke

The image of the diesel engine for many years was of a noisy, smoky machine, and to some extent this was justified. It is worth examining the causes of knock and smoke, both to see how they have been reduced in modern engines and to understand what causes them to get worse.

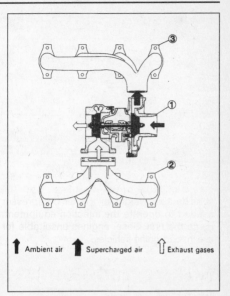

⬆ Ambient air   ⬆ Supercharged air   ⇧ Exhaust gases

Principle of turbocharging

1 Turbocharger   3 Inlet manifold
2 Exhaust manifold

There is inevitably a small delay (typically 0.001 to 0.002 sec) between the start of fuel injection and the beginning of proper combustion. This delay, known as ignition lag, is greatest when the engine is cold and idling. The characteristic diesel knock is caused by the sudden increase in cylinder pressure which occurs when the injected fuel has mixed with the hot air and starts burning. It is therefore an unavoidable part of the combustion process, though it has been greatly reduced by improvements in combustion chamber and injection system design. A defective injector (which is not atomising the fuel as it should for optimum combustion) will also cause the engine to knock.

Smoke is caused by incorrect combustion, but unlike knock it is more or less preventable. During start-up and warm-up a certain amount of white or blue smoke may be seen, but under normal running conditions the exhaust should be clean. The thick black smoke which is all too familiar from old or badly-maintained vehicles is caused by a lack of air for combustion, either because the air inlet is restricted (clogged air cleaner) or because too much fuel is being injected (defective injectors or pump). Causes of smoke are examined in more detail in the Reference Chapter.

Fuel supply and injection systems

Fuel supply

The fuel supply system is concerned with delivering clean fuel, free of air, water or other contaminants, to the injection pump. It always includes a fuel tank, a water trap and a fuel filter (which may be combined in one unit), and the associated pipework. Some arrangement must also be made for returning fuel leaked from the injection pump and injectors to the tank.

A fuel lift pump is fitted between the tank and the filter on vehicles which use an in-line injection pump, or where the fuel tank outlet is significantly lower than the injection pump. When a distributor injection pump is fitted and the tank outlet is at about the same level as the injection pump (as is the case with many passenger cars), a separate fuel lift pump is not

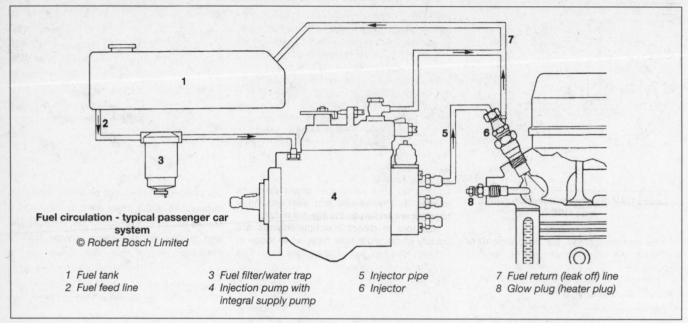

Fuel circulation - typical passenger car system

© Robert Bosch Limited

1 Fuel tank
2 Fuel feed line
3 Fuel filter/water trap
4 Injection pump with integral supply pump
5 Injector pipe
6 Injector
7 Fuel return (leak off) line
8 Glow plug (heater plug)

fitted. In this case a hand priming pump is often provided for use when bleeding the fuel system.

Additional refinements may be encountered. These include a fuel heater, which may be integral with the filter or on the tank side of it, to prevent the formation of wax crystals in the fuel in cold weather. A "water in fuel" warning light on the instrument panel may be illuminated by a device in the water trap when the water reaches a certain level.

The water trap and fuel filter are vital for satisfactory operation of the fuel injection system. The water trap may have a glass bowl, in which case water build-up can be seen, or it may as already mentioned have some electrical device for alerting the driver to the presence of water. Whether or not these features are present, the trap must be drained at the specified intervals, or more frequently if experience shows this to be necessary. If water enters the injection pump it can cause rapid corrosion, especially if the vehicle is left standing for any length of time.

The fuel filter may be of the disposable cartridge type, or it may consist of a renewable element inside a metal bowl. Sometimes a coarser pre-filter is fitted upstream of the main filter. Whatever the type, it must be renewed at the specified intervals. Considering the damage which can be caused to the injection equipment by the entry of even small particles of dirt, it is not worth using cheap replacement filters, which may not be of the same quality as those of reputable manufacture.

Fuel injection pump

The pump is a mechanical device attached to the engine. Its function is to supply fuel to the injectors at the correct pressure, at the correct moment in the combustion cycle and for the length of time necessary to ensure efficient combustion. The pump responds to depression of the accelerator pedal by increasing fuel delivery, within the limits allowed by the governor. It is also provided with some means of cutting off fuel delivery when it is wished to stop the engine.

Some kind of governor is associated with the injection pump, either integral with it or attached to it. All vehicle engine governors regulate fuel delivery to control idle speed and maximum speed; the variable-speed governor also regulates intermediate speeds. Operation

Sectional view of a typical fuel filter

1 Hand priming plunger
2 Fuel bleed screw (on outlet union)
3 Seals
4 Water drain tap
5 Through bolt
6 Through bolt seal
7 Filter element
8 Air bleed screw (on inlet union)

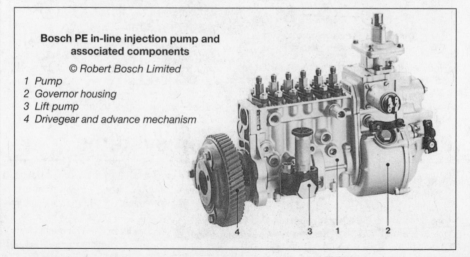

Bosch PE in-line injection pump and associated components

© Robert Bosch Limited

1 Pump
2 Governor housing
3 Lift pump
4 Drivegear and advance mechanism

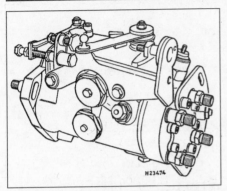

Lucas/CAV distributor injection pump, type DPC

of the governor may be mechanical or hydraulic, or it may be controlled by manifold depression.

Other devices in or attached to the pump include cold start injection advance or fast idle units, turbo boost pressure sensors and anti-stall mechanisms.

Fuel injection pumps are normally very reliable. If they are not damaged by dirt, water or unskilled adjustment they may well outlast the engine to which they are fitted.

Fuel injectors

One fuel injector is fitted to each cylinder. The function of the injector is to spray an evenly atomised quantity of fuel into the combustion or pre-combustion chamber when the fuel pressure exceeds a certain value, and to stop the flow of fuel cleanly when the pressure drops. Atomisation is achieved by a spring-loaded needle which vibrates rapidly against its seat when fuel under pressure passes it. The needle and seat assembly together are known as the injector nozzle.

Injectors in direct injection engines are usually of the multi-hole type, while those in indirect engines are of the pintle type. The "throttled pintle" injector gives a progressive build-up of injection, which is valuable in achieving smooth combustion.

The injector tips are exposed to the temperatures and pressures of combustion, so not surprisingly they will in time suffer from carbon deposits and ultimately from erosion and burning. Service life will vary according to factors such as fuel quality and operating conditions, but typically one could expect to clean and recalibrate a set of injectors after about 80 000 km (50 000 miles), and perhaps to renew them or have them reconditioned after 160 000 km (100 000 miles).

Injector pipes

The injector pipes are an important part of the system and must not be overlooked. The dimensions of the pipes are important and it should not be assumed that just because the end fittings are the same, a pipe from a different engine can be used as a replacement. Securing clips must be kept tight and the engine should not be run without them, as damage from vibration or fuel cavitation may result.

Introduction to the Peugeot diesel engine

The 1.9 litre diesel engine was first fitted to the Talbot Horizon in late 1982. Then in September 1983, the 1.7 litre version was fitted to the Peugeot 205. In October 1983 both engine sizes were available in the 305, and in August 1986 the 1.9 engine was available in the Peugeot 309. Both engine sizes were introduced on 405 models in August 1988, the 1.7 being turbocharged and the 1.9 being normally-aspirated. The 1.9 turbocharged version was introduced in October 1992.

Over the last decade the diesel engine has made a large impact on the saloon car market, due mainly to a marked improvement of its performance and economy, and a reduction in noise levels.

Routine maintenance tasks are few and easily carried out, although certain jobs will require the purchase or construction of special tools.

Outside the engine compartment, the vehicles to which these engines are fitted, are much the same as petrol engined versions. For complete coverage of a particular vehicle, the appropriate main manual, that includes petrol engined models will be needed.

Front three-quarter view of Peugeot XUD engine. Timing belt cover has been removed

1 Timing belt
2 Oil filler cap and ventilation hose
3 Injectors
4 Diagnostic socket
5 Temperature sensors
6 Fast idle thermo unit
7 Thermostat cover
8 Injection pump (Roto-Diesel)
9 Coolant hose to oil cooler
10 Drivebelt tension adjusting bolt
11 Flywheel
12 Alternator
13 Oil filter
14 Sump
15 Alternator drivebelt
16 Crankshaft pulley
17 Water pump
18 Timing belt intermediate roller
19 Injection pump sprocket
20 Timing belt tensioner
21 Right-hand engine mounting bracket
22 Camshaft sprocket

1 Engine . . . . Multigrade engine oil, viscosity SAE 15W/40

2 Manual transmission:

   Pre 1988 models . . . . Multigrade oil, viscosity SAE 15W/40, to
API SG/CD

     1988-on models . . . . Gear oil, viscosity SAE 75W/80W, to API GL5

3 Brake vacuum pump . . . . Multigrade oil, viscosity SAE 15W/40, to
API SG/CD

4 Brake hydraulic system . . . . Hydraulic fluid to SAE J1703 C or DOT 3

5 Clutch hydraulic system . . . . Hydraulic fluid to SAE J1703 C or DOT 3

6 Cooling system . . . . Ethylene glycol based antifreeze (9730.70)

Manual steering rack . . . . Molybdenum disulphide (MoS_2) grease

Power steering system . . . . Dexron type automatic transmission fluid (ATF)

Wheel bearings . . . . Multi-purpose grease

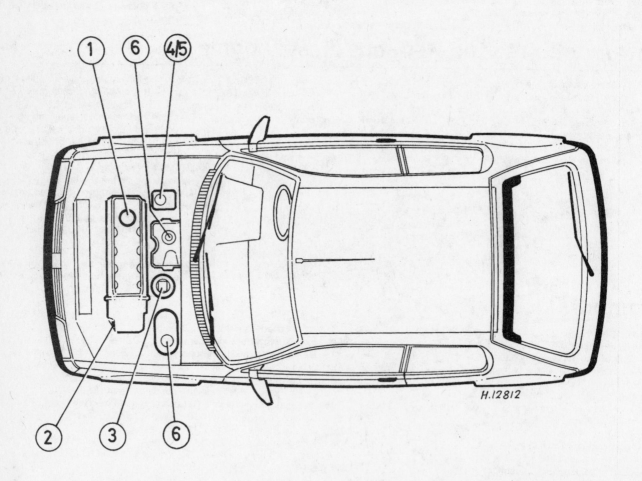

H.12812

Chapter 1
Routine maintenance and servicing

Contents

Degrees of difficulty

Easy, suitable for novice with little experience	**Fairly easy,** suitable for beginner with some experience	**Fairly difficult,** suitable for competent DIY mechanic	**Difficult,** suitable for experienced DIY mechanic	**Very difficult,** suitable for expert DIY or professional

Capacities

Cooling system:

205	8.3 litres
305	9.5 litres
309	8.5 litres

405:

Non Turbo	7.8 litres
Turbo	7.0 litres
Horizon	6.2 litres

Engine oil, drain and refill (including 0.5 litre for filter):

205 and 309 models (from 1993)	4.5 litres

405 models (from 1993):

XUD 9A (with air conditioning)	4.2 litres
XUD 9TE (without air conditioning)	4.6 litres
All other models	5.0 litres

Fuel tank:

205	50 litres
305	43 litres
309	55 litres
405	70 litres
Horizon	45 litres
Manual transmission oil	2.0 litres

Cooling

Antifreeze content (for protection down to -35ºC), all models	50%

Engine

Idle speed	800 rpm

Oil filter type:

All models	Champion F104

Air filter:

205:

Non-turbo models	Champion W117
Turbo models	Champion W233
305, 309 and Horizon	Champion W117
405	Champion U543

Fuel filter type:

205 and 309:

Pre April 1992 models:

Lucas/CAV pump	Champion L132
Bosch pump	Champion L135
May 1992 on models	Champion L141

305 and Horizon:

Lucas/CAV pump	Champion L131 or L137
Bosch pump	Champion L136

405:

Pre 1993 models:

Lucas/CAV pumps	Champion L132
Bosch pumps	Champion L135
1993-on models	Champion L141

Tyres

Pressures - bar (lbf/in^2):	Front	Rear
205:		
Except Van models	2.0 (29)	2.0 (29)
Van models	2.0 (29)	2.6 (38)
305	1.9 (28)	2.1 (30)
309:		
Except Turbo models	2.0 (29)	2.2 (32)
Turbo models	2.0 (29)	2.0 (29)
405:		
Saloon models	2.2 (32)	2.2 (32)
Estate models	2.2 (32)	2.6 ± 0.2 (38 ± 3)
Horizon	1.9 (28)	1.9 (28)

Torque wrench settings

	Nm	lbf ft
Fuel filter housing cover (405 models)	6	4
Fuel filter through-bolt	10	7
Power steering drivebelt tension:		
New belt	57	42
Used belt	30	22
Vacuum pump adjusting pivot (later models)	5	4

The maintenance schedules below are basically those recommended by us for vehicles driven daily. Servicing intervals are determined by mileage or time elapsed - this is because fluids and systems deteriorate with age as well as with use. Follow the time intervals if the appropriate mileage is not covered within the specified period.

Vehicles operating under adverse conditions may need more frequent maintenance. "Adverse conditions" include climatic extremes, full-time towing or taxi work, driving on unmade roads, and a high proportion of short journeys. The use of inferior fuel (such as may be found in some foreign countries) can cause early degradation of the engine oil.

Consult a dealer for full guidance.

Some of the procedures, where indicated, are described in detail in the relevant main manual for the vehicle. Refer to Haynes Manual No's. OWM 932 for 205 models, OWM 538 for 305 models, OWM 1266 for 309 models, OWM 1559 for 405 models and OWM 473 for Talbot Horizon models.

At weekly intervals, or before a long journey

- [ ] Check battery (Section 3)
- [ ] Check brake fluid level, investigate any sudden loss of fluid (Section 4)
- [ ] Check coolant level (Section 5)
- [ ] Check engine oil level (Section 6)
- [ ] Check operation of lights, wipers and horn (Section 7)
- [ ] Check tyre pressures and condition (including spare), (Section 8)
- [ ] Check washer fluid level(s) (Section 9)

Every 6000 miles (10 000 km) or 6 months, whichever comes first

Note: *On pre 1989 models, the mileage intervals were at 5000 miles (7500 km). The time intervals however, are the same.*

- [ ] Renew the engine oil and filter (Section 10)
- [ ] Check for any fluid leaks (Section 11)
- [ ] Drain water from fuel filter (Section 12)
- [ ] Check the steering gear and driveshaft components (Section 13)
- [ ] Check power steering pump fluid level (Section 14)

Every 12 000 miles (20 000 km) or 12 months, whichever comes first

Note: *On pre 1989 models, the mileage intervals were at 10000 miles (15000 km). The time intervals however, are the same.*
Along with the work specified in previous schedules, where applicable.

- [ ] Clean oil filler cap (where applicable), (Section 15)
- [ ] Examine exhaust system for corrosion and leakage (Section 16)
- [ ] Check idling speed (Section 17)
- [ ] Renew fuel filter (before winter, regardless of mileage) (Section 18)
- [ ] Lubricate clutch pedal and cable (Section 19)
- [ ] Check condition of the accelerator cable (Chapter 4)
- [ ] Check clutch adjustment (except Horizon) (refer to the relevant main manual)
- [ ] Check wheel bearings (refer to the relevant main manual)

Every 12 000 miles (20 000 km) or 12 months, whichever comes first (continued)

- [ ] Check seat belts and anchorages (refer to the relevant main manual)
- [ ] Check front wheel alignment (refer to the relevant main manual)
- [ ] Lubricate all controls, linkages, door locks and hinges (refer to the relevant main manual)

Every 18 000 miles (30 000 km) or 18 months, whichever comes first

Note: *On pre 1989 models, the mileage intervals were at 15000 miles (22500 km). The time intervals however, are the same.*
Along with the work specified in previous schedules, where applicable.

- [ ] Renew air cleaner element (refer to Chapter 4)
- [ ] Check drivebelt tension(s) (Section 20)
- [ ] Check vacuum pump (Section 21)
- [ ] Check rear brake shoes (refer to relevant main manual)
- [ ] Check handbrake adjustment (refer to relevant main manual)
- [ ] Check brake disc pads for wear (refer to the relevant main manual)

Every 30 000 miles (45 000 km) or 2 years, whichever comes first

Along with the work specified in previous schedules, where applicable.

- [ ] Renew coolant (Section 22)

Every 36 000 miles (60 000 km)

(Note: *The manufacturer recommends that the timing belt is changed every 72,000 miles (120 000km). However, we strongly advise that this belt is replaced sooner, as extensive damage may occur, if the belt fails under certain driving conditions)*

- [ ] Renew timing belt (refer to Chapter 2)
- [ ] Check transmission fluid level (manual transmission models) (Section 23)
- [ ] Renew brake fluid (refer to the relevant main manual)

1

Under-bonnet view of a Peugeot 205 GRD (air cleaner removed)

1 Brake fluid reservoir and filler cap	9 Coolant low level warning switch	18 Top hose	28 Vehicle lifting jack
2 Engine oil filler cap	10 Coolant filler/pressure cap	19 Fast idle thermostatic unit	29 Injection pump
3 Injectors	11 Expansion tank supply hose	20 Engine oil dipstick	30 Right hand engine mounting bracket
4 Speedometer cable	12 Preheater plug relay	21 Radiator	31 Timing cover
5 Inlet manifold	13 Reverse gear stop cable	22 Starter motor	32 Coolant bypass hose
6 Brake vacuum pump (exhauster)	14 Crankcase ventilation hose	23 Oil filter	33 Accelerator cable
7 Steering gear	15 Battery	24 Stop solenoid	34 Fuel filter
8 Expansion tank vent hose	16 Electric cooling fan relay	25 Fuel supply hose	
	17 Clutch relay lever	26 Fuel return hose	
		27 Alternator	

Front end underbody view of a Peugeot 205 GRD

1 Subframe
2 Final drive drain plug
3 Anti-roll bar guide rod
4 Exhaust pipe

5 Exhaust manifold resonator
6 Anti-roll bar
7 Tie rod
8 Lower suspension arm

9 Lower engine mounting torque link
10 Oil level sensor
11 Right hand driveshaft

12 Engine oil drain plug
13 Radiator
14 Transmission
15 Left hand driveshaft

Under-bonnet view of a Talbot Horizon LD (air cleaner removed)

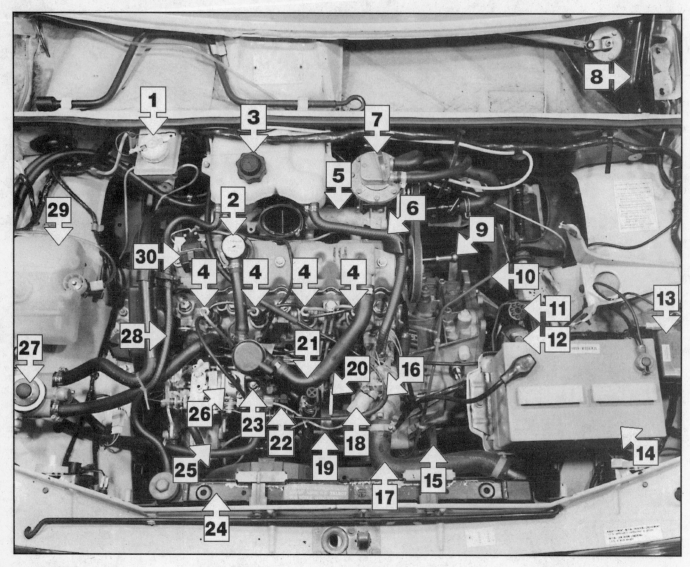

1 Brake fluid reservoir and filler cap	7 Brake vacuum pump (exhauster)	14 Battery	23 Stop solenoid
2 Engine oil filler cap	8 Windscreen wiper motor	15 Clutch release lever	24 Radiator
3 Coolant expansion tank and filler cap	9 Gearchange rod	16 Accelerator cable	25 Alternator
4 Injectors	10 Hydraulic clutch feed pipe	17 Top hose	26 Injection pump
5 Inlet manifold	11 Air cleaner mounting pad	18 Fast idle thermostatic unit	27 Fuel filter
6 Expansion tank supply hose	12 Left hand engine/transmission mounting	19 Starter motor	28 Expansion tank vent
	13 Preheater plug relay	20 Engine oil dipstick	29 Washer fluid reservoir
		21 Crankcase ventilation hose	30 Diagnostic socket
		22 Fast idle cable	

Front end underbody view of a Talbot Horizon LD

1 Torsion bar
2 Anti-roll bar
3 Gearchange control rods
4 Exhaust pipe
5 Crossmember
6 Track rod end

7 Lower suspension arm
8 Lower shock absorber
  mounting
9 Splash shield
10 Bottom hose

11 Lower engine mounting
   torque link
12 Electric cooling fan
13 Engine oil drain plug
14 Right hand driveshaft

15 Horn
16 Transmission
17 Final drive drain plug
18 Left hand driveshaft
19 Steering gear

Under-bonnet view of a Peugeot 309 GRD Turbo

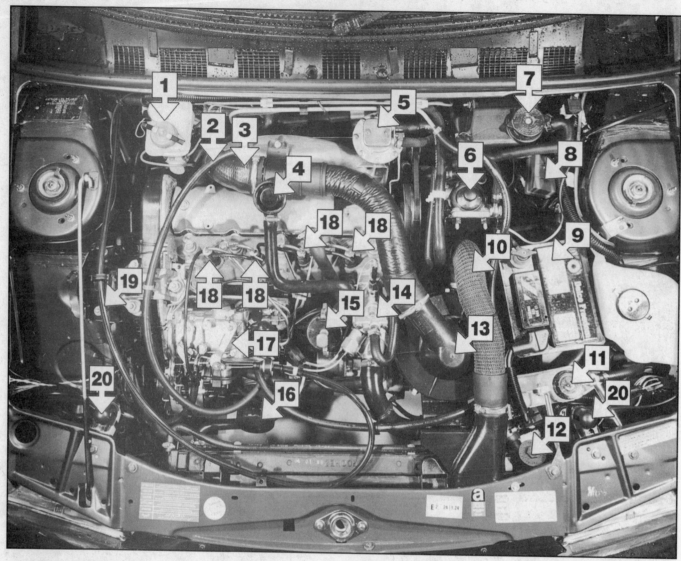

1 Brake fluid reservoir
2 Boost pressure hose
3 Air intake trunking
4 Crankcase ventilation oil trap
5 Vacuum pump

6 Fuel filter
7 Expansion tank filler cap
8 Heater plug relay
9 Battery
10 Air cleaner inlet hose

11 Power steering fluid reservoir
12 Radiator cap
13 Air cleaner
14 Thermostat housing
15 Engine oil dipstick/oil filler cap

16 Oil filter
17 Fuel injection pump
18 Fuel injectors
19 Throttle cable
20 Headlight beam adjusters

Under-bonnet view of a Peugeot 405 GRD Turbo (intercooler removed)

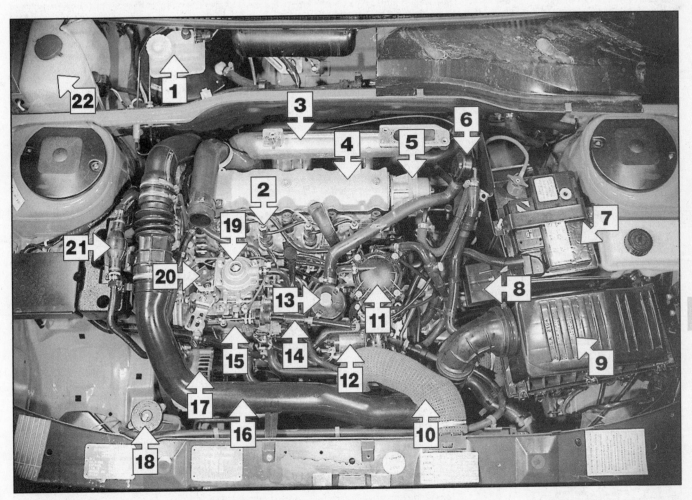

1 Brake fluid reservoir
2 Fuel injector
3 Inlet manifold
4 Valve cover
5 Brake vacuum pump
6 Crankcase ventilation system oil trap

7 Battery
8 Heater plug control unit
9 Air cleaner
10 Air inlet hose
11 Fuel filter unit
12 Starter motor

13 Engine oil dipstick/oil filler cap
14 Accelerator cable
15 Fuel injection pump
16 Air cleaner-to-turbo air hose
17 Alternator

18 Radiator filler cap
19 Richness limiter (Bosch pump)
20 Load lever position switch
21 Fuel system hand-priming bulb
22 Washer fluid reservoir

1 Introduction - general

1 This Chapter is designed to help the home mechanic maintain his/her vehicle for safety, economy, long life and peak performance.

2 The Chapter contains a master maintenance schedule, followed by Sections dealing specifically with each task in the schedule. Visual checks, adjustments, component renewal and other helpful items are included. Refer to the accompanying illustrations of the engine compartment and the underside of the vehicle for the locations of the various components.

3 Servicing your vehicle according to the mileage/time maintenance schedule and the following Sections will provide a planned maintenance programme, which should result in a long and reliable service life. This is a comprehensive plan, so maintaining some items but not others at the specified service intervals, will not produce the same results.

4 As you service your vehicle, you will discover that many of the procedures can - and should - be grouped together, because of the particular procedure being performed, or because of the proximity of two otherwise-unrelated components to one another. For example, if the vehicle is raised for any reason, the exhaust can be inspected at the same time as the suspension and steering components.

5 The first step in this maintenance programme is to prepare yourself before the actual work begins. Read through all the Sections relevant to the work to be carried out, then make a list and gather all the parts and tools required. If a problem is come across, seek advice from a parts specialist, or a dealers service department.

2 Intensive maintenance - general

1 If, from the time the vehicle is new, the routine maintenance schedule is followed closely and frequent checks made of fluid levels and high-wear items, as recommended, the engine will be kept in relatively good running condition. The need for additional work will be minimised.

2 It is possible that there will be times when the engine is running poorly due to the lack of regular maintenance. This is even more likely if a used vehicle, which has not received regular and frequent maintenance checks, is bought. In such cases, additional work may need to be carried out, outside of the regular maintenance intervals.

3 If engine wear is suspected, a compression test (refer to Chapter 2) will provide valuable information regarding the overall performance of the main internal components. Such a test can be used as a basis to decide on the extent of the work to be carried out. If, for example, a compression test indicates serious internal engine wear, conventional maintenance as described in this Chapter will not greatly improve the performance of the engine. It may also prove a waste of time and money, unless extensive overhaul work is carried out first.

4 The following series of operations are those most often required to improve the performance of a generally poor-running engine:

Primary operations

a) Clean, inspect and test the battery
b) Check all the engine related fluids
c) Check the condition and tension of the drivebelts
d) Check the condition of the air filter, and renew if necessary
e) Check the fuel filter
f) Check the condition of all hoses, and check for fluid leaks
g) Check the idle speed, anti-stall and mixture settings, as applicable

5 If the above operations do not prove fully effective, carry out the following secondary operations:

Secondary operations

6 All items listed under "Primary operations", plus the following:

a) Check the charging system
b) Check the preheating system
c) Check the fuel system

Weekly checks

3 Battery - check

⚠ **Warning: Read the 'Safety First' section in the front of this manual, before checking the battery.**

1 Make sure that the battery tray is in good condition and that the clamp is tight.

2 Corrosion on the tray, retaining clamp and the battery terminals, can be removed with a solution of water mixed with baking soda. Thoroughly rinse all cleaned areas with clean water. Any metal parts of the tray damaged by corrosion should be covered with a zinc-based primer, then painted.

3 Approximately every three months and definitely before the winter months, check the charge condition of the battery and (if applicable, the electrolyte levels).

4 Brake fluid - check

⚠ **Warning: Brake hydraulic fluid can harm your eyes and damage painted surfaces, so**

use extreme caution when handling and pouring it. Do not use fluid that has been standing open for some time, as it absorbs moisture from the air that can cause a dangerous loss of braking effectiveness.

1 The braking system is similar to that for petrol engine models. The brake master cylinder and fluid reservoir are mounted at the rear of the engine compartment, in front of the bulkhead.

> **HAYNES HiNT**
>
> **Make sure that your car is on level ground.**
>
> **The fluid level in the master cylinder will drop slightly as the brake linings wear down, but the fluid level must never be allowed to drop below the "MIN" mark.**

2 Before removing the reservoir cap, ensure that the surrounding area is clean. When adding fluid, pour it carefully and slowly into the reservoir, to avoid spilling it on surrounding painted surfaces. Use correct fluid, as listed in the Specifications. After filling to the correct level, ensure that the cap is refitted securely.

3 If the reservoir requires repeated topping-up this indicates a fluid leak somewhere in the system, that should be investigated immediately.

4 If a leak is suspected, the car should not be driven until the braking system has been checked. Never take any risks where brakes are concerned.

5 Coolant level - check

⚠ **Warning: DO NOT attempt to remove the expansion tank cap when the engine is hot, as there is a risk of scalding**

1 The cooling system fitted to these models is pressurised. As the engine temperature increases the coolant expands and the level in the expansion tank rises. As the engine cools the level drops.

2 The level in the tank should be between the "MIN" and "MAX" marks on the side of the expansion tank, when the engine is cold.

3 If the system needs topping-up, only when the engine cold, depress the filler cap and turn it anti-clockwise to remove it **(see illustration)**.

4 With sealed type cooling systems like these, regular topping-up should not be necessary. However if it is, there is likely to be a leak. Check the radiator, all hoses and sealing joints for signs of staining or indeed wetness and repair as necessary.

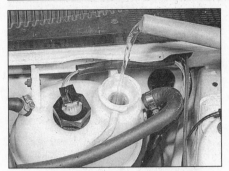

5.3 Filling the cooling system via the expansion tank

6 Engine oil level - check

1 The vehicle must be parked on level ground and the engine must have been stopped for approximately 10 minutes to allow oil in circulation to return to the sump.

2 Withdraw the dipstick from its tube, wipe the end with a piece of clean rag, re-insert it fully and then withdraw it again. Read the oil level on the end of the dipstick; it should be between the two cut-outs that represent the maximum and minimum oil levels **(see illustrations)**.

3 It is not strictly necessary to top-up the engine oil until it reaches the minimum cut-out, but on no account allow the level to fall any lower. The amount of oil needed to top-up from minimum to maximum is 1 litre for 1.7 models and approximately 1.5 litres for 1.9 models.

4 When topping-up is necessary, use clean engine oil of the specified type, preferably of the same make and grade as that already in the engine. Top up by removing the filler cap from the valve cover or the filler tube as applicable **(see illustration)**. Allow time for the oil to run down to the sump before rechecking the level on the dipstick. Refit the filler cap and dipstick on completion.

5 All engines use some oil, depending on the degree of wear and the pattern of use. Oil which is not being lost through external leaks is entering the cylinders and being burnt, however, the diesel engine is not so prone to this problem as its petrol counterpart since there is no inlet vacuum to suck oil past piston rings and inlet valve stems.

7 Lights, wipers and horn - check

1 Check the operation of all external lights. Use the reflection from a garage door or showroom window, to check brake and reverse lamps. Make sure that all direction indicators are working, including when hazard warning switch is on. Replace bulbs and fuses as necessary.

2 Turn on the wipers and spray the washers. Check that the glass is cleared without smearing or juddering. Replace wiper blades, if the rubbers are worn or damaged.

3 Sound the horn (during sociable hours). If it does not work, check the fuse, the wiring connections and the earth connections.

8 Tyre pressure and condition - check

1 It is very important that all tyres are in good condition and at the correct pressure. Consult the 'Specifications' or your owners handbook for tyre pressure recommendations.

2 Having a tyre failure at any speed is highly dangerous. Tyre wear is influenced by driving style. Harsh braking and acceleration, or fast cornering, will all produce more rapid tyre wear. As a general rule, the front tyres wear out faster than the rears. Interchanging the tyres from front to rear ("rotating" the tyres) may result in more even wear. However, if this is completely effective you may have the expense of replacing four tyres at once!

3 Remove any nails or stones embedded in the tread before they penetrate the tyre to cause deflation. If removal of a nail does reveal that the tyre has been punctured, refit the nail so that its point of penetration is marked. Then immediately change the wheel and have the tyre repaired, or replaced by a tyre dealer.

4 Regularly check the tyres for damage in the form cuts or bulges, especially in the sidewalls. Periodically remove the wheels the wheels and clean any dirt or mud from the inside and outside surfaces. Examine the wheel rims for signs of rusting, corrosion or other damage. Light alloy wheels are easily damaged by "kerbing" whilst parking. Steel wheels may also become dented or buckled. A new wheel is very often the only way to overcome severe damage.

5 New tyres should be balanced when they are fitted, but it may become necessary to re-balance them as they wear, or if the balance weights fitted to the wheel rim should fall off.

6 Unbalanced tyres will wear more quickly, as will the steering and suspension components.

7 Unbalanced wheels cause vibration, particularly at a certain speed (typically around 50 mph). If this vibration is only felt through the steering, it is likely that just the front wheels will need balancing. If however, the vibration is felt through the whole car, the rear wheels could also need balancing. Wheel balancing should be carried out by a tyre dealer or garage.

8 Check the security of the roadwheels. Ensure that all the bolts are tightened to their correct torque.

9 Washer fluid level - check

Ensure that the washer fluid is always topped-up after use. Modern screenwash additives not only prevent the fluid from freezing during winter months, but also reduces smearing, noticeable during night time driving at any time of year.

Clear the washer jets with a pin, if they become blocked. Ensure that the jets are directed toward the windscreen and not over the roof, to the vehicle behind.

6.2A Withdrawing the engine oil dipstick (XUD 7 engine)

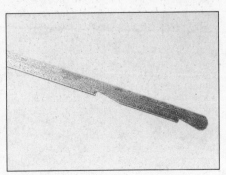

6.2B Minimum and maximum level cut-outs on the engine oil dipstick

6.4 Topping-up the engine oil

10 Engine oil and filter - renewal

Renewal

1 The engine oil should be replaced when hot (i.e. just after a run) with the vehicle parked on level ground.

2 Position a drain pan of adequate capacity beneath the sump. Wipe clean around the drain plug then unscrew it using a hexagon key and allow the oil to drain. The oil may be very hot, take precautions to avoid scalding **(see illustration)**.

3 Remove the oil filler cap and allow the oil to drain for at least 15 minutes.

4 Check and if necessary renew the drain plug washer then wipe the sump, refit the drain plug and tighten it.

5 Position the drain pan beneath the oil filter on the front of the cylinder block. Using a strap wrench, unscrew the filter and remove it **(see illustration)**. If a strap wrench is not available a screwdriver can be driven through the filter and used as a lever to remove it.

6 Wipe clean the filter seat on the cylinder block or oil cooler (as applicable). Smear a little clean engine oil on the sealing ring of the new oil filter then screw on the filter until it just touches the seat. Hand tighten the oil filter by a further two-thirds of a turn **(see illustration)**. Do not use any tools to tighten the filter.

7 Fill the engine with the correct grade and quantity of oil.

8 Start the engine and allow it to idle. Check that the oil pressure warning light goes out and also check that there is no oil leakage from the oil filter.

9 Switch off the engine and recheck the oil level.

10 Put the old oil into a sealed container and dispose of it safely. Do not pour old engine oil down a drain. Contact your local authority for further details.

10.2 Engine drain plug

OIL CARE
FOLLOW THE CODE

OIL BANK LINE
0800 66 33 66

Note: It is antisocial and illegal to dump oil down the drain. To find the location of your local oil recycling bank, call this number free.

11 Hose and fluid leak check

Engine

1 Visually inspect the engine joint faces, gaskets and seals for any signs of water or oil leaks. Pay particular attention to the areas around the camshaft cover, cylinder head, oil filter and sump joint faces. Remember that, over a period of time, some very slight seepage from these areas is to be expected - what you are really looking for is any indication of a serious leak. Should a leak be found, renew the offending gasket or oil seal by referring to the appropriate Chapters in this manual.

2 Also check the security and condition of all the engine related pipes and hoses. Ensure that all cable-ties or securing clips are in place, and in good condition. Clips that are broken or missing can lead to chafing of the hoses, pipes or wiring, which could cause more serious problems in the future.

Coolant

3 Carefully check the radiator hoses and heater hoses along their entire length. Renew any hose that is cracked, swollen or deteriorated. Cracks will show up better if the hose is squeezed. Pay close attention to the hose clips that secure the hoses to the cooling system components. Hose clips can pinch and puncture hoses, resulting in cooling system leaks. It is always beneficial to renew hose clips whenever possible.

4 Inspect all the cooling system components (hoses, joint faces, etc.) for leaks.

HAYNES
HINT

A leak in the cooling system will usually show up as white or rust coloured deposits on the area adjoining the leak.

5 Where any problems are found on system components, renew the component or gasket with reference to Chapter 3.

10.5 Unscrewing the oil filter with a strap wrench

10.6 Tighten the oil filter by hand only

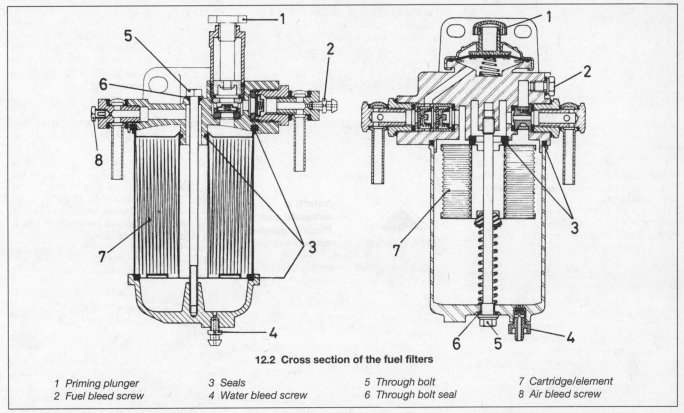

12.2 Cross section of the fuel filters

1 *Priming plunger*	3 *Seals*	5 *Through bolt*	7 *Cartridge/element*
2 *Fuel bleed screw*	4 *Water bleed screw*	6 *Through bolt seal*	8 *Air bleed screw*

Fuel system

6 With the vehicle raised, inspect the petrol tank and filler neck for punctures, cracks and other damage. The connection between the filler neck and tank is especially critical. Sometimes a rubber filler neck or connecting hose will leak due to loose retaining clamps or deteriorated rubber.

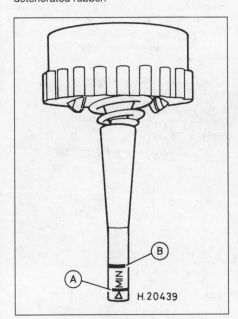

14.4 Filler cap level marks
a Minimum cold level   b Maximum hot level

7 Carefully check all rubber hoses and metal fuel lines leading away from the petrol tank. Check for loose connections, deteriorated hoses, kinked lines, and other damage. Pay particular attention to the vent pipes and hoses, which often loop up around the filler neck and can become blocked or kinked. Follow the lines to the front of the vehicle, carefully inspecting them all the way. Renew damaged sections as necessary.
8 From within the engine compartment, check the security of all fuel hose attachments and pipe unions, and inspect the fuel hoses and vacuum hoses for kinks, chafing and deterioration.

Power steering

9 Where applicable, check the condition of the power steering fluid hoses and pipes.

12 Water in fuel filter - drain

1 Position a small container beneath the filter.
2 Loosen the bleed screw on the bottom of the filter and allow any water to drain into the container. Where fitted, also loosen the air bleed screw on the filter head or inlet union bolt **(see illustration)**.
3 Tighten the lower bleed screw when fuel free of water flows. Retighten the air bleed screw where fitted.
4 Prime the fuel injection system as described in Chapter 4.

13 Steering gear and driveshaft - check

1 Check all swivel and ball joints for signs of excessive wear and replace worn or leaking components.
2 Ensure that the steering gear gaiters, driveshaft gaiters and balljoint rubbers show no signs of damage.
3 Check the fixings of all nuts and bolts on the steering gear and related components.
4 Replacement details, along with torque specifications can be found in the relevant main manual.

14 Power steering pump fluid level - check

1 Set the front wheels in the straight ahead position.
2 With the engine off, unscrew the pump reservoir filler cap and wipe the dipstick.
3 Refit and remove the cap and check the fluid level on the dipstick.
4 If the fluid is cold (i.e. after cooling for several hours), the level should be on the lower mark **(see illustration)**.
5 If the vehicle has been in use and the fluid is hot, the level should be on the upper mark.
6 If necessary, top-up the reservoir, then refit the cap.

17.1 Mark on the camshaft pump pulley for checking the idle speed with a timing light, operated by a petrol engine

15 Oil filler cap - clean

Note: *This procedure is only applicable to models with the cap fitted to the valve cover.*
1 Pull the oil filler cap from the top of the valve cover then loosen the clip and disconnect the crankcase ventilation hose.
2 Clean the wire mesh filter in paraffin and allow to dry. If it is blocked with sludge, however, renew the cap complete.
3 Refit the hose to the filler cap and fit the cap to the valve cover.

16 Exhaust system - examination

Examination

1 Inspect the exhaust system periodically for leaks, corrosion and damage, and check the security and condition of the mountings. Small leaks are more easily detected if an assistant temporarily blocks the tailpipe with a wad of cloth whilst the engine is idling.

2 Proprietary pastes and bandages are available for the repair of holes and splits. They work well in the short term, but renewal of the section concerned will probably prove more satisfactory in the long run.
3 Check the rubber mountings for deterioration, and renew them if necessary.

17 Idle speed - checking and adjustment

Checking

1 The usual type of tachometer (rev counter), which works from ignition system pulses, cannot be used on diesel engines. A diagnostic socket is provided for use of Peugeot test equipment, but this will not normally be available to the home mechanic. If it is not felt that adjusting the idle speed "by ear" is satisfactory, one of the following alternatives may be used:
  a) *Purchase or hire of an appropriate tachometer*
  b) *Delegation of the job to a Peugeot dealer or other specialist*
  c) *Timing light (strobe) operated by a petrol engine running at the desired speed. If the timing light is pointed at a mark on the camshaft pump pulley (see illustration), the mark will appear stationary when the two engines are running at the same speed (or multiples of that speed). The pulley will be rotating at half the crankshaft speed but this will not affect the adjustment, (in practice it was found impossible to use this method on the crankshaft pulley due to the acute viewing angle)*
2 Before making adjustments warm up the engine to normal operating temperature.
3 Check that the engine idles at the specified speed.

Adjustment

4 If adjustment is necessary on the Roto-Diesel pump, loosen the locknut on the fast idle lever then turn the adjustment screw as required and retighten the locknut **(see illustration)**.
5 If adjustment is necessary on a pre January 1984 Bosch pump, loosen the locknut and turn the stop screw, as required **(see illustration)**. Retighten the locknut on completion.
6 On later Bosch pumps, first loosen the locknut and unscrew the anti-stall adjustment screw until it is clear of the accelerator lever. Loosen the locknut and turn the idle speed adjustment screw, as required, then retighten the locknut. Adjust the anti-stall adjustment screw as described in Chapter 4.
7 Stop the engine and disconnect the instrument, as appropriate.

18 Fuel filter - removal and refitting

Note: *Although not essential, it is always beneficial to change this fuel just before winter, regardless of mileage.*
Pre-1993 models

Removal

1 The fuel filter is located on the right hand side of the engine compartment **(see illustration)**, except for 305 models, where it will be found on the left.
2 Place a container beneath the filter. Drain the fuel from the filter by opening the water bleed screw on the bottom of the filter and (where fitted), the air bleed screw. When the fuel has drained, remove the container and place some rags below the filter to catch any further spillage.

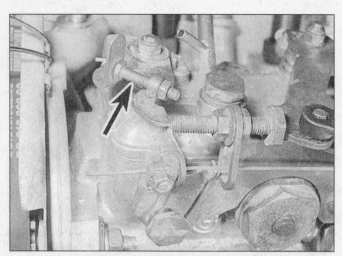

17.4 Idle speed adjustment screw (arrowed) on the Lucas CAV/Roto-Diesel

17.5 Idle speed adjustment screw (arrowed) on a pre January 1984 Bosch pump

18.1 Fuel filter on a Horizon model

3 Where applicable, disconnect the water detector wiring from the end cap or chamber.
4 Unscrew the through-bolt from the top (Lucas CAV/Roto-Diesel) or bottom (Bosch) of the filter. On the Lucas version this will release

the end cap and enable the cartridge and seals to be removed. On the Bosch version, remove the chamber, followed by the element and seals.

Refitting

5 Clean the filter head and end cap or chamber.
6 Make sure that the old seals are removed, then locate the new seals in position and fit the new cartridge or element using a reversal of the removal procedure.
7 Finally prime the fuel injection system as described in Chapter 4.

1993-on models

> ⚠️ **Warning: If the fuel is allowed to escape out of the fuel filter housing onto the engine, it will find its way into the clutch and possibly damage the linings.**

Removal

8 Models made from 1993 (except 205 and 309 Turbo models), the fuel filter is relocated in a housing on the cylinder head, above the thermostat and cylinder head coolant outlet housing. The new housing has a water detector and a water drain plug in its base. There is an external hand-priming bulb, and a double valve return system **(see illustration)**.
9 To remove the filter, first drain the housing by loosening the drain plug. If not already fitted, a plastic tube should be attached to the drain plug, and the fuel can then be directed into a container **(see illustration)**.
10 With the fuel drained, unscrew the cover bolts, remove the cover, and lift out the filter **(see illustrations)**.

1

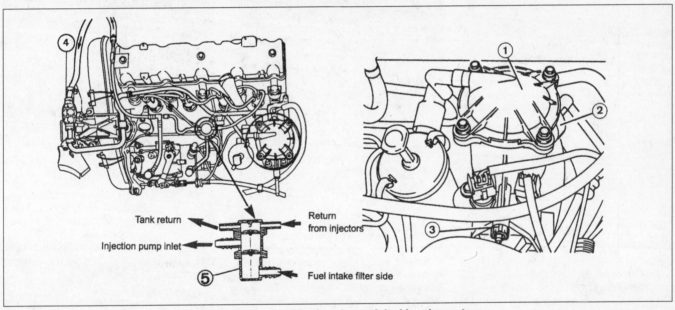

Tank return

Return from injectors

Injection pump inlet

Fuel intake filter side

18.8 Modified fuel filter housing and double valve system

1 Filter *2 Water detector* *3 Bleeding device* *4 To hand-priming pump* *5 Double valve*

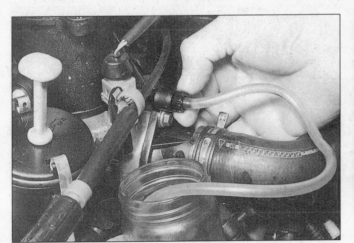

18.9 Draining the fuel from the fuel filter housing

18.10A Unscrew the cover bolts . . .

18.10B . . . remove the cover . . .

18.10C . . . and remove the filter

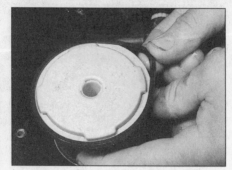

18.11A Checking the sealing rubber

Refitting

11 Check the sealing rubber before reversing the removal procedure, then priming the system as just described. Removal of the water detector is straightforward **(see illustrations)**.

 19 Clutch pedal and cable - lubrication

1 Lubricate the clutch pedal pivot with grease.
2 Also grease the operating rods and/or cable ends where they connect with the operating levers.
3 Removal of the air filter will enable easier access to the clutch cable at the transmission end.

18.11B Disconnecting the wiring plug . . .

18.11C . . . and removing the water detector (arrowed)

Every 18 000 miles or 18 months

 20 Drivebelt tension - checking and adjusting

Checking

1 To ensure maximum life from either the alternator, vacuum pump or the power steering pump (if applicable), the drivebelts need to be at the correct tension.
2 There should be approximately 6.0 mm deflection on the alternator drivebelt, when moderate thumb pressure is applied midway between the pulleys **(see illustration)**. The deflection on the vacuum or power steering pump, as applicable, should be marginally lower at approximately 5.0 mm.
3 Check the condition of the belt. If the belt is cracked, frayed or found to be slipping, it needs to be replaced.

Adjustment

Alternator

4 To adjust the tension, first check that the belt is correctly fitted over the pulleys.

5 With the alternator mountings loose, carefully lever the alternator outwards to tighten the drivebelt. Using a wooden lever will minimise the risk of damage to the alternator casing.
6 As mentioned previously the belt should be able to move by approximately 6.0 mm, with moderate thumb pressure midway between the pulleys.
7 Tighten the mounting bolts to the correct torque. Refer to Chapter 5, for details on renewal.

20.2 Checking the tension of the alternator drivebelt

Power steering pump

8 Adjust the tension by loosening the mounting and adjusting bolts, reposition the pump and retighten the bolts. Refer to paragraph 2.
9 On early models three slotted holes are provided in the bracket and on later models the pump pivots on a single bolt.
10 A torque wrench may be used on the later type to adjust the belt tension using the 12.7 mm (½ in) square hole provided **(see illustration)**. With both bolts loose, apply the torque given in the Specifications, then tighten the adjustment bolt, followed by the pivot bolt.

Vacuum pump (early models)

Note: *Later models have a revised mounting arrangement.*

11 On models fitted with a belt-driven brake vacuum pump, it is important to ensure that the drivebelt is correctly tensioned **(see illustration)**.
12 Loosen the mounting bolts and adjust the pump to the correct tension. Refer to paragraph 2.
13 When the drivebelt is at the correct tension, tighten the mounting bolts to the correct torque.

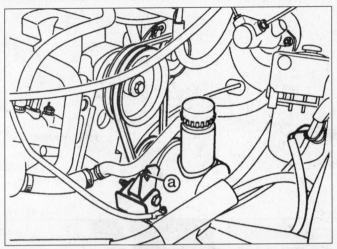

20.10 Square hole (a) for adjusting the belt tension on the later type pump

20.11 Checking the vacuum pump drivebelt tension

Vacuum pump drivebelt (later models)

14 The following paragraphs describe the adjustment procedure for later models, which have the revised mounting arrangement shown (see illustration).

15 Loosen the pivot and adjustment bolts on the vacuum pump.

16 A welded nut is fitted to the pivot bracket. Locate a socket and torque wrench on this nut, and apply the correct torque (see Specifications), so that the drivebelt is tensioned.

17 Hold the pivot bracket in this position and tighten the pivot and adjustment bolts. Remove the torque wrench.

1

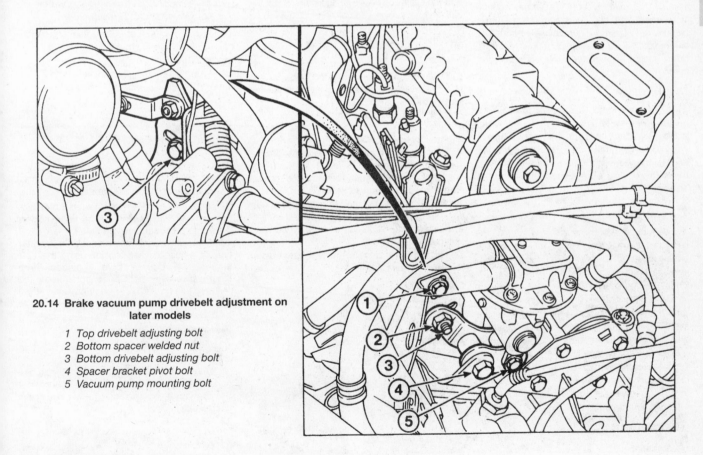

20.14 Brake vacuum pump drivebelt adjustment on later models

1 Top drivebelt adjusting bolt
2 Bottom spacer welded nut
3 Bottom drivebelt adjusting bolt
4 Spacer bracket pivot bolt
5 Vacuum pump mounting bolt

21 Vacuum pump - check

1 Examine the vacuum hose between the brake servo unit and vacuum pump for cracks, deterioration or damage. Renew if necessary.
2 Check the main body for signs of oil leakage.
3 Turn the engine, so that the mark on the vacuum pump pulley shoulder is in line with the mark on the pump (i.e. uppermost).
4 Unscrew the plug and check that the oil is level with the bottom of the hole **(see illustration)**. If not top-up with the specified oil.
5 Refit and tighten the plug.

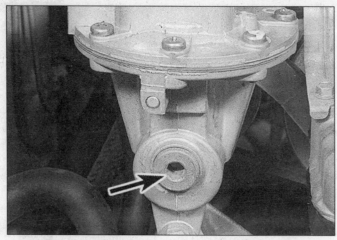

21.4 Filler/level plug (arrowed) on the vacuum pump

Every 30 000 miles or 2 years

22 Coolant - draining, flushing and filling

Note: *The coolant should be renewed at the first 12 000 miles (20 000 km), from new or from when the engine is renewed. This is necessary to flush out corrosive elements that can build up to high levels during the early life of the engine. There after renew as described in the maintenance schedule.*

Draining

1 Allow the engine to cool for at least 10 minutes after switching off.
2 Depress the filler cap and slowly turn it anti-clockwise until it can be removed. If the engine is hot cover the cap with a thick cloth before removing it as a precaution against scalding.
3 Position a container beneath the left-hand side of the radiator then unscrew the drain plug and allow the coolant to drain. If there is no drain plug fitted, disconnect the drain pipe on the left-hand side of the radiator or disconnect the bottom hose from the right-hand side.
4 When the radiator is completely drained refit the drain plug, pipe or hose then drain the block by unscrewing the drain plug located on the rear of the engine at the flywheel end. Refit the drain plug on completion.

Flushing

5 If the coolant is contaminated with rust and scale the complete system should be flushed as follows.
6 Drain the system as described earlier.
7 Remove the thermostat as described in Chapter 3.
8 If not already done disconnect the bottom hose from the radiator.
9 Insert a garden hose into the thermostat housing so that the water runs through the engine in the reverse direction to normal flow and comes out of the bottom hose. Continue until the water emerges clean.
10 Run the water through the radiator in the normal direction of flow by inserting the garden hose in the top hose. In severe cases of contamination it may be helpful to remove the radiator and reverse-flush it.
11 Chemical descalers or flushing agents should only be used as a last resort, in which case follow the instructions given by the manufacturers.
12 When flushing is complete, refit the thermostat and reconnect the hoses.

Filling

13 Make sure that the drain plugs are secure and that all hoses are in good condition and their clips tight.
14 Loosen or remove the bleed screws located on the thermostat housing cover, and where applicable, on the heater hose at the bulkhead **(see illustrations)**.

22.14A Bleed screws on the thermostat housing cover (arrowed)

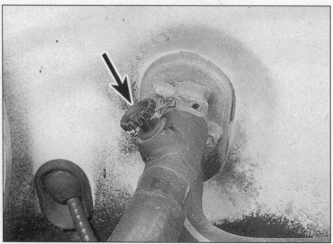

22.14B Bleed screws on the heater hose (arrowed)

15 Fill slowly with coolant through the filler neck and at the same time keep an eye on the bleed screw holes. When coolant free of air bubbles emerges refit and tighten the bleed screws.

16 Top up the radiator or expansion tank until it is full to the filler cap seating. There still remains air in the system which must be purged as follows.

17 Start the engine and run at a fast idle speed for several minutes. Stop the engine.

18 Top up the expansion tank to the maximum level. On some models this is marked on the outside of the expansion tank, but on others, a level plate or tube is visible through the filler neck. Both minimum and maximum levels are indicated **(see illustration)**.

19 Fit the filler cap.

20 Start the engine and run to normal operating temperature indicated by the electric cooling fan(s) cutting in then out after a few minutes.

21 Stop the engine and allow to cool for at least 1 hour.

22 Recheck the coolant level as described in Section 5 and top-up as necessary.

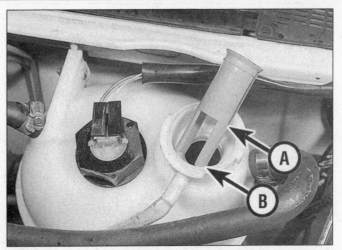

22.18 Showing the level tube removed from the expansion tank
A Maximum level   B Minimum level

Every 36 000 miles

23 Transmission fluid level (manual transmission models) - check

Pre 1987 models

1 Jack up the front of the vehicle and support on axle stands (see *"Jacking and vehicle support"*). Chock the rear wheels.

2 Two drain plugs are provided on early models - one for the transmission and one for the differential **(see illustration)**. On later models the transmission drain plug is deleted and it is important not to confuse the reverse gear shaft clamping screw with a drain plug.

3 Unscrew the drain plug(s) and drain the oil into a container. On completion refit and tighten the drain plug(s).

4 There is no provision for a level plug so the correct quantity of oil must be measured before refilling the transmission through the filler plug hole **(see illustration)**.

5 Lower the vehicle to the ground.

1987 - on models

6 On models built from 1987, an oil filler/level plug is fitted in the transmission end cover.

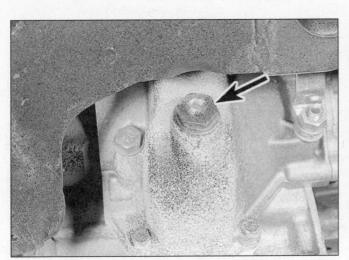

23.2 Differential drain plug (arrowed)

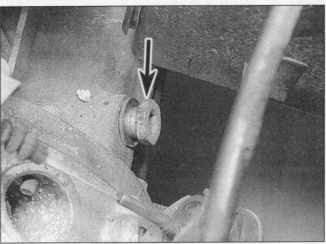

23.4 BE1 transmission filler plug (arrowed)

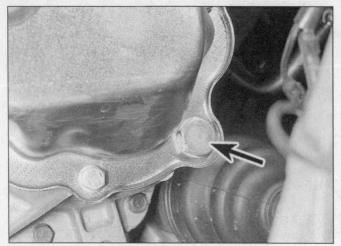

23.6 BE3 transmission oil filler/level plug (arrowed)

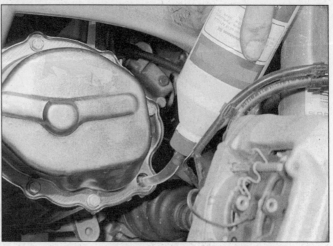

23.8 Topping-up the oil in the BE3 transmission

Access is easiest through the left-hand wheel arch **(see illustration)**. The vehicle should be parked on level ground for this check.

7 Having gained access to the oil level plug, clean around the plug before removing it. Check the oil level; with the vehicle level, the oil level must be up to the bottom of the plug hole.

8 Top-up if necessary with the specified oil **(see illustration)**. Add the oil slowly; the oil level is correct when the oil just begins to flow from the plug hole. Allow a few minutes for the oil level to stabilise, then refit and tighten the filler/level plug. Check for leaks if regular topping-up is required.

Chapter 2
Engine repair procedures

Contents

Degrees of difficulty

 Easy, suitable for novice with little experience   **Fairly easy,** suitable for beginner with some experience   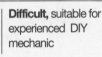 **Fairly difficult,** suitable for competent DIY mechanic   **Difficult,** suitable for experienced DIY mechanic   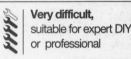 **Very difficult,** suitable for expert DIY or professional

2

Specifications

General

Type	Four-cylinder, in-line, four-stroke, overhead camshaft, compression-ignition, mounted transversely and inclined 30° to rear. Transmission mounted on left-hand end of engine.
Codes:	
205, 305 and models	XUD 7 and XUD 7L
205, 309 and 405 Turbo models	XUD 7T and XUD 7TE
305, 309, 405 and Horizon	XUD 9, XUD 9A and XUD 9L
405 Turbo models	XUD 9TE and XUD 9TEL
Engine size:	
XUD 7	1765 cc (1.7 litre)
XUD 9	1905 cc (1.9 litre)
Number of cylinders	4
Bore and stroke:	
XUD 7	80.0 x 88.0 mm
XUD 9	83.0 x 88.0 mm
Compression ratio:	
XUD 7	23.0 : 1
XUD 7TE/T	22.0 : 1
XUD 9	23.5 : 1
XUD 9A	23.0 : 1
XUD 9TE	21.8 : 1
Compression pressures (engine hot, cranking speed):	
Minimum	18 bar
Normal	25 to 30 bar
Maximum difference between any two cylinders	5 bar

Maximum torque (ISO):
   XUD 7 . . . .   110 Nm at 2200 rpm
   XUD 7T . . . .   157 Nm at 2100 rpm
   XUD 7TE . . . .   180 Nm at 2100 rpm
   XUD 9 . . . .   118 Nm at 2000 rpm
   XUD 9A . . . .   120 Nm at 2000 rpm
   XUD 9TE . . . .   196 Nm at 2250 rpm
Maximum power (ISO):
   XUD 7 . . . .   43.5 kW at 4600 rpm
   XUD 7T . . . .   57.5 kW at 4300 rpm
   XUD 7TE . . . .   66.0 kW at 4300 rpm
   XUD 9 . . . .   47.0 kW at 4600 rpm
   XUD 9A . . . .   51.0 kW at 4600 rpm
   XUD 9TE . . . .   67.5 kW at 4000 rpm
Maximum speed:
   Except XUD 7T/TE models:
      No load . . . .   5100 rpm
      Full load . . . .   4600 rpm
   XUD 7T models:
      No load . . . .   4900 rpm
      Full load . . . .   4300 rpm
   XUD 7TE models:
      No load . . . .   4800 rpm
      Full load . . . .   4300 rpm
Firing order . . . .   1-3-4-2 (No 1 at flywheel end)

Cylinder block

Cylinder bore diameter:
   XUD 7 . . . .   80.000 to 80.018 mm, or 80.030 to 80.048 mm
   XUD 9 . . . .   83.000 to 83.018 mm, or 83.030 to 83.048 mm

Pistons and piston rings

Piston diameter:
   XUD 7 . . . .   79.93 ± 0.008 mm, or 76.96 ± 0.008 mm
   XUD 9 . . . .   82.930 ± 0.009 mm, or 82.960 ± 0.009 mm
Piston ring end gaps (fitted):
   Top compression . . . .   0.20 to 0.40 mm
   2nd compression . . . .   0.15 to 0.35 mm
   Oil scraper . . . .   0.10 to 0.30 mm
Connecting rod small-end bush inner diameter . . . .   25.007 to 25.020 mm
Maximum weight difference between any two pistons . . . .   2.5 g
Maximum piston protrusion difference between any two pistons . . . . .   0.12 mm

Crankshaft

Endfloat . . . .   0.07 to 0.32 mm
Maximum journal/crankpin out-of-round . . . .   0.007 mm

Cylinder head

Warp limit . . . .   0.07 mm subject to camshaft turning freely
Refinishing limit (see text) . . . .   0.40 mm
Swirl chamber protrusion . . . .   0 to 0.03 mm
Cylinder head bolt maximum length (Torx head type - refer to text):
   Except XUD9TE . . . .   121.5 mm (or 124.5 including the guiding end piece)
   XUD9TE . . . .   146.5 mm (or 151.5 including the guiding end piece)

Valves

Seat angle (inclusive):
   Pre October 1986 models:
      Inlet . . . .   120°
      Exhaust . . . .   90°
   October 1986-on models :
      Inlet and exhaust . . . .   90°
Valve recess below cylinder head:
   Inlet . . . .   0.50 to 1.05 mm
   Exhaust . . . .   0.90 to 1.45 mm

Valve clearances (cold):	**Inlet**	**Exhaust**
XUD7	0.10 to 0.25 mm	0.25 to 0.40 mm
XUD9	0.15 to 0.25 mm	0.35 to 0.45 mm

Camshaft
Endfloat . . . .   0.07 to 0.16 mm

Lubrication system
Oil pressure
  Non-Turbo models (at engine temperature of 80°C):
    Minimum . . . .   2.0 bar at 800 rpm
    Maximum . . . .   3.5 to 5.0 bar at 4000 rpm
  Turbo models (at 80°C/170°F) . . . .   3.4 bars at 2000 rpm
Oil pressure switch operating pressures:
  On . . . .   0.58 to 0.44 bar
  Off . . . .   0.8 bar maximum

Oil pump
Type . . . .   Two gear
Pressure relief valve opens . . . .   4.0 bar
Gear endfloat . . . .   0.12 mm
Clearance between gear lobes and housing . . . .   0.064 mm

Torque wrench settings

	Nm	lbf ft
Big-end bearing cap:		
Stage 1	40	30
Stage 2, Slacken then	20	15
Stage 3	Angle tighten by a further 70°	
Camshaft bearing cap	18	13
Camshaft sprocket	35	26
Crankshaft pulley bolt:		
Stage 1	40	30
Stage 2	Angle tighten by a further 60°	
Cylinder head bolts:		
Up to September 1986:		
Stage 1	30	22
Stage 2	60	44
Stage 3 Loosen ¼ turn then	60	44
Stage 4 (refer to text). Loosen ¼ turn then	70	52
September 1986-on, except Torx head bolts):		
Stage 1	30	22
Stage 2	70	52
Stage 3	Angle-tighten a further 120°	
Torx head bolt type (refer to text):		
Stage 1	20	16
Stage 2	60	44
Stage 3:		
Except XUD 9TE	Angle-tighten a further 180°	
XUD 9TE	Angle-tighten a further 220°	
Engine mounting, left hand:		
Centre nut	35	26
Small nuts	18	13
Centre stud to transmission	50	37
Engine mounting bracket, right-hand lower	18	13
Engine mounting bracket, right-hand upper:		
To engine	35	26
To mounting rubber	28	21
Engine mounting, right-hand rubber to body	40	30
Flywheel/driveplate	50	37
Front housing	11	8
Injection pump bracket	20	15
Lower link mounting	35	26
Main bearing cap	70	52
Oil cooler	68	50
Oil gallery plug	28	21
Oil pressure switch	30	22
Oil pump cover	9	7
Oil pump mounting	13	10
Pump pulley to camshaft	35	26
Sump	19	14
Sump oil drain bracket	3	2.2
Timing belt intermediate roller	18	13
Timing belt tensioner	18	13
Timing cover, lower	12	9
Valve cover	2	1.5

2

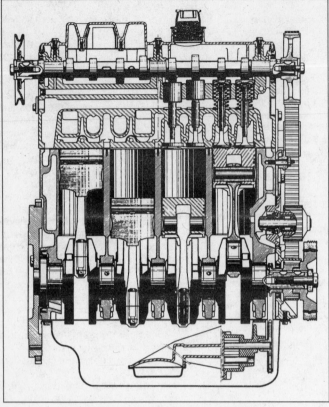

1.1A Engine longitudinal cross-section

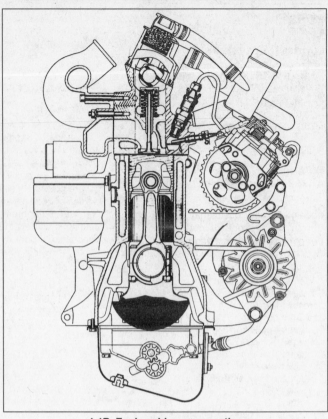

1.1B Engine side cross-section

1 Description - general

1 The engine is of four-cylinder overhead camshaft design, mounted transversely and inclined 30° to the rear, with the transmission mounted on the left-hand side **(see illustrations)**.
2 A toothed timing belt drives the camshaft, injection pump and water pump. Bucket tappets are fitted between the camshaft and valves, and valve clearance adjustment is by means of selective shims.

3 The camshaft is supported by three bearings machined directly in the cylinder head.
4 The crankshaft runs in five main bearings of the usual shell type. Endfloat is controlled by thrustwashers either side of No 2 main bearing.
5 The pistons are selected to be of matching weight, and incorporate fully floating gudgeon pins retained by circlips.
6 The oil pump is chain driven from the front of the crankshaft. An oil cooler is fitted to the 1.9 engine.
7 During 1988, a 1765 cc Turbo diesel (the XUD 7TE),was introduced to selected models.

8 From January 1991 on all XUD 7 Turbo models, a redesigned cylinder head is fitted, being strengthened in the area of the coolant channels **(see illustration)**. The new cylinder head was, however, supplied from Peugeot parts departments earlier than this date.

2 Compression and leakdown test - description and interpretation

Note: *A compression tester specifically designed for diesel engines must be used for this test*

Compression test

Description

1 When engine performance is down, or if misfiring occurs which cannot be attributed to the ignition or fuel systems, a compression test can provide diagnostic clues as to the engine's condition. If the test is performed regularly, it can give warning of trouble before any other symptoms become apparent.
2 A compression tester specifically intended for diesel engines must be used, because of the higher pressures this type of engine produces. The tester is connected to an adapter that screws into the glow plug or injector hole **(see illustration)**. It is unlikely to be worthwhile buying such a tester for

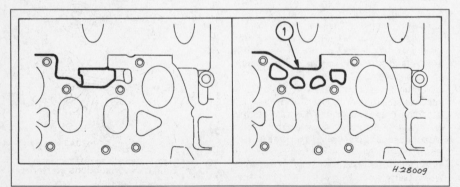

H.28009

1.8 Early (left) and later (right) cylinder head design
1 Modification on the exhaust side of the cylinder head

2.2 Performing a compression test

occasional use, but it may be possible to borrow or hire one. If not, have the test performed by a garage, or dealer.

3 Unless specific instructions to the contrary are supplied with the tester, observe the following points:

a) *The battery must be in a good state of charge, the air filter must be clean, and the engine must be at normal operating temperature.*

b) *All the injectors or glow plugs should be removed before starting the test. If removing the injectors, also remove the fire shield washers, otherwise they may be blown out.*

c) *The stop solenoid must be disconnected, to prevent the engine from running or fuel from being discharged.*

4 There is no need to hold the accelerator pedal down during the test, because the diesel engine air inlet is not throttled.

5 The actual compression pressures measured are not so important as the balance between cylinders. Values are given in the Specifications.

6 The cause of poor compression is less easy to establish on a diesel engine than a petrol driven one. The effect of introducing oil into the cylinders ('wet testing') is not conclusive, because there is a risk that oil will sit in the swirl chamber or in the recess on the piston crown instead of passing to the rings. However, the following can be used as a rough guide to diagnosis.

Interpretation

7 All cylinders should produce very similar pressures. Any difference greater than the specified indicates the existence of a fault. Note that the compression should build up quickly in a healthy engine. Low compression on the first stroke, followed by gradually increasing pressure on successive strokes, indicates worn piston rings. A low compression reading on the first stroke, which does not build up during successive strokes, indicates leaking valves or a blown head gasket (a cracked head could also be the cause). Deposits on the undersides of the valve heads can also cause low compression.

8 A low reading from two adjacent cylinders is almost certainly due to the head gasket having blown between them. The presence of coolant in the engine oil will confirm this.

9 If the compression reading is unusually high, the cylinder head surfaces, valves and pistons are probably coated with carbon deposits. If this is the case, the cylinder head should be removed and decarbonised.

Leakdown test

Description

10 A leakdown test measures the rate at which compressed air fed into the cylinder is lost. It is an alternative to a compression test, and in many ways is better, since the escaping air provides easy identification of where pressure loss is occurring (piston rings, valves or head gasket).

11 The equipment needed for leakdown testing is unlikely to be available to the home mechanic. If poor compression is suspected, have the test performed by a suitably equipped garage.

---

3 Major operations possible with the engine in the vehicle

The following operations can be carried out without having to remove the engine from the car:

a) *Timing belt - removal and refitting*
b) *Camshaft - removal and refitting*
c) *Cylinder head - removal and refitting*
d) *Camshaft oil seals - renewal*
e) *Crankshaft oil seals - renewal*
f) *Sump - removal and refitting*
g) *Oil pump - removal and refitting*
h) *Pistons and connecting rods - removal and refitting*
i) *Flywheel/driveplate - removal and refitting*

For almost any job involving work on the top of the engine (for example valve clearance adjustment) the intercooler must be removed. This is described in Chapter 4.

---

4 Timing belt - removal, refitting and tensioning

Removal

1 The timing belt drives the camshaft, injection pump, and water pump from a toothed sprocket on the front of the crankshaft. If it breaks in service the pistons are likely to hit the valve heads and result in an expensive repair.

2 The timing belt should be renewed at the intervals specified in Chapter 1. However, if it is contaminated with oil or if it is at all noisy in operation (a "scraping" noise due to uneven wear) it should be renewed earlier. Where a Bosch injection pump is fitted, excessive play in the front bearing can wear the sides of the timing belt.

3 Apply the handbrake, then jack up the front right-hand corner of the vehicle until the wheel is just clear of the ground. Support the vehicle

on an axle stand and engage 4th or 5th gear. This will enable the engine to be turned easily by turning the right-hand wheel.

4 Remove the engine splash guard from under the right-hand front wheel arch. On 405 models fitted with XUD 9TE engines, remove the air inlet duct, vibration damper and hand primer (refer to Chapter 4), to improve access.

5 For extra working space on 205, 305 and 309 models, drain the cooling system (detailed in Chapter 1) and disconnect the bottom hose from the water pump inlet. On 205 and 309 models, also remove the intermediate metal tube after removing the cross head screws.

6 Disconnect the battery negative lead.

7 Loosen the alternator pivot and adjustment bolts then unscrew the tension bolt until it is possible to slip the drivebelt from the pulleys.

8 With 4th or 5th gear selected on manual transmission models have an assistant depress the footbrake pedal, then unscrew the crankshaft pulley bolt. Alternatively the crankshaft can be locked, by unbolting the transmission cover plate and using a large screwdriver lock the starter ring gear. Note that the crankshaft pulley bolt is extremely tight.

9 Slide the pulley from the front of the crankshaft. Unbolt the bottom timing cover.

10 Support the weight of the engine using a hoist or trolley jack.

11 Unscrew the nuts and remove the right-hand engine mounting bracket. On Horizon models it will first be necessary to remove the centre timing cover section.

12 Pull up the front clip (early models), release the spring clips, and withdraw the two timing cover sections. Note that the spring clip is not fitted to later models, which have a modified cover and fastenings. On Horizon models first push the engine as far forward as possible **(see illustrations)**.

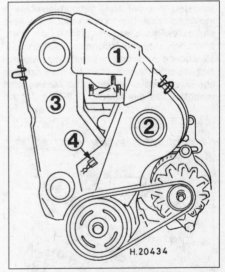

4.12A Timing cover sections on Horizon models

1 *Centre section*   3 *Right hand section*
2 *Left hand section*   4 *Clip*

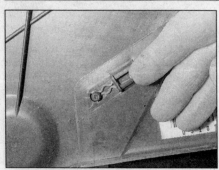

4.12B Timing cover front clip (early models) . . .

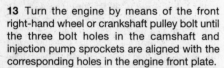

4.12C . . . and spring clips

13 Turn the engine by means of the front right-hand wheel or crankshaft pulley bolt until the three bolt holes in the camshaft and injection pump sprockets are aligned with the corresponding holes in the engine front plate.

14 Insert an 8.0 mm diameter metal dowel rod or drill through the special hole in the left-hand rear flange of the cylinder block by the starter motor. Then carefully turn the engine either way until the rod enters the TDC hole in the flywheel **(see illustration)**.

15 Insert three M8 bolts through the holes in the camshaft and injection pump sprockets and screw them into the engine front plate finger-tight **(see illustration)**.

16 Loosen the timing belt tensioner pivot nut and adjustment bolt, then turn the bracket anti-clockwise to release the tension and retighten the adjustment bolt to hold the tensioner in the released position. If available use a 3/8 inch square drive extension in the

4.14 Using a twist drill to enter the TDC hole in the flywheel

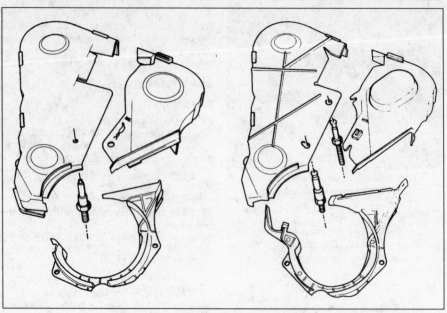

4.12D Earlier and later type of timing belt covers

hole provided to turn the bracket against the spring tension.

17 Mark the timing belt with an arrow to indicate its normal direction of turning then remove it from the camshaft, injection pump, water pump and crankshaft sprockets.

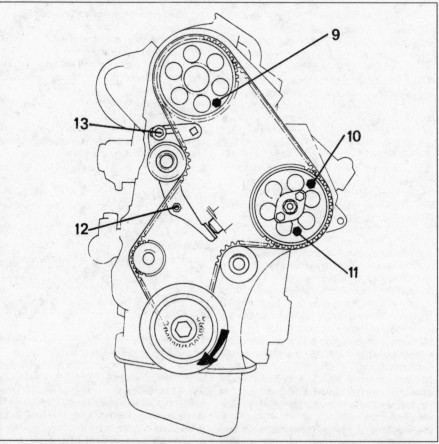

4.15 Holding camshaft and injection pump sprockets in position using M8 bolts
9, 10 and 11 M8 bolts   12 Tensioner pivot nut   13 Tensioner adjustment bolt

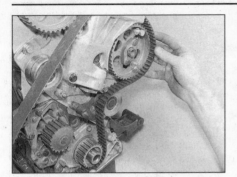

4.20A Fitting the timing belt over the injection pump sprocket . . .

4.20B . . . the camshaft sprocket . . .

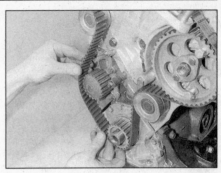

4.20C . . . and the water pump sprocket

Refitting

18 Inspect the belt for cracks, fraying, and damage to the teeth. Pay particular attention to the roots of the teeth. If any damage is evident or if the belt is contaminated with oil it must be renewed and any oil leak rectified.

19 Begin refitting by locating the timing belt on the crankshaft sprocket, making sure that, where applicable, the rotation arrow is facing the correct way.

20 Hold the timing belt engaged with the crankshaft roller sprocket then feed it over the roller and onto the injection pump, camshaft, and water pump sprockets and over the tensioner. To ensure correct engagement, locate only a half width on the injection pump sprocket before feeding the timing belt onto the camshaft sprocket keeping the belt taut and fully engaged with the crankshaft sprocket. Locate the timing belt fully onto the sprockets **(see illustrations)**.

Tensioning

21 With the pivot nut loose, slacken the tensioner adjustment bolt while holding the bracket against the spring tension. Slowly release the bracket until the roller presses against the timing belt. Retighten the adjustment bolt.

22 Remove the bolts from the camshaft and injection pump sprockets. Remove the metal dowel rod from the cylinder block.

23 Rotate the engine two complete turns in its normal direction. Do not rotate the engine backwards as the timing belt must be kept tight between the crankshaft, injection pump and camshaft sprockets.

24 Loosen the tensioner adjustment bolt to allow the tensioner spring to push the roller against the timing belt, then tighten both the adjustment bolt and pivot nut.

25 Recheck the engine timing as described in paragraphs 14 and 15, then remove the metal dowel rod.

26 Refit the timing cover sections and secure with the special clip and spring clips. as applicable. Also refit the bottom timing cover and tighten the bolts.

27 Refit the right-hand engine mounting bracket and tighten the nuts. On Horizon models, refit the centre timing cover section.

28 Remove the trolley jack or hoist.

29 Slide the pulley onto the front of the crankshaft.

30 Apply three drops of locking fluid on the threads of the crankshaft pulley bolt then insert it and tighten to the specified torque while holding the crankshaft stationary using the method described in paragraph 8.

31 Refit the alternator drivebelt and tension it as described in Chapter 1.

32 Reconnect the battery negative lead.

33 Refit the engine splash-guard under the right-hand front wheel arch.

34 Where applicable, reconnect the bottom hose, intermediate metal tube and refill the cooling system (as described in Chapter 1).

35 Lower the vehicle to the ground.

5 Timing belt tensioner - removal and refitting

Removal

1 Apply the handbrake, then jack up the front right-hand corner of the vehicle until the wheel is just clear of the ground.

2 Support the vehicle on an axle stand and engage 4th or 5th gear so that the engine may be rotated by turning the right-hand wheel.

3 Support the weight of the engine using a hoist or trolley jack.

4 Unscrew the nuts and remove the right-hand engine mounting bracket. On Horizon models, it will first be necessary to remove the centre timing cover section.

5 Disconnect the battery negative lead.

6 Pull up the special clip (early models), release the spring clips and withdraw the two timing cover sections.

7 On Horizon models first push the engine as far forward as possible.

8 Turn the engine by means of the front right-hand wheel or crankshaft pulley bolt until the three bolt holes in the camshaft and injection pump sprockets are aligned with the corresponding holes in the engine front plate.

9 Insert an 8.0 mm diameter metal dowel rod or drill through the special hole in the left-hand rear flange of the cylinder block by the starter motor.

10 Carefully turn the engine either way until the rod enters the TDC hole in the flywheel.

11 Insert three M8 bolts through the holes in the camshaft and injection pump sprockets and screw them into the engine front plate finger-tight.

12 Loosen the timing belt tensioner pivot nut and adjustment bolt, then turn the bracket anti-clockwise until the adjustment bolt is in the middle of the slot and retighten the bolt. If available use a 3/8 inch square drive extension in the hole provided to turn the bracket against the spring tension.

13 A tool must now be obtained to hold the tensioner plunger in the mounting bracket. The tool shown **(see illustration)**, is designed to slide in the two lower bolt holes of the mounting bracket and it should be quite easy to fabricate a similar tool out of sheet metal using long bolts instead of metal dowel rods.

14 Unscrew the two lower bolts then fit the special tool. Grease the inner surface of the tool to prevent any damage to the end of the tensioner plunger.

15 Unscrew the pivot nut and adjustment bolt and withdraw the tensioner bracket, complete with roller.

16 Unbolt the engine mounting bracket noting that the uppermost bolt is on the inside face of the engine front plate (except on Horizon models).

17 Compress the tensioner plunger into the mounting bracket, remove the special tool then withdraw the plunger and spring.

Refitting

18 Refitting is a reversal of removal, but refer to Section 4, paragraphs 21 to 25 for details of the timing belt adjustment procedure.

5.13 Peugeot tool for holding the tensioner plunger

2

6 Timing belt intermediate roller - removal and refitting

Removal

1 Follow the procedure given in paragraphs 1 to 12 of Section 5.
2 Remove the engine splash guard from under the right-hand front wheel arch. For extra working space on 205, 305 and 309 models, drain the cooling system (Chapter 1), and disconnect the bottom hose from the water pump inlet. On 205 and 309 models, also remove the intermediate metal tube after removing the cross-headed screws.
3 Disconnect the battery negative lead.
4 Loosen the alternator pivot and adjustment bolts then unscrew the tension bolt until it is possible to slip the drivebelt from the pulleys.
5 With 4th or 5th gear selected have an assistant depress the footbrake pedal, then unscrew the crankshaft pulley bolt. Alternatively, the crankshaft can be locked by unbolting the transmission cover plate and using a wide-bladed screwdriver to lock the starter ring gear.
6 Slide the pulley from the front of the crankshaft.
7 Unbolt the lower timing cover.
8 Remove the spacer from the stud (two studs on later models), for the upper timing cover sections. Note the position of the stud(s), then unscrew and remove it.
9 Unscrew the remaining bolts securing the intermediate roller bracket to the cylinder block noting that the upper bolt also secures the engine mounting bracket.
10 Slightly loosen the remaining engine mounting bracket bolts then slide out the intermediate roller and bracket.

Refitting

11 Refitting is a reversal of removal, but note the following additional points:
a) *Tighten all bolts to the specified torque*
b) *Apply three drops of locking fluid to the threads of the crankshaft pulley bolt before inserting it*
c) *Tension the alternator drivebelt as described in Chapter 1*
d) *Adjust the timing belt as described in Section 4, paragraphs 21 to 25*

7 Camshaft - removal and refitting

Removal

1 Follow the procedure given in paragraphs 1 to 12 of Section 5.
2 Remove the timing belt from the camshaft sprocket and tie it to one side without bending it excessively.
3 Unscrew the M8 bolt holding the camshaft sprocket in the timing position. Where applicable, remove the brake vacuum pump from the end of the camshaft (refer to Chapter 7).

4 Remove the oil filler cap/breather from the valve cover and position it to one side. On some models, it will be necessary to remove the air distribution box or intercooler, as applicable (details in Chapter 4).
5 Disconnect the battery negative lead and disconnect the air inlet hose from the inlet manifold and air cleaner.
6 Loosen the pivot and adjustment bolts of the brake vacuum pump, swivel the unit forwards, and disconnect the drivebelt from the pulleys. Where applicable also disconnect the drivebelt the power steering pump drivebelt.
7 Disconnect the crankcase ventilation hose from the valve cover **(see illustration)**. Also disconnect the wiring for the diagnostic socket or oil level sensor.
8 Unbolt and remove the valve cover. Remove the gasket **(see illustrations)**.
9 Hold the camshaft stationary with a spanner on the special lug between the 3rd and 4th cams or by using a lever in the sprocket holes then unscrew the camshaft sprocket bolt and withdraw the sprocket **(see illustrations)**. Recover the Woodruff key if it is loose. Do not rotate the camshaft otherwise the valves will strike the pistons of Nos 1 and 4 cylinders. If necessary turn the engine one quarter turn to position all the pistons halfway down the cylinders to prevent any damage, however, release the timing belt from the injection pump sprocket first.
10 Mark the position of the camshaft bearing caps numbering them from the flywheel end and making the marks on the manifold side.

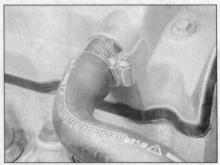

7.7 Crankcase ventilation hose

7.8A Unbolt the valve cover . . .

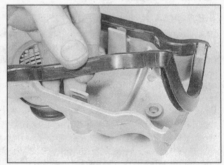

7.8B . . . and remove the gasket

7.9A Special lug (arrowed) for holding the camshaft

7.9B Removing the camshaft sprocket

7.13 Using a puller to remove the pump pulley from the camshaft

7.17 The DIST marking must be at the timing belt end

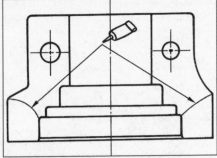

7.19A Areas on camshaft end bearing caps to apply sealing compound

7.19B Fitting a camshaft end bearing cap

11 Progressively unscrew the nuts then remove the bearing caps.

12 Lift the camshaft and withdraw it through the front engine plate. Remove the oil seal from the timing end of the camshaft.

13 Hold the camshaft stationary with a spanner on the special lug between the 3rd and 4th cams, then unscrew the bolt and remove the pump pulley from the flywheel end of the camshaft. Use a puller if it is tight **(see illustration)**. Recover the Woodruff key if it is loose.

14 Remove the oil seal from the flywheel end of the camshaft.

15 Clean all the components including the bearing surfaces in the cylinder head. Examine the components carefully for wear and damage, in particular check the surface of the cams for scoring and pitting. Renew components as necessary and obtain new oil seals.

Refitting

16 Begin reassembly by lubricating the cams and bearing journals with engine oil.

17 Locate the camshaft on the cylinder head, passing it through the engine front plate and with the tips of cams 4 and 6 facing downwards and resting on the bucket tappets. The cast DIST marking on the camshaft should be at the timing belt end of the cylinder head **(see illustration)** and the key slot for the camshaft sprocket should be facing upwards.

18 Fit the centre bearing cap the correct way round as previously noted then screw on the nuts and tighten them two or three turns.

19 Apply sealing compound to the end bearing caps on the areas as shown. Fit them in the correct positions and tighten the nuts two or three turns **(see illustrations)**.

20 Tighten all the nuts progressively to the specified torque making sure that cams 4 and 6 remain facing downwards **(see illustration)**. Check that the camshaft endfloat is as given in the Specifications using feeler blades **(see illustration)**. The only answer if it is not correct is to renew the cylinder head.

21 If the original camshaft is being refitted and it is known that the valve clearances are correct, go on to paragraph 22, otherwise check and adjust the valve clearances as described in Section 8. Note that as the timing belt is disconnected at this stage, the crankshaft must be turned one quarter turn either way from the TDC position so that all the pistons are halfway down the cylinders. This will prevent the valves striking the pistons when the camshaft is rotated. Release the timing belt from the injection pump sprocket while turning the engine as the timing bolts are still in position.

22 Smear the lips of the oil seals with oil then fit them over each end of the camshaft, open end first, and press them in until flush with the end faces of the end caps. Use an M10 bolt, washers and a socket to press in the oil seals **(see illustration)**.

23 Fit the Woodruff key and pump pulley to the flywheel end of the camshaft, insert the bolt and tighten it while holding the camshaft stationary.

24 Fit the Woodruff key and camshaft sprocket to the timing end of the camshaft. Apply locking fluid to the threads then insert the bolt and tighten it to the specified torque while holding the camshaft stationary.

25 Refit the valve cover, together with a new gasket, and tighten the bolts. Reconnect the wiring.

26 Refit the crankcase ventilation hose.

27 Locate the drivebelt on the camshaft and vacuum pump pulleys. Press the pump rearwards until the deflection of the belt, midway between the two pulleys is approximately 5.0 mm under firm thumb pressure. Tighten the adjustment bolt followed by the pivot bolt. Similarly refit the power steering pump drivebelt, where applicable.

28 Reconnect the battery negative lead and the air inlet hose.

29 Refit the oil filler cap/breather. Replace the brake vacuum pump, where applicable.

30 Align the holes and refit the M8 timing bolt to the camshaft sprocket.

31 If the crankshaft was turned a quarter turn from TDC as in paragraphs 9 and 21, turn the crankshaft back the quarter turn so that pistons 1 and 4 are again at TDC. Do not turn the engine more than a quarter turn otherwise pistons 2 and 3 will pass their TDC positions and will strike valves 4 and 6.

32 Refit the TDC dowel rod to the flywheel.

33 Refit and adjust the timing belt, referring to Section 4, paragraphs 20 to 25. The remaining procedure is a reversal of removal.

2

7.20A Tightening the camshaft bearing cap nuts

7.20B Checking the camshaft endfloat

7.22 Using a socket and bolt to fit a camshaft oil seal

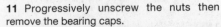

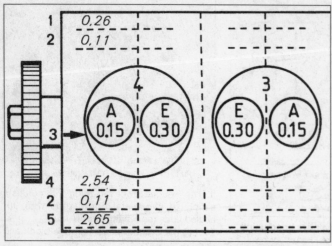

8.8 Example of valve shim thickness calculation

8.10 Checking the valve clearances with feeler blades

8 Valve clearances - checking and adjustment

Checking

1 Apply the handbrake, then jack up the front right-hand corner of the vehicle until the wheel is just of the ground.
2 Support the vehicle on an axle stand and engage 4th or 5th gear so that the engine may be rotated by turning the right-hand wheel.
3 Disconnect the battery negative lead.
4 Remove the oil filler cap/breather and position it to one side.
5 Disconnect the air inlet hose from the inlet manifold and air cleaner.
6 Disconnect the crankcase ventilation hose from the valve cover. Also disconnect the wiring for the diagnostic plug or oil level sensor.
7 Unbolt and remove the valve cover. Remove the gasket.
8 On a piece of paper draw the outline of the engine with the cylinders numbered from the flywheel end and showing the position of each valve, together with the specified valve clearance. Above each valve draw two lines for noting (1) the actual clearance and (2) the amount of adjustment required **(see illustration)**.
9 Turn the engine until the inlet valve of No 1 cylinder (nearest the flywheel) is fully closed and the apex of the cam is facing directly away from the bucket tappet.
10 Using feeler blades measure the clearance between the base of the cam and the bucket tappet **(see illustration)**. Record the clearance on line (1).
11 Repeat the measurement for the other seven valves, turning the engine as necessary so that the cam lobe in question is always facing directly away from the particular bucket tappet.

12 Calculate the difference between each measured clearance and the desired value and record it on line (2). Since the clearance is different for inlet and exhaust valves make sure that you are aware which valve you are dealing with. The valve sequence from either end of the engine is:

Inlet - Exhaust - Exhaust - Inlet - Inlet - Exhaust - Exhaust - Inlet

13 If all the clearances are within tolerance, refit the valve cover using a new gasket if necessary. If any clearance measured is outside the specified tolerance, adjustment must be carried out as described below.

Adjustment

14 Remove the camshaft as described in Section 7.
15 Withdraw the first bucket tappet and its shim. Be careful that the shim does not fall out of the tappet. Clean the shim and measure its thickness with a micrometer **(see illustration)**.
16 Refer to the clearance recorded for the valve concerned. If the clearance was more than the amount required the shim thickness must be increased by the difference recorded (2), if too small the thickness must be decreased.
17 Draw three more lines beneath each valve on the calculation paper, as described in

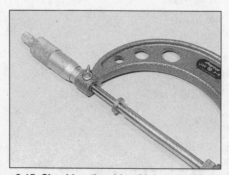

8.15 Checking the shim thickness with a micrometer

paragraph 8. On line (4) note the measured thickness of the shim then add or deduct the difference from line (2) to give the final shim thickness required on line (5).
18 Shims are available in thicknesses between 2.425 mm and 3.550 mm in steps of 0.075 mm. Clean new shims before measuring or fitting them.
19 Repeat the procedure given in paragraphs 15 to 17 on the remaining valves keeping each tappet identified for position.
20 When reassembling, oil the shim and fit it on the valve stem first with the size marking facing downwards then oil the bucket tappet and lower it onto the shim. Do not raise the tappet after fitting as the shim may become dislodged.
21 When all the tappets are in position with their shims, refit the camshaft referring to Section 7, but recheck the clearances to make sure they are correct.

9 Cylinder head (except 405 models) - removal and refitting

Note: *Models produced after September 1986, are fitted with revised cylinder head bolts, having different tightening procedures (refer to Specifications), refer also to text. The revised head bolts MUST be replaced, with their washers, when refitting the cylinder head. Refer to paragraphs 42 and 43 if Torx type head bolts are fitted. Peugeot recommend the use of Molycote G Rapid Plus grease (available from a Peugeot dealer) on cylinder head bolts, when refitting. However if not available, use a good quality high-melting-point grease. On XUD 7TE Turbo models, if replacing the cylinder head, with a modified version (refer to Section 1), a new exhaust manifold and gasket will be needed.*

Removal

1 Follow the procedure given in paragraphs 1 to 12 of Section 5.

9.19 Disconnecting the inlet manifold-to-injection pump hose

2 Remove the timing belt from the camshaft sprocket and carefully secure it to one side, without bending it excessively.

3 Drain the cooling system as described in Chapter 1. On Horizon models, remove the expansion tank.

4 Remove the air cleaner assembly, as described in Chapter 4.

5 Unscrew the M8 bolt holding the camshaft sprocket in the timing position. Also unscrew the tensioner adjustment bolt and the one or two upper bolts from the engine mounting bracket. On Horizon models, unscrew the rear bolt securing the front plate.

6 At this stage, the right-hand engine mounting bracket may be temporarily fitted and the hoist or trolley jack removed.

7 Disconnect the heater hose from the flywheel end of the cylinder head.

8 Disconnect the two small hoses from the thermostat housing then unbolt the housing from the cylinder head and position it to one side.

9 Remove the oil filler cap/breather and position it to one side.

10 Disconnect the air inlet hose from the inlet manifold.

11 Remove the brake vacuum pump, as described in Chapter 7. Where applicable disconnect the power steering pump drivebelt.

12 Disconnect the crankcase ventilation hose from the valve cover. Also disconnect the wiring for the diagnostic socket or oil level sensor.

13 Unbolt and remove the valve cover. Remove the gasket.

14 Unscrew the union nuts securing the injection pipes to the injectors and fuel injection pump, and remove the pipes as two assemblies.

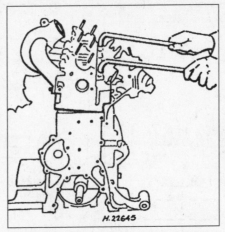

9.23 Removing the cylinder head using angled dowel rods

15 Unbolt the left-hand engine lifting bracket.

16 Disconnect the wiring from the glow plugs.

17 Disconnect the fuel leak off pipe from the injection pump.

18 Hold the camshaft stationary with a spanner on the special lug between the 3rd and 4th cams or by using a lever in the sprocket holes, then unscrew the camshaft sprocket bolt and withdraw the sprocket. Recover the Woodruff key if it is loose. Do not rotate the camshaft otherwise the valves will strike the pistons of Nos 1 and 4 cylinders. If necessary release the timing belt from the injection pump sprocket and turn the engine one quarter turn in either direction to position all the pistons halfway down the cylinders to prevent any damage.

19 On Turbo models, remove the following:
a) *Turbo oil feed and return pipes (see Chapter 4).*
b) *Inlet manifold-to-injection pump hose (see illustration).*
c) *Fuel preheater (where fitted).*

20 The turbocharger itself may be removed with the manifolds.

21 Unscrew the exhaust manifold to downpipe bolts. Recover the springs and collars.

22 Progressively unscrew the cylinder head bolts in the reverse order to that shown for tightening (refer to paragraph 34). Remove the washers.

23 Release the cylinder head from the cylinder block and location dowel by rocking

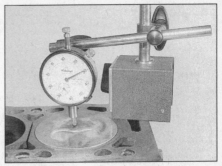

9.27 Checking the piston protrusion

it. The Peugeot tool for doing this consists simply of two metal dowel rods with 90° angled ends **(see illustration)**.

24 Lift the cylinder head from the block and remove the gasket.

25 Do not dispose of the old gasket until a new one has been obtained. The correct thickness of gasket is determined after measuring the protrusion of the pistons at TDC.

Refitting

26 Clean the gasket faces of the cylinder head and cylinder block, preferably using a soft blunt instrument to prevent damage to the mating surfaces. Clean the threads of the cylinder head bolts and the corresponding holes in the cylinder block.

27 Check that the timing belt is clear of the injection pump sprocket, then turn the engine until pistons 1 and 4 are at TDC. Position a dial test indicator on the cylinder block and zero it on the block face. Transfer the probe to the centre of piston 1 then slowly turn the crankshaft back and forth past TDC noting the highest reading on the indicator **(see illustration)**. Record this reading.

28 Repeat this measurement procedure on piston 4 then turn the crankshaft half a turn (180°) and repeat the procedure on pistons 2 and 3.

29 If a dial test indicator is not available, piston protrusion may be measured using a straight-edge and feeler blades or vernier calipers, however, these methods are inevitably less accurate and cannot therefore be recommended.

30 Ascertain the greatest piston protrusion measurement and use this to determine the correct cylinder head gasket from the following chart:

Piston protrusion	Gasket identification
0.54 to 0.65 mm	1 notch or 1 hole
0.65 to 0.77 mm	2 notches or 2 holes
0.77 to 0.82 mm	3 notches or 3 holes
0.84 mm plus	4 notches or holes (fitted to some reconditioned engines)

31 The notch on the centre line of the gasket **(see illustration)** identifies the gasket for use only on the 1.7 engine (type XUD 7) and has no significance for the gasket thickness. The head gasket for the turbo engine is identified by having two notches on the centre-line.

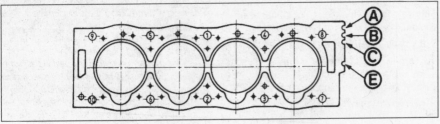

9.31 Head gasket thickness identification notches

A = 1.49 mm (0.059 in)
A + B = 1.61 mm (0.063 in)

A + B + C = 1.73 mm (0.068 in)
E = 1.7 engine identification

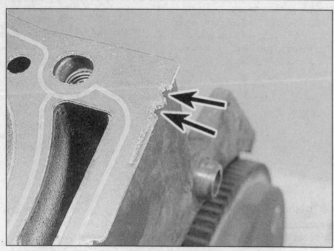

9.33 Cylinder head gasket identification notches (arrowed)

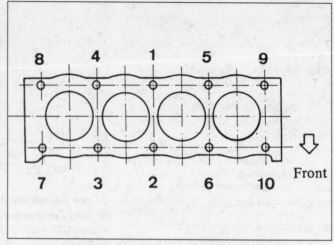

9.34 Cylinder head bolt tightening sequence

32 Turn the crankshaft clockwise (viewed from the timing belt end) until pistons 1 and 4 pass bottom dead centre (BDC) and start to rise, then position them halfway up their bores. Pistons 2 and 3 will also be at their mid-way positions, but descending their bores.

33 Fit the correct gasket the right way round on the cylinder block with the identification notches or holes at the flywheel/driveplate end **(see illustration)**. Make sure that the location dowel is in place at the timing end of the block.

34 The tightening sequence is the same for all models **(see illustration)**. Measure the length of each bolt. If any bolt is greater than the length shown if the Specifications, renew complete with new washers. If in any doubt, renew the complete set. Models produced after September 1986 are fitted with revised cylinder head bolts and have a different tightening procedure. If built before this date, continue on to next paragraph, otherwise go to paragraph 39 or 42, as applicable.

Pre September 1986 models

35 The original head bolts, fitted to these early models, have a plain shank **(see illustration)**.

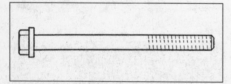

9.35 Early type plain shank cylinder head bolt

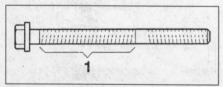

9.39 Later type hexagonal cylinder head bolt
1 Coarse spiral groove

36 Lower the cylinder head onto the block.

37 Grease the threads and contacts faces of the bolts, with Molycote G Rapid Plus (or equivalent). Then insert them, together with their washers (convex side uppermost) and tighten them in the sequence shown, in the stages and at the correct torque, as shown in the Specifications. Before tightening the bolts to their final stage, run the engine for 10 minutes at 3000 rpm and then allow the engine to cool for around two and a half hours (with the bonnet open). Depressurise the cooling system, by depressing the filler cap and slowly turn it anti-clockwise until it can be removed. Tighten the bolts to Stage 4, as shown in the Specifications.

38 Continue on to paragraph 44.

September 1986-on models

39 Models produced after September 1986 are fitted with revised cylinder head bolts and have a different tightening procedure. These bolts can be identified by having a coarse spiral grooving on the upper shank **(see illustration)**.

40 Carefully clean the threaded holes in the cylinder head, using a M12 x 1.5 tap.

41 Coat the threads and contact faces of the **new** cylinder head bolts with Molycote G Rapid Plus (or equivalent), and fit the new washers. Insert the bolts and tighten them in the order shown, in stages and to their correct torque/angle, as shown in the Specifications. Further retightening is not necessary. Continue on to paragraph 44.

Torx type head bolts

42 During 1989, the hexagon-head bolts were replaced by Torx-head bolts. These bolts are tightened through a larger angle than the hexagon-head bolts **(see illustration)**.

43 Torx-head bolts need not be renewed provided that they have not stretched excessively. The maximum permissible length of the bolt (from the underside of the bolt head to the tip) is given in the Specifications.

Even if the bolts are re-usable, new washers must be fitted. Carefully clean the threaded holes in the cylinder head, using a M12 x 1.5 tap. Coat the threads and contact faces of the **new** cylinder head bolts with Molycote G Rapid Plus (or equivalent), and fit the new washers. Insert the bolts and tighten them in the order shown, in stages and to their correct torque/angle, as shown in the Specifications. Further retightening is not necessary.

All models

44 Recheck the valve clearances, referring to Section 8 and adjust them as necessary. Do this even if the clearances have been adjusted with the cylinder head removed, as there may be minor differences.

45 Lubricate the exhaust manifold-to-downpipe contact surfaces with heat resistant grease, then reconnect them and fit the bolts, together with the springs, cups and self-locking nuts. On 1.9 engines the bolts incorporate a shoulder to ensure that the springs are compressed correctly. However, on 1.7 engines, tighten the nuts progressively until approximately four threads are visible and the springs are compressed to 23.5 mm in length.

46 Check that the Woodruff key is in place on the camshaft then fit the camshaft sprocket and bolt. Tighten the bolt to the specified

9.42 Angle-tightening a Torx-type cylinder head bolt, using a commercially-available angle gauge

torque while holding the camshaft stationary with a spanner on the special lug between the 3rd and 4th cams.

47 Turn the camshaft until the tips of cams 4 and 6 (counting from the flywheel end) are facing downwards.

48 Turn the crankshaft a quarter turn clockwise until pistons 1 and 4 are at TDC, and fit the TDC dowel rod to the flywheel. Do not turn the crankshaft anti-clockwise otherwise pistons 2 and 3 will pass their TDC positions and will strike valves 4 and 6.

49 Align the hole and refit the M8 timing bolt to the camshaft sprocket. Refit the valve cover, together with a new gasket.

50 Apply locking fluid to the threads then refit and tighten the two upper bolts to the right-hand engine mounting bracket. Also refit the tensioner adjustment bolt and tighten it. Loosen the tensioner pivot nut.

51 Refit and adjust the timing belt, referring to Section 4, paragraphs 20 to 25.

52 Reconnect the fuel leak off pipe to the injection pump. On Turbo models refit the inlet manifold to injection pump hose.

53 Reconnect the glow plug wiring and fuel preheater (where fitted).

54 Refit the left-hand engine lifting bracket. Refit the injection pipes and tighten the union nuts.

55 Reconnect the crankcase ventilation hose to the valve cover. Reconnect the wiring for the diagnostic socket or oil level sensor.

56 Refit the brake vacuum pump as described in Chapter 7. Where applicable, also reconnect and adjust the power steering pump drivebelt.

57 Reconnect the air inlet hose to the inlet manifold.

58 Refit the oil filler, cap/breather. Reconnect the Turbo oil feed and return pipes, if applicable.

59 Clean the thermostat housing mating faces then refit it, together with a new gasket, and tighten the bolts. Refit the two small hoses.

60 Reconnect the heater hose to the cylinder head.

61 Refit the timing cover sections. On Horizon models, insert and tighten the front plate bolt.

62 Refit the right-hand engine mounting bracket and tighten the nuts. Remove the hoist or trolley jack.

63 Refit the air cleaner (Chapter 4).

64 Reconnect the battery negative lead.

65 Refit the coolant expansion tank (Horizon models).

66 Refill the cooling system (Chapter 1).

67 Lower the vehicle to the ground.

68 On Turbo models, after refitting and before initial start-up, prime the turbo lubrication circuit by disconnecting the stop solenoid lead at the fuel pump, and cranking the engine on the starter for three ten-second bursts.

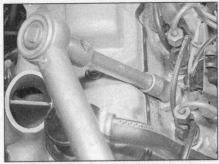

9.71 Retightening the cylinder head bolts

On pre September 1986 models only

69 Before retightening the head bolts, run the engine at 3000 rpm for 10 minutes then switch off the ignition and let the engine cool for at least three and a half hours.

70 Remove the filler cap from the cooling system expansion tank to release any remaining pressure, then refit it.

71 Working on each cylinder head bolt in turn in the correct sequence first loosen the bolt 90° then retighten to the final torque given in the Specifications **(see illustration)**.

---

10 Cylinder head (405 models) - removal and refitting

Note: The following paragraphs describe the removal and refitting procedure of the cylinder head on the XUD9 engine; the procedure for the XUD7 turbo engine in 405 models is very similar.

Removal

1 Apply the handbrake, then jack up the front of the vehicle and support it on axle stands (see "*Jacking and vehicle support*").

2 Drain the cooling system.

3 Remove the intercooler (Turbo models) or the air inlet distribution box (non-Turbo models).

4 Unbolt and remove the vibration damper from the top of the engine right-hand mounting.

5 Remove the battery and the battery tray.

6 Identify all hoses and wires connected to the cylinder head, then disconnect them.

7 Unbolt and remove the engine left-hand lifting eye.

8 Drain the fuel filter (see Chapter 1). Unbolt the cover, then remove the fuel filter. Unscrew the bolt in the bottom of the fuel filter housing, and lift off the housing **(see illustration)**. Recover the O-ring from the groove in the bottom of the housing.

9 Unscrew the bolts, and remove the coolant outlet elbow.

10 Bring the engine to TDC, No 4 cylinder (timing belt end) on compression. The engine may be turned by removing the right-hand front wheel and pulling back the inner plastic cover for access to the crankshaft pulley bolt.

Make sure that the engine is on TDC compression for No 4 cylinder by unscrewing the access plug next to No 4 injector and checking for pressure as the engine is turned. Remember to refit and tighten the plug after making the check.

11 Insert a length of 8.0 mm diameter metal dowel rod or a drill through the block flange (behind the starter motor) and into the flywheel. This locks the engine in the TDC position. Turn the engine back and forth slightly if necessary to enable the rod to enter the hole.

12 Support the weight of the right-hand side of the engine, using a trolley jack and interposed piece of wood beneath the sump. Where fitted, remove the rubber stop located near the engine right-hand mounting.

13 Unscrew the nuts and remove the engine right-hand mounting top bracket.

14 Remove the timing belt with reference to Chapter 2.

15 Unbolt and remove the valve cover, and remove the gasket.

16 Note the position of the camshaft sprocket for reference when refitting; make alignment marks if necessary. Hold the camshaft sprocket stationary, then unscrew the bolt and remove the sprocket from the end of the camshaft. Recover the Woodruff key, if it is loose. If a special tool to hold the sprocket is not available, use a spanner on the lug between the 3rd and 4th cams. Another method is to use a lever in one of the sprocket holes, but this is not recommended, as it is possible to damage the cylinder head.

17 Unscrew the bolts holding the front end bracket and tensioner to the cylinder head.

XUD 9TE (Turbo) engine

18 Remove the centralising pin from the timing end of the cylinder head and through the front end bracket **(see illustration)**. Peugeot technicians use a special removal tool, consisting of a sleeve and bolt that is screwed into the pin. However, a sleeve may easily be made out of metal tubing, and a bolt used to draw the pin out **(see illustration)**.

19 Pull the engine forwards as far as possible, and wedge a block of wood between the body and the engine at the right-hand mounting.

10.8 Fuel filter housing mounting bolt (arrowed)

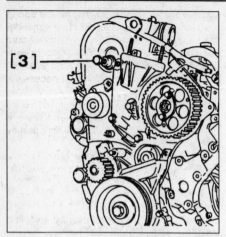

10.18A Using an extractor (3) to remove the cylinder head centralising pin on Turbo models

20 Loosen (but do not remove) the lower centre bolt securing the inlet manifold to the turbocharger (see illustration). The inlet manifold is slotted, to allow its removal without completely removing this bolt.

21 Unbolt the inlet manifold and remove it from the cylinder head. Remove the gasket.

22 Unscrew and remove the bolts securing the turbocharger to the exhaust manifold. The turbocharger remains in position while the cylinder head is being removed.

XUD 9A engine

23 Disconnect the exhaust downpipe from the manifold.

24 Remove the expansion chamber.

All engines

25 Progressively unscrew the cylinder head bolts in the reverse order to that described in Section 9, paragraph 41. Remove the washers.

26 Rock the cylinder head to release it from the cylinder block and its location dowel. Refer to Section 9, for details of the Peugeot tool for doing this.

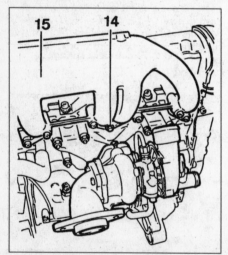

10.20 Loosen but do not remove the bolt (14) securing the inlet manifold (15)

10.18B Cylinder head centralising pin fitting tool

27 Lift the cylinder head from the block, and remove the gasket.

28 Do not dispose of the old gasket until a new one has been obtained. The correct thickness of gasket is determined after measuring the protrusion of the pistons at TDC. (In practice it is probably acceptable to fit a new gasket of the same thickness as the old one, provided that no work has been carried out which could affect piston protrusion and that there is no reason for suspecting the thickness of the old gasket of being incorrect.)

Refitting

29 Clean the faces of the cylinder head and cylinder block, and check the protrusion of the pistons with reference to Section 9, paragraph 26. Do not forget to remove the rod or drill from the flywheel before turning the engine.

30 Ascertain the greatest piston protrusion measurement, and use this to determine the correct cylinder head gasket from the following table.

Piston protrusion	Gasket identification
0.54 to 0.77 mm	2 notches
0.77 to 0.82 mm	3 notches

31 The cylinder head gasket notch identification for the various engines is as given in the table below (see illustration).

Engine	A	B	Thickness
XUD9A	None	2	1.16 mm
XUD9A	None	3	1.73 mm
XUD9TE	3	2	1.54 mm
XUD9TE	3	3	1.64 mm

32 Check the cylinder head bolts for damage and wear. They may be re-used, provided that they have not stretched beyond the maximum length given in the Specifications. However, new washers must be used every time.

33 Turn the engine as necessary, and re-insert the drill or rod into the flywheel.

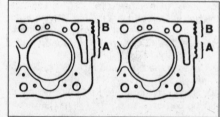

10.31 Cylinder head gasket identification
For A and B, see text

34 Fit the correct gasket the right way round on the cylinder block, with the identification notches or holes at the flywheel end. Make sure that the location dowel is in place at the timing end of the block.

35 Check that the camshaft and sprocket are in the position noted during removal by offering the sprocket to the end of the camshaft. The reference marks made during removal should be aligned; if not, turn the camshaft and sprocket until they are. (If the camshaft position is wrong, there is a risk of piston-to-valve contact.)

36 Lower the cylinder head onto the block.

37 When applicable, make sure that the cylinder head centralising pin hole is correctly aligned, so that the pin may be inserted later.

38 Refer to Section 9, paragraphs 34 to 43, for details on head bolt refitting or renewal.

39 Insert the bolts, and tighten them in the three stages given in the Specifications, in the sequence shown in the Specifications.

XUD 9A engine

40 Refit the expansion chamber, and reconnect the exhaust downpipe to the manifold.

XUD9TE (Turbo) engine

41 Fit a new gasket, then insert the bolts securing the turbocharger to the exhaust manifold, and tighten them to the specified torque.

42 Refit the inlet manifold with a new gasket and tighten the bolts.

43 Tighten the lower centre bolt securing the inlet manifold to the turbocharger.

44 Remove the wedge of wood from the right-hand mounting.

45 Refit the cylinder head centralising pin. If the special Peugeot tool is being used, first screw in the stud together with its nut, then refit the centralising pin and remove the stud. A stud can easily be made instead of the Peugeot tool.

All engines

46 Refit the bolts holding the front end bracket and tensioner to the cylinder head.

47 Check that the Woodruff key is in place on the camshaft, then fit the camshaft sprocket and bolt. Tighten the bolt to the specified torque, while holding the camshaft stationary as during removal.

48 Apply sealant to the four corners of the cylinder head where the valve cover will seat.

49 Refit the valve cover together with a new gasket, and tighten the bolts.

50 Refit the timing belt with reference to Section 4.

51 Refit the engine right-hand mounting top bracket, and tighten the nuts.

52 When applicable, refit the rubber stop on the engine right-hand mounting.

53 Remove the trolley jack from under the engine.

54 Remove the metal dowel rod or drill from the flywheel.

55 Refit the coolant outlet elbow together with a new gasket, and tighten the bolts.

56 Refit the fuel filter housing, using a new O-ring, and tighten the mounting bolt.
57 Insert the fuel filter, then refit the cover and tighten the bolts.
58 Refit the engine left-hand lifting eye, and tighten the bolts.
59 Reconnect all hoses and wiring to the cylinder head.
60 Refit the battery and its support bracket.
61 Refit the vibration damper to the top of the engine right-hand mounting.
62 Refit the intercooler or air inlet distribution box, as applicable.
63 Prime the fuel system as described in Chapter 4.
64 Refill the cooling system, referring to Chapter 1.
65 Lower the vehicle to the ground.

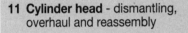

11 Cylinder head - dismantling, overhaul and reassembly

Note: *All engines with suffix L (i.e. XUD 7T/L) are fitted with inlet and exhaust valve stem oil seals. These seals should be renewed as a matter of course whenever the valves are removed.*

Dismantling

1 With the head removed as described in the previous Section remove the camshaft, referring to Section 7.

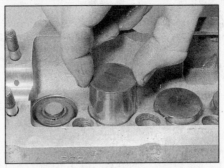

11.2 Removing the bucket tappets

2 Withdraw the bucket tappets, together with their respective shims, keeping them all identified for location **(see illustration)**.
3 Disconnect the remaining leak off pipes and unscrew the injectors. Remove the special washers.
4 Disconnect the wiring and unscrew the glow plugs.
5 Unscrew the nuts and bolts, and remove the inlet and exhaust manifolds from the cylinder head. Remove the exhaust manifold gaskets. The turbocharger, if applicable, must be removed at the same time as the manifolds.
6 Using a valve spring compressor, depress one valve spring retainer to gain access to the collets. The valves are deeply recessed, so the end of the compressor may need to be extended with a tube or box section with a "window" for access. Remove the collets and release the compressor. Recover the retainer,

large and small valve springs, and the spring seat, then withdraw the valve from the cylinder head. **(see illustrations)**. Repeat the procedure to remove the other seven valves, keeping each valve and components identified for position. Remove the timing probe blank if necessary. From around September 1988, single valve springs are fitted instead of the double ones used previously. If the old double springs are to be renewed, a set of the new single springs may be fitted.
7 Dismantling of the cylinder head is now complete. Refer to Section 12 for decarbonisation procedures.

Overhaul

8 Clean all the components and examine them for wear. Obtain new gaskets for the cylinder head, manifolds, valve cover and thermostat housing. Inspect the head for cracks or other damage.
9 Check the head gasket face for distortion (warp) using a straight-edge and feeler blades diagonally and along the edge **(see illustration)**. Do not position the straight-edge over the swirl chambers, as they may be proud of the cylinder head face. Distortion more than that specified may be corrected by machining ("skimming") within a specified limit. This is a specialist's job: the valve seats and swirl chambers must also be machined, and washers fitted under the valve springs. A head that cannot be reclaimed by machining, or any head in which the camshaft does not turn freely, must be renewed.

2

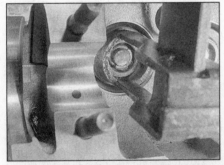

11.6A Depress the retainer with a valve spring compressor and remove the collets, retainer . . .

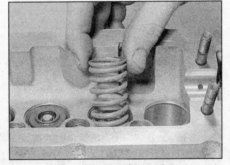

11.6B . . . large valve spring . . .

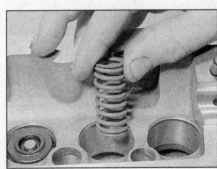

11.6C . . . small valve spring . . .

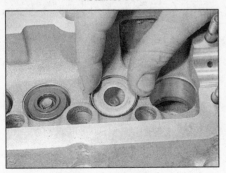

11.6D . . . spring seat . . .

11.6E . . . and valve

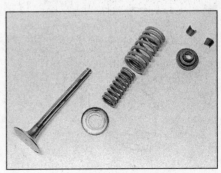

11.6F Valve components

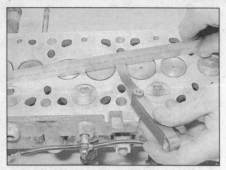

11.9 Checking the cylinder head for distortion

10 Inspect the valve seats and swirl chambers for burning or cracks **(see illustration)**. Both can be renewed but the work should be entrusted to a specialist. From late 1992, all engines are fitted with the same exhaust valves and seats as fitted to the XUD 9TE model. To accommodate the thicker exhaust valve head and maintain the same compression ratio, the exhaust valve seats are recessed by 2.5 mm instead of 2.0 mm **(see illustration)**. Cylinder heads fitted with the new exhaust valves and seats can be identified by a 9.0 mm diameter drilling in the boss above the glow plug instead of the previous 7.0 mm diameter drilling.

11 Using a dial test indicator check that the swirl chamber protrusion is within the limits given in the Specifications **(see illustrations)**.

12 Check each valve for straightness, freedom from burning or cracks, and for an acceptable fit in its guide. Excessive play in the guide may be

11.11A Zero the dial test indicator . . .

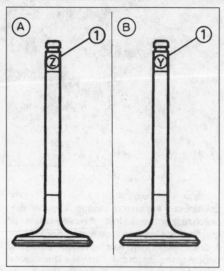

11.10A Exhaust valve identification (1) for engines manufactured from late 1992 onwards

A Non-Turbo engines   B Turbo engines

caused by wear in either component. Measure the valve stem with a micrometer, or try the fit of a new valve, if available, to establish whether it is the valve or the guide that is worn.

13 The valve guides can be renewed, but this is a job for a specialist.

14 Minor surface pitting or carbon build-up on the valve heads and seats may be removed by grinding, but if refacing or recutting is required, consideration must be given to the final height of the valve head in relation to the cylinder head surface. A dial test indicator will be required to check that the valve head is within the specified limits **(see illustration)**.

15 New or refaced valves and seats should be ground together as follows (the coarse paste may be omitted if the fit is already good).

16 Invert the head and support it securely. Smear a little coarse grinding paste around the sealing area of the valve head. Insert the valve in its guide and grind it to the seat using a valve grinding stick and rubber sucker. The stick is held between the hands and rotated first in one direction then in the opposite direction **(see illustration)**. Lift the valve occasionally to redistribute the grinding paste.

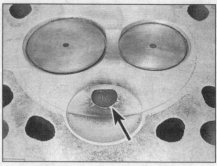

11.10B This swirl chamber shows the initial stages of cracking and burning (arrowed)

17 Wipe the paste from the valve and seat occasionally to check progress. When the sealing faces are unbroken and all pitting is removed, repeat the procedure using fine grinding paste.

18 After all the valves have been ground in, clean away all traces of grinding paste, first with a paraffin-soaked rag then with clean dry rags, finally with compressed air if available. Do not overlook the valve guides. It will be obvious that even a small quantity of grinding paste remaining in the engine could cause extremely rapid wear.

19 Examine the valve springs for signs of fatigue and if possible compare their length with a new spring. It is worth renewing all the springs if the engine has completed a high mileage.

20 Examine the tappets and their bores for scoring or other damage.

21 Examine the camshaft bearing surfaces in the cylinder head and bearing caps. Also examine the camshaft, referring to Section 7.

22 Inspect the studs for the manifolds and camshaft bearing caps. Renew them if necessary by using a proprietary stud extractor, or lock two nuts together on the exposed threads. Studs that have come out by mistake should be cleaned up and refitted using thread locking fluid.

Reassembly

23 Begin reassembly by oiling a valve stem and inserting it into its guide. With the cylinder head on its side, fit the spring seat followed by the two springs (either way up) and the retainer.

11.11B . . . then check the swirl chamber protrusion

11.14 Checking the valve head height

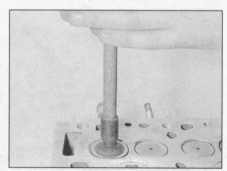

11.16 Grinding in the valves

24 Compress the springs (or spring) with the compressor and fit the collets. A smear of grease on the collets will hold them in place on the valve stem groove. Carefully release the compressor and remove it.

25 Repeat the procedure to fit the other seven valves. Refit the timing probe blank if removed.

26 Refit the inlet and exhaust manifolds with new gaskets and progressively tighten the nuts.

27 Insert and tighten the heater plugs to the specified torque (Chapter 4). Reconnect the wiring.

28 Insert and tighten the injectors with their washers to the specified torque (Chapter 4). Reconnect the leak off pipes.

29 Oil and insert the bucket tappets, together with their respective shims, making sure that they are fitted in the correct locations, and with the size markings downwards. Make a note of the shim thickness fitted at each position, if not already done, for reference when checking the valve clearances.

30 Refit the camshaft, referring to Section 7.

12 Cylinder head and pistons - decarbonisation

1 With the cylinder head removed as described in Section 9 or 10, as applicable, the carbon deposits should be removed from the valve heads and surrounding surfaces of the head. Use a blunt scraper or wire brush and take care not to damage the valve heads.

2 Where a more thorough job is to be carried out, the cylinder head should be dismantled as described in the previous Section so that the valves may be ground in and the parts cleaned, brushed and blown out after the manifolds have been removed. Also clean the manifolds, particularly the exhaust manifold where an accumulation of carbon is most likely.

3 Before grinding-in a valve, remove the carbon and deposits completely from its head and stem. With an inlet valve this is usually simply a matter of scraping off the carbon with a blunt knife and finishing with a wire brush. With an exhaust valve the deposits are much harder to remove. One method of cleaning valves quickly is to mount them in the chuck of an electric drill using a piece of card or foil to protect the surface of the stem. A scraper or wire brush may then be used carefully to remove the carbon.

4 An important part of the decarbonising operation is to remove the carbon deposits from the piston crowns. To do this, turn the crankshaft so that two pistons are at the top of their stroke and press some grease between these pistons and the cylinder walls. This will prevent carbon particles falling down into the piston ring grooves. Cover the other two bores and the cylinder block internal oil and water channels with newspaper taped down securely.

5 Using a blunt scraper remove all the carbon from the piston crowns, taking care not to score the soft alloy. Thoroughly clean the combustion spaces that are recessed in the piston crowns.

6 Remove the newspaper then rotate the crankshaft half a turn and repeat the cleaning operation on the remaining two pistons. Wipe away the grease from the top of the bores.

7 Finally clean the top surface of the cylinder block.

13 Oil seals - renewal

Note: *The procedures described here are for renewal with the engine in the vehicle - with the engine removed, the steps taken to gain access may be ignored.*

Camshaft (timing belt end)

Removal

1 Follow the procedure given in paragraphs 1 to 12 of Section 5.

2 Remove the timing belt from the camshaft sprocket and tie it to one side without bending it excessively.

3 Unscrew the M8 bolt holding the camshaft sprocket in the timing position.

4 Hold the camshaft sprocket stationary using a large screwdriver (or similar tool), through two of the holes **(see illustration)**. A tool may be made out of flat metal bar and two long bolts. Alternatively a strap wrench as used for removing oil filters may be used to hold the sprocket.

5 Unscrew the bolt and withdraw the sprocket from the camshaft. Do not rotate the camshaft otherwise the valves will strike the pistons of Nos 1 and 4 cylinders. Recover the Woodruff key if it is loose.

6 Pull out the oil seal using a hooked instrument.

Refitting

7 Clean the oil seal seating.

8 Smear the lip of the new oil seal with oil then fit it over the end of the camshaft, open end first, and press it in until flush with the end face of the cylinder head. Use an M10 bolt, washers and a socket to press it in **(see illustration)**.

9 Fit the Woodruff key (if removed) and the camshaft sprocket to the camshaft, insert the bolt and tighten it while holding the camshaft stationary.

10 Refit the M8 timing bolt to the camshaft sprocket.

11 Refit and adjust the timing belt, referring to Section 4, paragraphs 20 to 25. The remaining procedure is a reversal of removal.

Camshaft (flywheel end)

Removal

12 Remove the air cleaner.

13 Remove the inlet ducting as necessary.

14 Loosen the pivot and adjustment bolts of the brake vacuum pump, swivel the unit upwards, and disconnect the drivebelt from the pulleys.

2

13.4 Using a home made tool to prevent the camshaft sprocket from turning

13.8 Socket, bolt and washer for fitting the camshaft oil seals

13.18 Camshaft oil seal flush with the end face of the cylinder head

15 Unscrew the centre bolt and remove the pump pulley from the camshaft. If the centre bolt is very tight it will be necessary to remove the timing covers and hold the camshaft sprocket stationary while the bolt is loosened (to prevent damage to the timing belt). Recover the Woodruff key if it is loose.
16 Pull out the oil seal using a hooked instrument.

Refitting

17 Clean the oil seal seating.
18 Smear the lip of the new oil seal with oil then fit it over the end of the camshaft, open end first, and press it in until flush with the end face of the cylinder head **(see illustration)**. Use a bolt, washers and a socket to press it in.
19 Refit the Woodruff key (if removed) and the pump pulley to the camshaft and tighten the centre bolt.
20 Locate the drivebelt on the camshaft pulley and pump pulley then press the pump downwards until the deflection of the belt

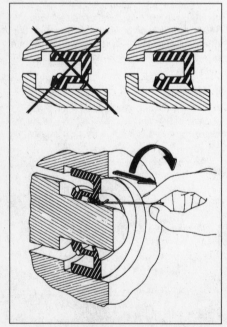

13.33A Correct fitting of the crankshaft flywheel end oil seal

13.26 Fitting the timing belt end oil seal to the crankshaft with a plastic protector

midway between the two pulleys is approximately 5.0 mm under firm thumb pressure. Tighten the adjustment bolt followed by the pivot bolt.
21 Refit the air cleaner.
22 Refit the inlet ducting.

Crankshaft (timing belt end)

Removal

23 Remove the timing belt as described in Section 4.
24 Slide the timing belt sprocket from the crankshaft and recover the Woodruff key if it is loose.
25 Note the fitted depth then pull the oil seal from the housing using a hooked instrument. Alternatively drill a small hole in the oil seal and use a self-tapping screw to remove it.

Refitting

26 Clean the housing and crankshaft then dip the new oil seal in engine oil and press it in (open end first) to the previously noted depth. A piece of thin plastic is useful to prevent damage to the oil seal **(see illustration)**.
27 Refit the Woodruff key and timing belt sprocket.
28 Refit the timing belt, referring to Section 4.

Crankshaft (flywheel end)

Removal

29 Remove the flywheel/driveplate as described in Section 18.
30 Using vernier calipers measure the fitted depth of the oil seal and record it.
31 Pull out the oil seal using a hooked

13.33B Fitting the flywheel end oil seal to the crankshaft with a plastic protector

instrument. Alternatively drill a small hole in the oil seal and use a self-tapping screw to remove it.

Refitting

32 Clean the oil seal seating and crankshaft flange.
33 Dip the new oil seal in engine oil, locate it on the crankshaft open end first, and press it in squarely to the previously noted depth using a metal tube. A piece of thin plastic is useful to prevent damage to the oil seal. When fitted note that the outer lip of the oil seal must point outwards; if it is pointing inwards use a piece of bent wire to pull it out **(see illustrations)**.
34 Refit the flywheel/driveplate, referring to Section 18.

14 Sump - removal and refitting

Removal

1 Chock the rear wheels then jack up the front of the car and support on axle stands. (see "*Jacking and vehicle support*")
2 Position a container beneath the engine.
3 Unscrew the drain plug and allow the oil to drain from the sump.
4 Wipe clean the drain plug and refit it.
5 Note the location of the sump bolts, then unscrew them.
6 Remove the sump and gasket **(see illustration)**. The sump will probably be stuck in position in which case it will be necessary to cut it free using a thin knife.

Refitting

7 Clean all remains of gasket from the sump and block and wipe dry.
8 Apply a little sealing compound where the front housing abuts the block on both sides.
9 Position a new gasket on the sump then lift the sump into position and insert the bolts in their correct locations.
10 Tighten the bolts evenly to the specified torque.
11 Lower the car to the ground and refill the engine with the correct quantity and grade of oil.

14.6 Removing the sump

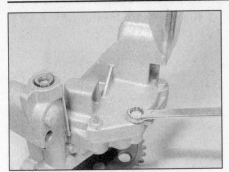

15.9A Unscrew the oil pump bolts . . .

15.9B . . . separate the halves . . .

15.9C . . . and remove the relief valve spring . . .

15.9D . . . and plunger

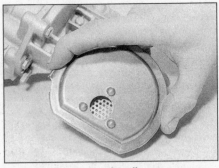

15.10A Removing the oil pump cap . . .

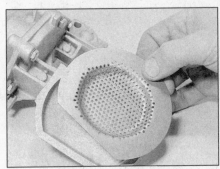

15.10B . . . and strainer

15 Oil pump - removal, inspection and refitting

Note: *From April 1987, the oil pump spacer and location dowel are no longer fitted. The height of the pump is increased to compensate. A new pump may be fitted in place of an old one, provided that the spacer and dowel are discarded. Thicker washers must be fitted under the heads of the oil pump bolts. On XUD 7T engines, a thin spacer is still fitted between the oil pump and the block.*

Removal

1 Remove the timing belt (Section 4).
2 Slide the timing belt sprocket from the crankshaft and recover the Woodruff key if it is loose.
3 Remove the sump as described in Section 14.

4 Unscrew the bolts and remove the front oil seal housing. Remove the gasket.
5 Unscrew the three bolts securing the oil pump to the crankcase. Identify them for position as all three are of different lengths.
6 Withdraw the L-shaped spacer from beneath the oil pump, if applicable.
7 Remove the location dowel (if fitted) and disengage the oil pump sprocket from the chain. Withdraw the oil pump.
8 Remove the chain and sprocket from the nose of the crankshaft and recover the Woodruff key if it is loose.
9 Remove the six bolts which hold the two halves of the oil pump together. Separate the halves, being prepared for the release of the relief valve spring and plungers **(see illustrations)**.
10 If necessary remove the strainer by prising off the cap, then clean all components **(see illustrations)**.

Inspection

11 Inspect the gears and the housings for wear and damage. Check the endfloat of the gears using a straight-edge and feeler blades, also check the clearance between the tip of the gear lobes and the housing **(see illustrations)**. If any of these clearances exceeds the specified limit, renew the pump. Note that except for the relief valve spring and plunger, individual components are not available.
12 If the pump is to be renewed it is wise to renew the chain and the crankshaft sprocket also.

Refitting

13 Lubricate the gears with engine oil then reassemble the oil pump in reverse order and tighten the six bolts evenly to the specified torque.

2

15.11A Oil pump rotors and housing

15.11B Checking the rotor endfloat

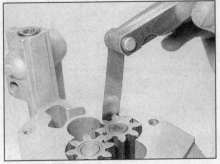

15.11C Checking the rotor side clearance

15.18 Tightening the oil pump mounting bolts
(Longest bolt arrowed. Next longest bolt being tightened)

14 Locate the Woodruff key on the nose of the crankshaft and refit the sprocket, teeth end first. Engage the chain with the sprocket.
15 Prise the oil seal from the front housing. Refit the housing to the cylinder block, together with a new gasket, and tighten the bolts evenly to the specified torque.
16 Fit a new oil seal to the housing, referring to Section 13.
17 Check that the location dowel is fitted to the block. Engage the oil pump sprocket with the chain and slide the L-shaped spacer into position, making sure that its open end engages the dowel.
18 Insert the bolts in their correct locations. The longest bolt through the dowel and the next longest by the oil return hole. Tighten the bolts evenly to the specified torque **(see illustration)**.
19 Refit the sump, referring to Section 14.
20 Refit the Woodruff key and timing belt sprocket.
21 Refit the timing belt, referring to Section 4.

16 Oil cooler - general, removal and refitting

General

1 From late 1990, the oil cooler mounting is improved, to ensure that the oil cooler remains stationary while the oil filter is being removed **(see illustration)**. A retaining lug is provided on the cylinder block, which engages with a fork on the oil cooler.
2 On earlier engines not fitted with the modified retaining lug, it is possible to obtain an anti-rotation bracket that may be bolted to the cylinder block. The bracket effectively stops the oil cooler from rotating.

Removal

3 To remove the oil cooler, first remove the oil filter.
4 Remove the cooling system filler/pressure cap (engine cold). Disconnect the coolant hoses from the filter. Be prepared for coolant spillage, and plug the open ends of the hoses to prevent further coolant loss.
5 Unscrew the oil filter mounting stub, then withdraw the oil cooler from the engine.

Refitting

6 Refitting is a reversal of removal, remembering the following points:
a) *When refitting the oil cooler, ensure that the fork on the cooler engages with the lug on the cylinder block (or, if applicable, locates beneath the anti-rotation bracket on the side of the cylinder block).*
b) *Before refitting the oil filter mounting stub, thoroughly clean the threads, and coat them with thread-locking compound.*

c) *Tighten the mounting stub to the specified torque.*

17 Pistons and connecting rods - removal and refitting

Removal

1 Remove the cylinder head as described in Section 9 or 10, as applicable.
2 Remove the oil pump (Section 15).
3 If there is a pronounced wear ridge at the top of any bore, it may be necessary to remove it with a scraper or ridge reamer to avoid piston damage during removal. Such a ridge may indicate that reboring is necessary, which will entail new pistons in any case.
4 Check that each connecting rod and cap is marked for position and, if not, mark them with a centre punch on the oil filter side, number one at the flywheel end.
5 Turn the crankshaft to bring pistons 1 and 4 to BDC (bottom dead centre). Unscrew the nuts from No 1 piston big-end bearing cap, then take off the cap and recover the bottom half bearing shell **(see illustration)**.
6 Using a hammer handle push the piston up through the bore and remove it from the block. Loosely refit the shell bearings and cap to ensure correct reassembly.
7 Remove No 4 piston in the same manner then turn the crankshaft 180° to bring pistons 2 and 3 to BDC (bottom dead centre) and remove them.
8 If new piston rings are to be fitted to old bores, the bores must be deglazed to allow the new rings to bed-in properly. Protect the big-end journals by wrapping them in masking tape, then use a piece of coarse emery paper to produce a cross-hatch pattern in each bore. A flap wheel in an electric drill may be used, but beware of spreading abrasive dust. When deglazing is complete wash away all abrasive particles and unwrap the big-end journals.

Refitting

9 Begin refitting by laying out the assembled pistons and rods in order, with the bearing shells, connecting rod caps and nuts.

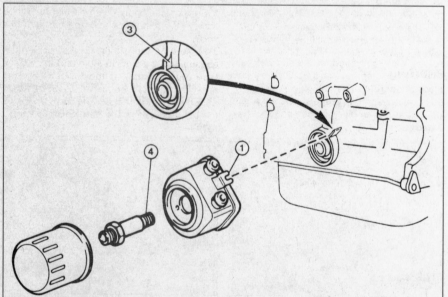

16.1 Oil cooler fitted to models from late 1990
1 Oil cooler fork   3 Cylinder block lug   4 Oil filter mounting stub

17.5 Removing a big-end bearing cap

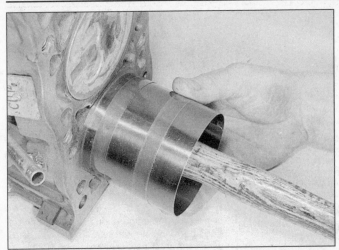

17.13 Using a hammer handle to tap the piston through the ring compressor

17.14 Tightening the big-end bearing cap nuts

10 Arrange the piston ring gaps 120° from each other.

11 Clean the bearing shells, caps and rods then press the shells into position so that the locating tangs engage in the grooves.

12 Oil the bores, pistons, crankpins and shells. Fit a piston ring compressor to No 1 piston. With Nos 1 and 4 crankpins at BDC insert No 1 piston in the bore nearest the flywheel, making sure that the clover leaf cut-out on the piston crown is towards the oil filter side of the engine.

13 Using a hammer handle tap the piston through the ring compressor and into the bore **(see illustration)**. Guide the connecting rod onto the crankpin and fit the cap, together with its shell bearing, making sure it is the correct way round.

14 Fit the nuts and tighten them to the specified torque **(see illustration)**. Turn the crankshaft to check for free movement.

15 Repeat the procedure to fit the other three pistons.

16 Refit the oil pump, referring to Section 15.

17 Refit the cylinder head, referring to Section 9 or 10, as applicable.

18 Flywheel/driveplate - removal and refitting

Removal

1 Either remove the engine and transmission and separate them (described in the following Sections), or remove the transmission alone as described in the appropriate main manual.

2 Make alignment marks then slacken the clutch pressure plate bolts progressively and remove the pressure plate and driven plate **(see illustration)**.

3 Hold the flywheel/driveplate stationary with a screwdriver or bar inserted between the teeth of the starter ring gear and the transmission location dowel, then unscrew and remove the bolts and lift the flywheel/driveplate from the crankshaft. Alignment marks are not required as there is a location dowel on the crankshaft flange. Obtain new bolts for reassembly.

Refitting

4 Begin refitting by cleaning the mating surfaces of the crankshaft and flywheel/driveplate.

5 Locate the flywheel/driveplate on the crankshaft dowel.

6 Apply locking fluid to the threads of the bolts, insert them, and tighten them to the specified torque while holding the flywheel/driveplate stationary **(see illustrations)**.

7 On manual transmission models refit the clutch driven and pressure plates.

8 Refit the transmission and the engine, if removed.

19 Engine/transmission mountings - removal and refitting

Right-hand mounting

Removal

1 Support the engine with a hoist or with a trolley jack and block of wood beneath the sump.

2 Make up a tool similar to that shown, to engage with the slots in the rim of the rubber **(see illustrations)**. If the rubber is being renewed, the new component can be used as a guide when making the tool. Unscrew the old rubber from the body using the tool.

18.2 Removing the clutch pressure plate and driven plate

18.6A Apply locking fluid to the flywheel bolts . . .

18.6B . . . then insert and tighten them

On Horizon models, first remove the centre timing cover.

3 Unscrew the nuts and remove the right-hand mounting bracket, noting the location of any shims.

Refitting

4 Refitting is a reversal of removal. Tighten the rubber firmly to the body using the tool, to the specified torque. With the weight of the engine on the mounting, the clearance between the mounting bracket and each rubber stop should be 1.0 ± 0.7 mm. If necessary adjust the clearance by means of shims positioned under the stops.

Left-hand mounting

Removal

5 Support the transmission with a hoist or with a trolley jack and block of wood.

6 Remove the air cleaner and trunking.

7 Remove the battery and battery tray.

8 Unscrew the nut and remove the rubber mounting. On Horizon models, first knock back the locking tab. Also unscrew the nuts or bolts and remove the mounting bracket.

9 If necessary unscrew the mounting stud from the transmission casing.

Refitting

10 Refitting is a reversal of removal, but before fitting the mounting stud, clean the threads and apply a little locking fluid. Tighten the nuts and bolts to the specified torque. On Horizon models, lock the bolt by bending the lock tab.

Lower mounting

Removal

11 Jack up the front of the car and support on axle stands (see "*Jacking and vehicle support*").

12 Unscrew and remove both bolts from the torque link and withdraw the link.

Refitting

13 Drive or press the mounting from the housing.

14 Drive or press the new mounting into position then refit the torque link and tighten the bolts to the specified torque.

15 Lower the car to the ground.

20 Engine, methods of removal
- general

The engine is removed together with the transmission by lowering from the engine compartment.

It is possible to remove the transmission alone from under the vehicle, after which it would, in theory, be possible to remove the engine separately. However, this method is not recommended as it involves the extra work of disconnecting the transmission which, if required is best carried out with the engine and transmission removed from the vehicle.

19.2A Home-made tool for removing the engine mounting rubber

19.2C Using the tool to unscrew the rubber

21 Engine and transmission (except 405 models) - removal and refitting

Removal

1 Either remove the bonnet, or raise it to the highest position. On 205 models, unbolt the strut from the right-hand suspension tower, raise the bonnet and retain it by inserting U-bolts thorough special holes in the bonnet hinges.

2 If available, on 309 models, fit Peugeot special cables (No.'s 0903) to the front suspension struts as described in the main manual. Loosen the strut mounting nuts.

3 Apply the handbrake then jack up the front of the vehicle and support on axle stands (see "*Jacking and vehicle support*"). Allow at least 60cm between the bumper and the ground for

21.5 Using a hexagonal key to unscrew the transmission oil drain plug

19.2B Engine mounting rubber in position, showing slots

19.2D Removing the engine mounting rubber

removing the engine and transmission. Remove both front wheels.

4 Drain the cooling system as described in Chapter 1.

5 Using a hexagonal key, unscrew the drain plug and drain the transmission oil into a container **(see illustration)**. When completely drained refit and tighten the drain plug.

6 Drain the engine oil, as described in Chapter 1.

7 Remove the air cleaner assembly, as described in Chapter 4.

8 Disconnect the battery leads (negative lead first), then unscrew the clamp bolt and remove the battery and tray **(see illustration)**.

9 Remove the radiator, as described in Chapter 3.

10 Disconnect the top hose from the thermostat housing and the expansion hose(s) from the expansion tank and thermostat housing **(see illustrations)**.

21.8 Battery clamp (205 models)

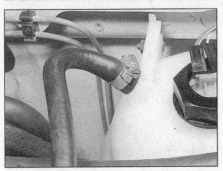

21.10A Disconnect the expansion hose from the expansion tank . . .

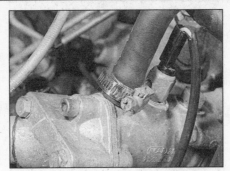

21.10B . . . and thermostat housing . . .

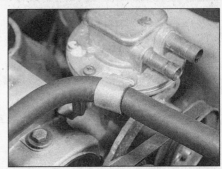

21.10C . . . and release it from the clip

11 Disconnect the heater hoses at the bulkhead (see illustration).
12 Where applicable, remove the power steering pump, without disconnecting the hoses, and secure it to one side.

13 Working under the right-hand wheel arch, remove the engine shield. Where applicable, disconnect the wiring for the front disc pad warning system (see illustrations).
14 Disconnect the bottom hose from the

block and, where fitted, remove the metal pipe from the right-hand inner wing panel (see illustration).
15 Disconnect the heater supply hose from the rear of the cylinder head (see illustration).

21.11 Heater hose location on the bulkhead (205 models)

21.13A Front disc pad warning system wiring connector (205 models)

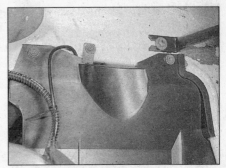

21.13B Engine shield . . .

2

21.13C . . . and mounting bolt removal (205 models)

21.13D Engine shield side mounting bolt (arrowed) . . .

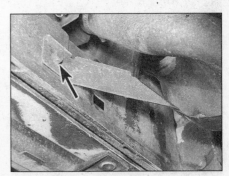

21.13E . . . front mounting bolt (arrowed) . . .

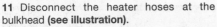

21.13F . . . and rear mounting bolt (arrowed), (Horizon models)

21.14 Coolant intermediate metal pipe (205 models)

21.15 Heater supply hose on rear of cylinder head

21.16A Bypass hose on the water pump inlet (arrowed)

21.16B Bypass hose retaining clips (arrowed)

21.16C Disconnecting the bypass hose from the cylinder head

16 Unclip and disconnect the bypass hose from the water pump inlet and front of the cylinder head **(see illustrations)**.

17 On Horizon models, unbolt and remove the coolant expansion tank **(see illustration)**.

The expansion tank may also be removed from other models, to provide additional work space.

18 Disconnect the engine wiring harness, located next to where the battery is normally

fitted, and release the securing clip on the transmission **(see illustrations)**.

19 Disconnect the wiring from the following:-
a) *Starter motor*
b) *Alternator*
c) *Water temperature switch (see illustrations)*
d) *Oil level switch (see illustration)*
e) *Oil pressure switch (see illustration)*
f) *Reversing lamp switch (see illustration)*
g) *Heater plugs*
h) *Stop solenoid on the injection pump*
i) *Diagnostic socket (see illustration)*

20 Unbolt the earth cable(s) from the transmission **(see illustrations)**.

21 On Horizon models, unbolt the clutch slave cylinder and position it to one side **(see illustration)**.

21.17 Coolant expansion tank on Horizon models

21.18A Engine wiring harness connector . . .

21.18B . . . and harness clip (205 models)

21.19A Water temperature switch (arrowed)

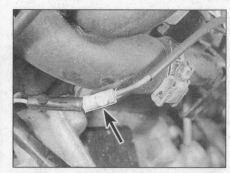

21.19B . . . and wiring connector (arrowed)

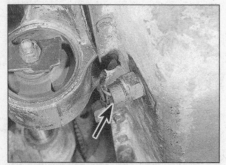

21.19C Oil level switch (205 models)

21.19D Oil pressure switch

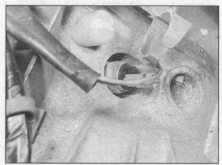

21.19E Reversing lamp switch

21.19F Diagnostic socket - arrowed (Horizon models)

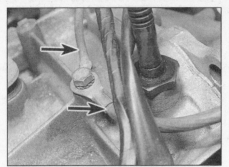

21.20A Earth cables - arrowed (205 models)

21.20B Earth cable - arrowed (Horizon models)

22 On other models, disconnect the clutch cable and recover the pushrod **(see illustration)**.

23 Disconnect the speedometer cable from the transmission.

24 Disconnect the accelerator cable from the injection pump and secure it one side.

25 Disconnect the vacuum hose from the vacuum pump and brake servo unit. Also disconnect the discharge hose from the pump

and inlet manifold.

26 Disconnect the fuel supply and return hoses from the injection pump.

27 Where fitted, unscrew the nut and remove the reverse gear stop cable from the top of the transmission **(see illustrations)**. Position the cable to one side.

28 Disconnect the gearchange control rods at the transmission end. A small open ended spanner will prove useful in prising off the rods **(see illustrations)**.

29 Unscrew and remove the exhaust manifold to downpipe bolts, together with the springs and collars **(see illustrations)**.

30 Unscrew the bolts and nuts securing the front lower suspension arms to the hub carriers **(see illustration)**. Unbolt the anti-roll bar links on 305 models.

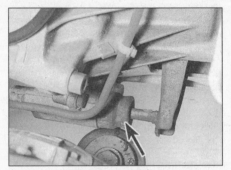

21.21 Clutch slave cylinder - arrowed (Horizon models)

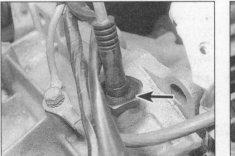

21.22 Clutch cable - arrowed (except Horizon models)

2

21.27A Unscrew the nut (arrowed) . . .

21.27B . . . and remove the reverse gear stop cable

21.28A Disconnecting the gearchange engagement rod (205 models)

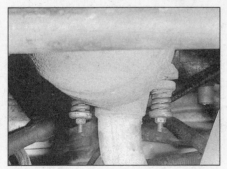

21.28B Disconnecting the gearchange selection rod (205 models)

21.28C Gearchange control rods on Horizon models

21.29A Exhaust manifold to downpipe bolts

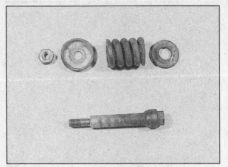

21.29B Exhaust manifold-to-downpipe bolt, spring and collars

21.30 Lower suspension arm to hub carrier bolt (arrowed)

21.33 Removing the left-hand driveshaft

31 On models other than the Horizon, use a lever to move the suspension arms down in turn, so that the balljoints are removed from the bottom of the hub carriers. Retrieve the balljoint protectors, if fitted.

32 On Horizon models, use a balljoint separator tool to release the balljoints, but leave them in the suspension arms, at this stage.

33 Have an assistant pull the left-hand hub carrier outwards while the left-hand driveshaft is levered from the differential side gear **(see illustration)**. Use a block of wood to hold the hub carrier out.

34 On models built before July 1984, the left-hand differential side gear must be supported using a dowel, preferably wooden. If this precaution is not taken, the side gears may become misaligned when the right-hand driveshaft is removed.

35 On models, other than the Horizon, loosen the two nuts retaining the right-hand driveshaft intermediate bearing in the lower engine mounting bracket bolted to the rear of the cylinder block and turn the bolt heads through 90° in order to release the bearing **(see illustrations)**.

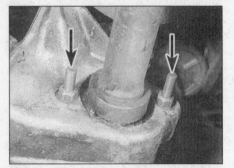

21.35A Right-hand driveshaft intermediate bearing bolts - arrowed (except Horizon models)

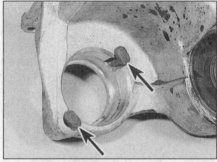

21.35B Special bolt heads (arrowed) on the right-hand driveshaft intermediate bearing (except Horizon models)

36 On Horizon models, unscrew the nuts and remove the clamp retaining the right-hand driveshaft intermediate bearing in the lower engine mounting bracket bolted to the rear of the cylinder block **(see illustration)**.

37 Have an assistant pull the right-hand hub carrier outwards while the right-hand driveshaft is levered from the differential side gear **(see illustration)**. Use a block of wood to hold the hub carrier out.

38 Unscrew the nuts from the lower engine mounting torque link bolts at the mounting and the crossmember, noting the location of any spacers **(see illustrations)**.

39 Unscrew the bolts and lever the lower engine mounting from the dowels on the block **(see illustration)**.

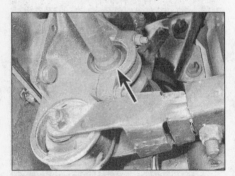

21.36 Right-hand driveshaft intermediate bearing on Horizon models (arrowed)

21.37 Removing the right-hand driveshaft

21.38A Lower engine mounting (except Horizon models)

21.38B Removing a spacer from the lower engine mounting

21.38C Removing the lower engine mounting torque link (not Horizon models)

21.38D Lower engine mounting bracket
(Horizon models)

21.39 Removing the lower engine
mounting bracket from the dowels

21.40A Remove the bracket . . .

40 On models, other than the Horizon, remove the bracket, swivel the right-hand driveshaft to the front and tie it to the front towing eye (see illustrations).

41 On Horizon models, tie the driveshaft to the rear.

42 Connect a hoist to the engine lifting brackets (see illustration), so that the engine

and transmission are supported in a horizontal position. Take the weight of the assembly.

43 Unscrew the nuts and remove the right-hand engine mounting bracket (see illustrations). On Horizon models, first remove the centre timing cover section.

44 Unscrew the nut/bolt from the left-hand engine mounting (see illustration). On Horizon models, first knock back the locking tab. Unscrew the nut(s) and remove the mounting rubber (see illustration).

45 Lower the engine and transmission to the ground, taking care not to damage the surrounding components in the engine compartment (see illustrations).

46 Withdraw the assembly from under the vehicle.

21.40B . . . and tie the right-hand
driveshaft to the front towing eye (except
Horizon models)

21.40C Lower engine mounting bracket
removed

2

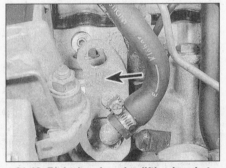

21.42 Right-hand engine lifting bracket
(arrowed)

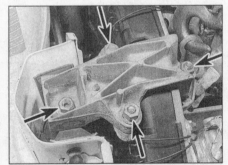

21.43A Unscrew the nuts (arrowed)

21.43B . . . and remove the right-hand
engine mounting bracket

21.43C Right-hand engine mounting
bracket on Horizon models

21.44A Left-hand engine mounting (except
Horizon models)

21.44B Left-hand engine mounting
(Horizon models)

21.45A Lower the engine and transmission to the ground . . .

21.45B . . . and remove from under the vehicle

47 If the vehicle must be moved with the engine and transmission out, reconnect the suspension arms to the hub carriers, refit the roadwheels and support the driveshafts in their normal position with wire, so that they can rotate without damage.

Refitting

48 Refitting is the reversal of the removal procedure, but note the following additional points:

a) *Use a final drive oil seal protector (Chapter 6) when inserting the right-hand driveshaft. Remove the protector when the driveshaft is fitted*

b) *Refill the transmission and engine with oil*

c) *Adjust the accelerator and fast idle cables, referring to Chapter 4*

d) *On XUD 7 models, tighten the exhaust manifold-to-downpipe bolts, referring to Section 9, paragraph 45*

e) *Refit the engine/transmission mountings, referring to Section 19*

f) *Adjust the clutch cable (not Horizon models)*

g) *Refill the cooling system (Chapter 1)*

h) *Check the injection pump timing if necessary*

49 On turbo models, prime the turbo lubrication circuit before start-up by disconnecting the stop solenoid lead at the fuel pump and cranking the engine on the starter for three ten-second bursts.

22 Engine and transmission (405 models) - removal and refitting

Note: *The engine is removed downwards from the engine compartment. This Section describes the removal and refitting procedure for an XUD9 engine; the procedure for an XUD7 turbo engine is very similar.*

Removal

1 Apply the handbrake, then jack up the front of the vehicle and support it on axle stands (see "*Jacking and vehicle support*"). Remove both front wheels.

2 Drain the cooling system.

3 Unscrew the drain plug from the gearbox, and drain the oil into a container. Clean the plug, and refit it on completion.

4 If necessary, drain the engine oil.

5 Disconnect the battery (if not already done) and remove the preheater control unit.

6 Remove the intercooler or the air distribution box.

7 Remove the battery and battery tray.

8 Remove the air cleaner and bracket, and the air inlet hoses **(see illustration)**.

9 Unbolt the vibration damper from the top of the engine right-hand mounting.

10 Disconnect the fuel pipe from the fuel system hand-priming pump by removing the collar **(see illustration)**.

11 Identify the location of all hoses, wiring and cables connected to the engine and gearbox; disconnect them, and where necessary release them from their clips. Do not forget to disconnect the wiring connector box and the in-line connector on the left-hand side of the engine compartment **(see illustrations)**.

12 Working under the vehicle, unbolt and remove the engine right-hand rear mounting torque reaction link from the underbody and engine bracket **(see illustration)**.

22.8 Removing an air inlet hose

22.10 Fuel system hand-priming pump connection

22.11A Wiring connection to the temperature sensor

22.11B Thermal sender wiring connection

22.11C Engine wiring connector box

22.12 Engine right-hand rear mounting

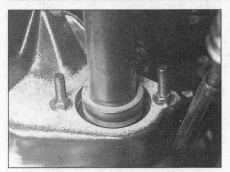

22.13 Right-hand driveshaft intermediate shaft bearing retaining nuts

22.14 Anti-roll bar mounting bolt on the front lower suspension arm

22.18 Lower suspension arm-to-steering knuckle mounting nut

13 Loosen (but do not remove) the nuts securing the right-hand driveshaft intermediate shaft bearing to the bracket on the engine **(see illustration)**. Turn the bolts through 90° and release them from the bracket.
14 On each side of the vehicle, unscrew the bolt securing the anti-roll bar to the front lower suspension arm **(see illustration)**.
15 Working on each side in turn, unscrew the lower screws and move the splash shield to one side. Tie the shields to hold them out of the way.

16 Remove the power steering pump (where applicable), leaving the fluid pipes and hoses still connected. Tie the pump to one side.
17 Remove the air conditioning compressor (where applicable), leaving the pipes and hoses still connected. Tie the compressor to one side.
18 Working on each side in turn, unscrew the nut securing the suspension lower arm to the steering knuckle. Separate the arm from the knuckle using a balljoint separator **(see illustration)**.
19 With the help of an assistant, pull the

steering knuckles outwards, and pull the driveshafts out of the differential side gears in the gearbox. Tie the driveshafts to one side.
20 Disconnect the gearbox gearchange rods **(see illustration)**.
21 Unbolt the exhaust downpipe from the exhaust manifold **(see illustration)**.
22 Disconnect the speedometer cable from the gearbox.
23 Disconnect the clutch cable from the gearbox.
24 On Turbo models, loosen the clip and remove the air inlet hose and bracket located near the engine right-hand mounting.
25 On Turbo models, remove the rubber stop (where fitted) from the top of the engine right-hand mounting.
26 Connect a hoist to the engine and gearbox, and take the weight of the assembly.
27 Unbolt and remove the engine right-hand mounting **(see illustrations)**.
28 Unscrew and remove the nut from the engine left-hand mounting.
29 Carefully lower the engine and gearbox assembly onto the floor, taking care not to damage any surrounding components in the engine compartment.

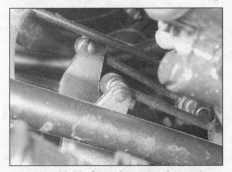

22.20 Gearchange rods

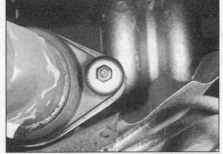

22.21 Exhaust downpipe mounting

22.27A Engine right-hand mounting outer nuts. . .

22.27B . . . and inner nut (arrowed)

2

Refitting

30 Refitting is a reversal of the removal procedure, but note the following points:

a) *If necessary, renew the driveshaft oil seals located in each side of the gearbox casing.*

b) *Tighten all nuts and bolts to the specified torque.*

c) *Check and if necessary adjust the clutch pedal travel.*

d) *Refill the gearbox with the correct quantity and grade of oil.*

e) *Refill the cooling system (see illustration).*

f) *Refill the engine with oil (see illustration).*

g) *Prime the fuel system if necessary, as described in Chapter 4*

22.30A Refilling the cooling system

22.30B Refilling the engine with oil

---

23 Engine and transmission - separation and reconnection

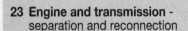

Separation

1 With the engine and transmission removed from the vehicle clean away all external dirt.

2 Slacken the bolts and remove the TDC sensor **(see illustration)**. Remove the bolts and withdraw the sensor holder.

3 Unbolt and remove the starter motor using a hexagonal key.

4 Unbolt the bottom cover from the transmission **(see illustration)**.

5 Support the engine then unscrew the bolts and lift the transmission from the engine.

Reconnection

6 Support the engine then lift the transmission into position. Turn the unit as required until the splined input shaft enters the clutch driven plate.

7 Push the transmission onto the location dowels and insert the bolts in their correct locations as previously noted. Tighten the bolts to the specified torque (Chapter 6).

8 Refit the bottom cover and tighten the bolts.

9 Refit the starter motor, tighten the bolts, and reconnect the wiring.

10 Refit the TDC sensor and holder and tighten the bolts. When the TDC sensor is fitted new it incorporates three legs that are 1.0 mm long and these automatically set the sensor 1.0 mm from the flywheel/driveplate. When fitting an old sensor the legs should be filed off - the unit can then be fully inserted until it touches the flywheel/driveplate and then withdrawn by 1.0 mm before tightening the bolts.

24 Engine overhaul - preparation

Note: Many components are specific to Turbo models. Although the parts may appear to be the same they are not all interchangeable.

1 Clean the engine thoroughly using a water-soluble grease solvent or similar product. Keep dirt and water out of vulnerable components such as the fuel injection pump and the alternator.

2 When possible the engine should be dismantled on a workbench or strong table. If an engine dismantling stand is available, so much the better. Avoid working directly on a concrete floor, as grit presents a serious problem. If there is no alternative to working on the floor, cover it with an old piece of lino or carpet.

3 As well as the usual selection of tools, have available some wooden blocks for propping up the engine. A notebook and pencil will be needed, as will a couple of segmented boxes or a good supply of plastic bags and labels.

4 A waterproof marker pen is useful for making alignment marks, without having to use to punches or chisels, however, take care that the marks are not erased during cleaning.

5 Whenever possible, refit nuts, washers etc. to the components from where they were removed. This makes reassembly much easier.

6 Spills of oil, fuel and coolant are bound to occur during dismantling. Have rags and newspapers handy to mop up the mess.

7 Do not throw away old gaskets immediately, but save them for comparison with new ones or for use as patterns if new gaskets have to be made.

8 Before starting reassembly, make sure that all parts are clean and that the new components required have been obtained. A full set of oil seals and gaskets must be bought - refer to Section 9 or 10, as applicable, for selection of the correct head gasket.

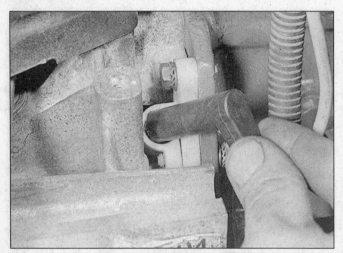

23.2 Removing the TDC sensor

23.4 Transmission bottom cover

25.3A Removing the left timing cover section

25.3B . . . and the right timing cover section

9 Renew any nuts, bolts or studs with damaged threads.
10 A dial test indicator and stand (preferably magnetic) will be needed, also an oil can filled with clean engine oil to lubricate working parts as they are assembled.
11 Small quantities of grease, thread locking compound, anti-seize compound and various types of sealant will be called for.
12 Have ready a good quantity of lint-free rags for wiping excess oil off hands and engine parts.

25 Engine overhaul - dismantling

Note: *Refer to Section 24, before this procedure.*
1 If not already done, drain the engine oil.
2 Remove the brake vacuum pump as described in Chapter 7.
3 Pull up the special clip (if fitted), release the

25.4 Diagnostic socket and mounting bolt

25.5 Removing the pump pulley from the flywheel end of the camshaft

spring clips, and withdraw the two timing cover sections **(see illustrations)**.
4 Unbolt and remove the diagnostic socket and bracket where fitted **(see illustration)**.
5 Unscrew the bolt and withdraw the pump pulley from the flywheel end of the camshaft **(see illustration)**. If it is tight due to corrosion, use a two or three-legged puller to remove it. Recover the Woodruff key.

6 Note the location of the fuel pipes from the injection pump to the injectors then unscrew the union nuts and remove the pipe assemblies. Cover the pipe ends, the injectors and the injection pump outlets to prevent entry of dust and dirt. Small plastic bags and elastic bands are ideal for this **(see illustrations)**.
7 Pull the leak-off hoses from the injectors.

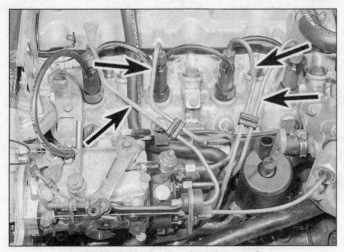

25.6A Fuel pipe locations (arrowed)

25.6B Small plastic bags can be used to protect the injectors from dust and dirt

25.8 Engine lifting bracket

25.13 Sump inlet and crankcase ventilation hose

8 Unbolt the engine lifting bracket from the cylinder head **(see illustration)**.
9 Remove the alternator (Chapter 5) and bracket.
10 Unscrew the oil filter cartridge using a strap wrench if necessary.
11 Where fitted, disconnect the hoses from the oil cooler. Unscrew the centre stud and remove the oil cooler from the block. Disconnect the oil cooler hoses.
12 Disconnect the bottom hose from the water pump inlet, if not already done so.
13 Disconnect the crankcase ventilation hoses from the valve cover and sump inlet

(see illustration). Remove the clip and slide the oil separator from the dipstick tube.
14 Remove the oil filler cap and ventilation hose if fitted.
15 Unscrew the bolts and remove the inlet manifold from the cylinder head. There are no gaskets.
16 Unscrew the nuts and withdraw the exhaust manifold and gaskets from the studs, complete with turbo, if applicable.
17 Slacken the bolt and remove the clamp from the end of the fast idle cable. Unscrew the locknut and remove the fast idle outer cable from the bracket on the injection pump.

18 Unscrew and remove the oil level sensor from the cylinder block, if fitted **(see illustrations)**. Unscrew the oil temperature sensor, if fitted. This can be found just above the oil filter.
19 Unscrew and remove the oil pressure switch **(see illustration)**.
20 Unbolt the thermostat housing from the cylinder head, complete with the fast idle thermo-unit and temperature sensor(s) **(see illustrations)**.
21 Unbolt the water pump inlet and remove the gasket. Also unbolt the coolant tube from the cylinder block **(see illustrations)**.
22 Unscrew the nuts securing the inlet bracket to the sump. Remove the bracket and gasket **(see illustrations)**.
23 Have an assistant hold the flywheel/driveplate stationary with a screwdriver or bar inserted between the teeth of the starter ring gear and the transmission location dowel, then unscrew the crankshaft pulley bolt. Slide the pulley from the front of the crankshaft **(see illustration)**.
24 Unbolt the bottom timing cover **(see illustration)**.
25 Turn the engine by the flywheel/driveplate until the three bolt holes in the camshaft and injection pump sprockets are aligned with the corresponding holes in the engine front plate.

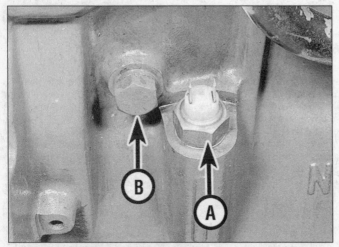

25.18A Oil level sensor (A) located in the cylinder block. Coolant drain plug (B) is adjacent

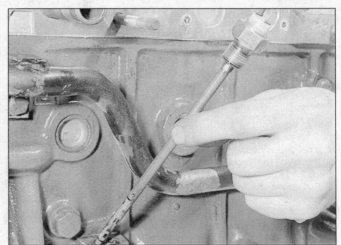

25.18B Removing the oil level sensor

25.19 Removing the oil pressure switch

25.20A Unscrew the bolts . . .

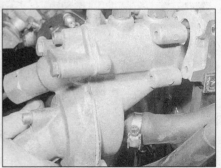

25.20B . . . and remove the thermostat housing

25.21A Removing the water pump inlet

25.21B Coolant tube mounting on the rear of the cylinder block

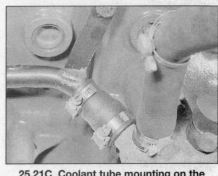

25.21C Coolant tube mounting on the front of the cylinder block

26 Insert an 8.0 to 8.5 mm diameter metal dowel rod or twist drill through the special hole in the left-hand rear flange of the cylinder block. Then carefully turn the engine either way until the rod enters the TDC hole in the

flywheel/driveplate **(see illustration)**.
27 Insert three M8 bolts through the holes in the camshaft and injection pump sprockets and screw them into the engine front plate finger tight.

28 Loosen the timing belt tensioner pivot nut and adjustment bolt, then turn the bracket anti-clockwise to release the tension and retighten the adjustment bolt to hold the tensioner in the released position.
29 Mark the timing belt with an arrow to indicate its normal direction of turning then remove it from the camshaft, injection pump, water pump, and crankshaft sprockets.
30 Unbolt and remove the valve cover. Remove the gasket.
31 With the injection pump sprocket held stationary by the timing bolts, unscrew the central nut to release the sprocket from the pump shaft taper. Remove the timing bolts and the pump sprocket with its nut and puller, and recover the Woodruff key if it is loose **(see illustrations)**. The puller is incorporated in the sprocket by means of the plate bolted over the nut, and the nut has an outer shoulder that bears against the plate.

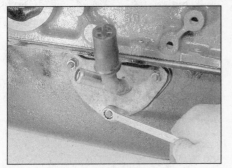

25.22A Unscrew the nuts . . .

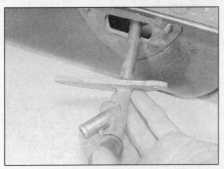

25.22B . . . and remove the inlet bracket . . .

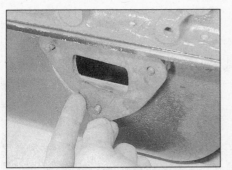

25.22C . . . and gasket

25.23 Removing the crankshaft pulley

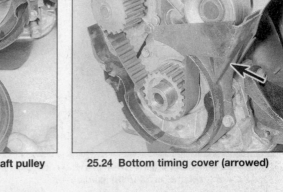

25.24 Bottom timing cover (arrowed)

25.26 Using a twist drill to enter the TDC hole in the flywheel

25.31A Unscrew the nut . . .

25.31B . . . and remove the injection pump sprocket

2

25.36 Injection pump mounting bracket

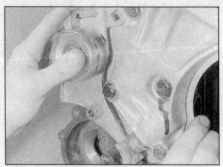

25.37 Removing the tensioner arm and roller

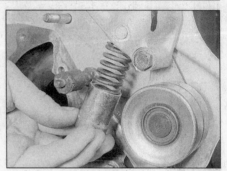

25.38 Removing the tensioner plunger and spring

32 Similarly unscrew the bolt from the camshaft sprocket and withdraw the sprocket.

33 Slide the sprocket from the crankshaft and recover the Woodruff key if it is loose.

34 Unscrew the bolts and remove the water pump from the cylinder block. Remove the gasket.

35 Mark the injection pump in relation to the mounting bracket. Unscrew the nuts and bolt and withdraw the injection pump.

36 Unbolt and remove the mounting bracket **(see illustration)**.

37 Unscrew the timing belt tensioner adjustment bolt and pivot nut. A tool may now be used to hold the tensioner plunger as described in Section 5 while the tensioner arm and roller is removed. However, it is possible to remove the arm and roller by keeping the arm pressed against the plunger **(see illustration)**.

38 Remove the plunger and spring **(see illustration)**.

39 Unscrew the bolts and remove the engine mounting bracket and the timing belt intermediate roller and bracket **(see illustrations)**.

40 Unbolt the engine front plate **(see illustration)**.

41 Progressively unscrew the cylinder head bolts in the reverse order to that shown. Remove the washers.

42 Release the cylinder head from the cylinder block and location dowel by rocking it. Lift the head from the block and remove the gasket.

43 Remove the clutch if applicable then hold the flywheel/driveplate stationary with a screwdriver or bar inserted between the teeth of the starter ring gear and the transmission location dowel. Then unscrew and remove the bolts and lift the flywheel/driveplate from the crankshaft.

44 Invert the engine and unbolt the sump. Remove the gasket.

45 Unscrew the three bolts securing the oil pump to the crankcase. Identify them for position as all three are of different lengths.

46 Withdraw the L-shaped spacer from beneath the oil pump (if fitted), **(see illustration)**.

47 Remove the location dowel (if fitted), and disengage the oil pump sprocket from the chain. Withdraw the oil pump **(see illustration)**.

48 Unscrew the bolts and remove the front oil seal housing **(see illustration)**. Remove the gasket.

49 Remove the oil pump chain followed by the sprocket. Recover the Woodruff key if it is loose **(see illustrations)**.

50 Check that each connecting rod and cap is marked for position and, if not, mark them with a centre punch on the oil filter side, number one at the flywheel end.

25.39A Right-hand engine mounting bracket (except Horizon models)

25.39B Timing belt intermediate roller and bracket

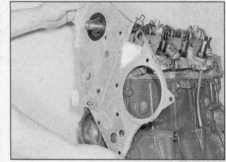

25.40 Removing the engine front plate

25.46 Withdrawing the oil pump spacer

25.47 Removing the oil pump

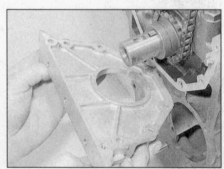

25.48 Removing the crankshaft front oil seal housing

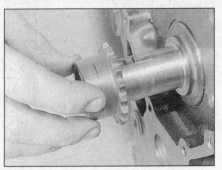

25.49A Slide off the oil pump sprocket . . .

25.49B . . . and remove the Woodruff key

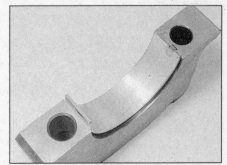

25.56 Main bearing cap and lower half bearing shell

25.57A Lift out the crankshaft . . .

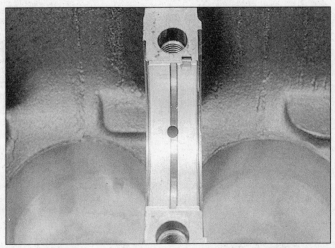

25.57B . . . and remove the upper half bearing shells

2

51 Position the cylinder block either on its side or on the flywheel end.

52 Turn the crankshaft to bring pistons 1 and 4 to BDC (bottom dead centre). Unscrew the nuts from No 1 piston big-end bearing cap then take off the cap and recover the bottom half bearing shell.

53 Using a hammer handle push the piston up through the bore and remove it from the block. Loosely refit the shell bearings and cap to ensure correct reassembly.

54 Remove No 4 piston in the same manner then turn the crankshaft 180° to bring pistons 2 and 3 to BDC and remove them.

55 The main bearing caps should be numbered 1 to 5 from the flywheel end. If not mark them accordingly. Also note the fitted depth of the rear oil seal.

56 Invert the engine then unbolt and remove the main bearing caps. Recover the lower half bearing shells keeping them with their respective caps **(see illustration)**. Also recover the thrustwashers.

57 Lift out the crankshaft. Discard the rear oil seal. Recover the upper half bearing shells and keep them together with their respective caps, however, identify them as the upper shells **(see illustrations)**. Also recover and identify the upper thrustwashers.

26 Engine overhaul - reassembly

Note: *Refer to Section 24, before this procedure.*

1 Position the block upside down on the bench. Wipe clean the main bearing shell seats in the block and caps.

2 Wipe any protective coating from the new bearing shells. Fit the top half main bearing shells (with the oil grooves) to their seats in the block. Make sure that the locating tangs on the shells engage with the recesses in the seats.

3 Fit the thrustwashers on each side of No 2 main bearing, grooved side outwards. Use a smear of grease to hold them in position **(see illustration)**.

4 Lubricate the top half shells and lower the crankshaft into position **(see illustration)**.

5 Fit the plain bottom half main bearing shells to their caps, making sure that the locating tangs engage with the recesses. Oil the shells.

6 Fit the thrustwashers on each side of No 2 main bearing cap using a smear of grease to hold them in position.

26.3 No 2 main bearing and thrustwashers

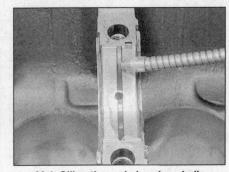

26.4 Oiling the main bearing shells

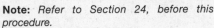

26.8 Fitting No 5 main bearing cap

26.9 Applying thread locking fluid to the No 1 main bearing cap joint face

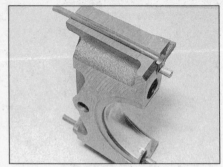

26.10A Sealing strips fitted to No 1 main bearing cap

7 Before fitting the caps check that the crankshaft endfloat is within the specified limits using a dial test indicator on the crankshaft nose.

8 Fit the main bearing caps Nos 2 to 5 to their correct locations **(see illustration)** and the right way round (the bearing shell tang locations in the block and caps must be on the same side). Insert the bolts loosely.

9 Apply a small amount of thread locking fluid to the No 1 main bearing cap face on the block around the sealing strip holes **(see illustration)**.

10 Press the sealing strips in the grooves on each side of No 1 main bearing cap **(see illustration)**. It is now necessary to obtain two thin metal strips of 0.25 mm thickness or less to prevent the strips moving when the cap is being fitted. Peugeot dealers use the tool shown **(see illustration)** which acts as a clamp, however, metal strips can be used provided all burrs that may damage the sealing strips are first removed.

11 Oil both sides of the metal strips and hold them on the sealing strips. Fit the No 1 main bearing cap, insert the bolts loosely, then carefully pull out the metal strips with a pair of pliers in a horizontal direction **(see illustrations)**.

12 Tighten the main bearing bolts evenly to the specified torque **(see illustration)**.

13 Check that the crankshaft rotates freely - there must be no tight spots or binding.

14 Dip the new rear oil seal in engine oil, locate it on the crankshaft open end first, and press it squarely to the previously noted depth using a metal tube slightly less than 102 mm diameter. A piece of thin plastic is useful to prevent damage to the oil seal **(see illustration)**. Make sure that the outer lip of the oil seal points outwards and if necessary use a piece of bent wire to pull it out.

15 Position the cylinder block either on its side or on the flywheel end.

16 Lay out the assembled piston and rods in order with the bearing shells, connecting rod caps and nuts.

17 Check that the piston ring gaps are arranged 120° from each other.

18 Clean the bearing shells, caps and rods then press the shells into position so that the locating tangs engage in the grooves.

19 Oil the bores, pistons, crankpins and shells. Fit a piston ring compressor to No 1 piston. With Nos 1 and 4 crankpin at BDC insert No 1 piston in the bore at the flywheel end, making sure that the clover leaf cut-out on the piston crown is towards the oil filter side of the engine.

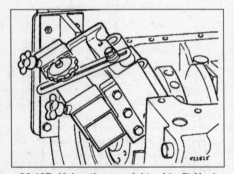

26.10B Using the special tool to fit No 1 main bearing cap

26.11A Slide the No 1 main bearing cap and metal strips into position . . .

26.11B . . . insert the bolts . . .

26.11C . . . then carefully pull out the metal strips

26.12 Tightening the main bearing bolts

26.14 Fitting the crankshaft rear oil seal with a plastic protector

26.23 Checking the crankshaft turning torque

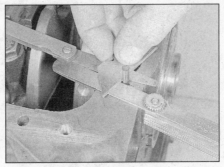

26.24 Cutting the sealing strips on No 1 main bearing cap

26.25 Fitting the chain to the oil pump sprocket

20 Using a hammer handle tap the piston through the ring compressor and into the bore. Guide the connecting rod onto the crankpin and fit the cap, together with its shell bearing, making sure it is the correct way round.

21 Fit the nuts and tighten them to the specified torque. Turn the crankshaft to check for free movement.

22 Repeat the procedure to fit the other three pistons.

23 Temporarily refit the pulley bolt to the nose of the crankshaft then, using a torque wrench, check that the torque required to turn the crankshaft does not exceed 41 Nm (30 lbf ft) **(see illustration)**. Any excessive tightness must be investigated before proceeding.

24 Using feeler blades and a knife, cut the sealing strips on No 1 main bearing cap to 1.0 mm above the sump gasket mating surface **(see illustration)**.

25 Fit the Woodruff key to the groove in the crankshaft and refit the oil pump sprocket, teeth end first. Engage the chain with the sprocket and tie it up or to one side so that it remains engaged **(see illustration)**.

26 Prise the oil seal from the front housing. Check that the two dowels are located in the front of the cylinder block then refit the front housing, together with a new gasket, and tighten the bolts evenly to the specified torque **(see illustration)**.

27 Check that the dowel is fitted to the bottom of the block. Engage the oil pump sprocket with the chain and slide the L-shaped spacer under the pump (if applicable), making sure that its open end engages the dowel.

28 Insert the oil pump bolts in their correct location, the longest bolt through the dowel and the next longest by the oil return hole. Tighten the bolts evenly to the specified torque.

29 Dip the front oil seal in engine oil then press it into the front housing until flush with the outer face.

30 Apply a little sealing compound where the front housing abuts the block on both sides. Position a new gasket on the block and refit the sump **(see illustrations)**. Note the correct location of the bolts as shown. Tighten the bolts evenly to the specified torque. Remove the sump drain plug, renew the washer, then refit and tighten the plug.

31 Locate the flywheel/driveplate on the crankshaft dowel.

32 Apply locking fluid to the threads of the bolts, insert them, and tighten them to the specified torque while holding the flywheel/driveplate stationary with a screwdriver or bar inserted between the teeth of the starter ring gear and the transmission location dowel.

33 Position the cylinder block upright on the bench.

34 Check that the cylinder head bolt holes in the block are clear preferably using an M12 x 1.5 tap **(see illustration)**.

35 Locate the correct cylinder head gasket (see Section 9 or 10) in the block the right way round with the identification notches or holes at the flywheel/driveplate end. Check that the location dowel is fitted **(see illustration)**.

36 Turn the crankshaft clockwise (from timing belt end) until pistons 1 and 4 pass

2

26.26 Tightening the front oil seal housing bolts

26.30A Apply sealing compound here . . .

26.30B . . . then fit the new sump gasket

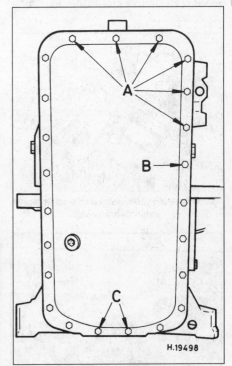

H.19498

26.30C Sump bolt locations

A 6 socket-head bolts
B 15 bolts (16 mm in length)
C 2 bolts (14 mm in length)

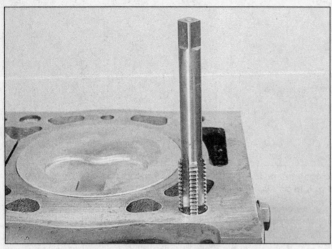

26.34 Cleaning the cylinder head bolt holes with a tap

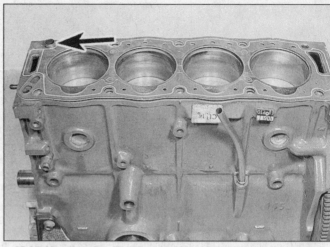

26.35 Head gasket fitted to cylinder block with location dowel arrowed

BDC and begin to rise. Then position them halfway up their bores. Pistons 2 and 3 will also be at their mid-way positions, but descending their bores. The Woodruff key groove on the nose of the crankshaft will be at the 9 o'clock position.

37 Check that the camshaft is set to TDC with the Woodruff key position facing upwards and the tips of cams 4 and 6 resting on the bucket tappets.

38 Lower the cylinder head onto the block **(see illustration)**. Refer to Section 9, paragraphs 34 to 43 or to Section 10, as applicable.

39 Grease the threads and contact faces of the cylinder head bolts, then insert them and tighten them in the stages as given in Specifications **(see illustrations)**.

40 Recheck the valve clearances, referring to Section 8 and adjust them if necessary. Do this even if the clearances have been adjusted with the cylinder head removed as there may be minor differences.

41 Refit the engine front plate followed by the timing belt intermediate roller and bracket, and the engine mounting bracket. Tighten all the bolts. Do not forget the mounting bracket bolt on the inside face of the engine front plate **(see illustration)**.

42 Insert the timing belt tensioner spring and plunger in the mounting bracket. Press the tensioner arm against the plunger and refit the bracket and roller onto the pivot stud. Alternatively compress the plunger with the tool described in Section 5. Fit the adjustment bolt and pivot nut, and tighten the bolt with the tensioner in the released position (i.e. spring compressed) **(see illustrations)**.

43 Refit the injection pump mounting bracket and tighten the bolts.

44 Refit the injection pump, align the previously made marks then tighten the nuts followed by the bolt.

26.38 Lowering the cylinder head onto the block

26.39A Insert the cylinder head bolts

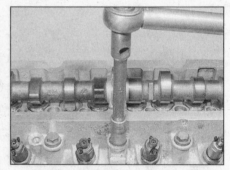

26.39B . . . and tighten them to the specified torque

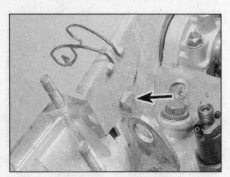

26.41 Inner bolt location for the engine mounting bracket (arrowed)

26.42A Turn the tensioner bracket anti-clockwise . . .

26.42B . . . and tighten the bolt to hold the tensioner in the released position

26.46 Fitting the sprocket to the crankshaft

26.47 Tightening the camshaft sprocket bolt with the timing bolt in position

26.48 Tightening the injection pump sprocket bolt with the timing bolts in position

26.49 Tightening the special puller to the injection pump sprocket

26.55 Tightening the tensioner adjustment bolt

2

45 Refit the water pump together with a new gasket and tighten the bolts to the specified torque (Chapter 3).

46 Locate the Woodruff key in the groove then slide the sprocket onto the front of the crankshaft **(see illustration)**.

47 Fit the camshaft sprocket to the camshaft. Apply locking fluid to the threads then insert and tighten the bolt to the specified torque, while holding the camshaft sprocket stationary. A tool made out of metal bar and two bolts may be used to hold the sprocket, or alternatively the timing bolt may be screwed into the head **(see illustration)**.

48 Unbolt the special puller from the injection pump sprocket. Refit the Woodruff key, then fit the sprocket to the injection pump shaft. Refit the nut and tighten it while holding the sprocket stationary using either method described in paragraph 47 **(see illustration)**.

49 Refit the special puller onto the sprocket then insert and tighten the bolts **(see illustration)**.

50 Refit the valve cover, together with a new gasket, and tighten the bolts.

51 Check that the camshaft and injection pump sprockets are at their TDC positions with the three timing bolts inserted in the front plate.

52 Insert an 8.0 mm diameter metal dowel rod through the special hole in the left-hand

rear flange of the cylinder block. Then turn the crankshaft slowly clockwise (from the timing belt end) until the rod enters the TDC hole in the flywheel/driveplate. It is only necessary to turn the crankshaft a quarter turn as Nos 1 and 4 pistons are already halfway up their bores. Do not turn the crankshaft more than this otherwise pistons 2 and 3 will strike valves 4 and 6.

53 Locate the timing belt on the crankshaft sprocket making sure where applicable that the rotation arrow is facing the correct way.

54 Hold the timing belt engaged with the crankshaft sprocket then feed it over the roller and onto the injection pump, camshaft, and water pump sprockets and over the tensioner roller. To ensure correct engagement locate only a half width on the injection pump sprocket before feeding the timing belt onto the camshaft sprocket, keeping the belt taut and fully engaged with the crankshaft sprocket. Locate the timing belt fully onto the sprockets.

55 With the pivot nut loose, slacken the tensioner adjustment bolt while holding the bracket against the spring tension, then slowly release the bracket until the roller presses against the timing belt. Retighten the adjustment bolt **(see illustration)**.

56 Remove the bolts from the camshaft and injection pump sprockets. Remove the metal dowel rod from the cylinder block.

57 Rotate the engine two complete turns in its normal direction. Do not rotate the engine backwards as the timing belt must be kept tight between the crankshaft, injection pump and camshaft sprockets.

58 Loosen the tensioner adjustment bolt to allow the tensioner spring to push the roller against the timing belt, then tighten both the adjustment bolt and pivot nut.

59 Recheck the engine timing by turning the engine until the sprocket bolt holes are aligned, and check that the metal dowel rod can be inserted into the flywheel/driveplate.

60 Refit the bottom timing cover and tighten the bolts **(see illustration)**.

26.60 Bottom timing cover fitted

26.62A Apply locking fluid to the crankshaft pulley bolt before fitting it

26.62B Tightening the crankshaft pulley bolt

61 Fit the pulley to the front of the crankshaft over the Woodruff key.

62 Apply locking fluid to the threads of the pulley bolt. Then insert it and tighten to the specified torque while an assistant holds the flywheel/driveplate stationary with a screwdriver inserted between the teeth of the starter ring gear and the transmission location dowel. Note that after tightening to the initial torque, the bolt must be angle tightened a further 60° that is the equivalent of one flat on the bolt head. Alternatively mark the flat extremities on the socket together with a starting datum on the pulley **(see illustrations)**.

63 Locate a new gasket on the side of the sump, refit the inlet bracket, and tighten the nuts evenly.

64 Refit the water pump inlet together with a new gasket and tighten the bolts.

65 Bolt the coolant tube to the cylinder block and fit the hoses.

66 Refit the thermostat housing, together with a new gasket, and tighten the bolts.

67 Insert the oil pressure switch in the block and tighten.

68 Insert the oil level sensor and tighten.

69 Refit the fast idle cable to the injection pump, referring to Chapter 4.

70 Refit the exhaust manifold, together with new gaskets, and tighten the nuts evenly.

71 Refit the inlet manifold and tighten the bolts evenly. There are no gaskets.

72 Refit the oil filler cap and ventilation hose if fitted.

73 Slide the oil separator onto the dipstick tube **(see illustration)** and secure with the clip. Reconnect the crankcase ventilation hoses to the valve cover and sump inlet.

74 Reconnect the bottom hose to the water pump inlet.

75 Where applicable, reconnect the oil cooler hoses and refit the oil cooler, tightening the centre stud to the specified torque **(see illustrations)**.

76 Smear a little engine oil on the sealing ring of the oil filter cartridge then refit it and tighten by hand only.

77 Refit the alternator (Chapter 5).

78 Refit the engine lifting bracket to the cylinder head, also refit the lower rear engine mounting bracket.

79 Reconnect the leak off hoses to the injectors.

80 Refit the fuel pipe assemblies to the injectors and injection pump and tighten the union nuts to the specified torque (Chapter 4).

81 Slide the pump pulley onto the flywheel end of the camshaft. Insert the bolt and tighten it to the specified torque **(see illustration)**.

26.62C Markings necessary in order to angle-tighten the crankshaft pulley bolt by 60°

26.73 Oil separator located on the dipstick tube (where applicable)

26.75A Oil cooler . . .

26.75B . . . and coolant hose connections

26.81 Tightening the pump pulley bolt on the camshaft

82 Where applicable refit the diagnostic socket and bracket and tighten the bolt.
83 Refit the two timing cover sections and press down the special clip and spring clips to secure, if applicable.
84 Refit the brake vacuum pump, as described in Chapter 7.
85 Refit the clutch on manual transmission models.

27 Engine overhaul examination and renovation - general

1 With the engine completely dismantled, all components should be cleaned and examined as detailed in the appropriate Sections of this Chapter.
2 Most components can be cleaned with rags, a soft brush and paraffin, or some other solvent. Do not immerse parts with oilways in solvent since it can be very difficult to remove and if left will contaminate the oil. Clean oilways and water channels with a piece of wire and blow through with compressed air if available.
3 When faced with a borderline decision whether to renew a particular part, take into consideration the expected future life of the engine and the degree of trouble or expense that will be caused if the part fails before the next overhaul.
4 If extensive overhauling is required, estimate the likely cost and compare it with the cost of a complete reconditioned engine. The difference may not be great, and the reconditioned engine will have a guarantee.

28.9 Big-end bearing shell

28.13 Checking the crankshaft endfloat

28 Engine components - overhaul

Cylinder block and bores

Overhaul

1 Check the cylinder block casting for any damage or cracking.
2 If necessary unscrew the two plugs from the rear of the block and from the flange beneath the oil filter location, and clean the oil gallery. Refit and tighten the plugs on completion. The water channels may be cleaned by removing the inspection plate from the rear of the block. On Turbo models, remove the piston cooling jets. Clean them and inspect them for damage or wear and replace them if necessary.
3 Check the core plugs for signs of leakage and if necessary renew them. It may be possible to remove the old plugs by drilling a small hole and using a self-tapping screw to pull them out. Alternatively, use a hammer to drive a chisel through the old plugs and prise them out. Clean the seating then apply a little sealing compound and tap the new plug into position with the flat face of a hammer. Spread the core plug by striking the centre with a ball face hammer.
4 If cracks in the block are suspected it may be necessary to have it crack-tested professionally. There are various ways of doing this, some involving special dyes and chemicals, some using ultrasonic or electromagnetic radiation.
5 Bore wear is indicated by a wear ridge at the top of the bore. For accurate assessment a bore micrometer is required, however, a rough measurement can be made by inserting feeler blades between a piston (without rings) and the bore wall. Compare the clearance at the bottom of the bore, which should be unworn, with that just below the wear ridge. No wear limits are specified, but out-of-round or taper more than 0.1 mm would normally be considered grounds for a rebore. Scuffs, scores and scratches must also be taken into account.

6 If reboring is undertaken the machine shop will normally obtain the oversize pistons and rings at the same time.
7 Where the degree of wear does not justify a rebore, the fitting of proprietary oil control rings may be considered.

Crankshaft and bearings

Overhaul

8 Check the crankshaft for damage or excessive wear.
9 Examine the bearing shells for wear and scratches on the working surfaces. New shells should be fitted in any case, unless the old ones are obviously in perfect condition and are known to have covered only a nominal mileage **(see illustration)**. Refitting used shells is false economy.
10 Examine the bearing journals on the crankshaft for scoring or other damage, which if present will probably mean that regrinding or renewal is necessary. If a micrometer is available, measure the journals in several places to check for out-of-round and taper. No limits are specified but typically 0.025 mm is the maximum acceptable.
11 Note that the crankshaft may already have been reground, and that the makers only specify one stage of regrinding.
12 Main and big-end bearing clearances can be measured using Plastigage thread. The journal and bearing shell are wiped dry before placing the thread across the journal. After tightening the bearing cap onto the Plastigage it is removed and a special gauge used to determine the running clearance. The makers do not specify any clearances but typically it would be between 0.025 and 0.050 mm.
13 Check the crankshaft endfloat using a feeler blade between the No 2 thrustwashers and crankshaft web. If this is more than the specified amount obtain new thrustwashers. Alternatively a dial gauge on the end of the crankshaft may be used for the check **(see illustration)**.

Pistons, piston rings and connecting rods

Overhaul

14 The piston rings may be removed from each piston with the aid of some old feeler blades or similar thin metal strips. Carefully spread the top ring just far enough to slide the blades in between the ring and the piston, then remove the ring and blades together **(see illustration)**. Be careful not to scratch the piston with the ends of the ring.
15 Repeat the process to remove the second and third rings, using the blades to stop the rings falling into the empty grooves. Note that the third ring incorporates an expander. Always remove the rings from the top of the piston. Keep each set of rings with its piston if the old rings are to be re-used.
16 Measure the end gaps of the rings by fitting them, one at a time, to their bores. Check the gaps with the rings either at the

28.14 Removing the piston rings with an old feeler blade

2

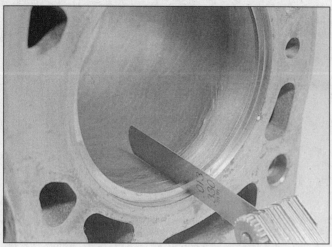

28.16 Measuring the piston ring end gaps

28.22A Prising out the gudgeon pin circlip

extreme top or bottom of the bores, where the wear is minimum, using feeler blades **(see illustration)**.

17 If the rings are renewed the bores must be deglazed as described in Section 17.

18 Examine the pistons for damage, in particular for burning on the crown and for scores or other signs of "picking-up" on the skirts and piston ring lands. Scorch marks on the sides show that blow-by has occurred.

19 If the pistons pass this preliminary inspection clean all the carbon out of the ring grooves using a piece of old piston ring. Protect your fingers - piston rings are sharp. Do not remove any metal from the ring grooves.

20 Roll each ring around its groove to check for tight spots. Any excessive clearance not due to worn rings must be due to piston wear and, unless the piston can be machined to accept special rings, renewal is required.

21 If renewing pistons without reboring make sure that the correct size is obtained. Piston class is denoted by either an "A1" mark or no

mark at all on the centre of the crown. The identical code appears also on the corner of the cylinder block at the timing belt end. The piston weight class is stamped on the crown and must be identical on all pistons in the same engine.

22 To separate a piston from its connecting rod, prise out the circlips and push out the gudgeon pin **(see illustrations)**. Hand pressure is sufficient to remove the pin. Identify the piston and rod to ensure correct reassembly.

23 Wear between the gudgeon pin and the connecting rod small-end bush can be cured by renewing both the pin and bush. Bush renewal, however, is a specialist job because press facilities are required and the new bush must be reamed accurately.

24 New gudgeon pins and circlips are supplied when buying new pistons. The connecting rods themselves should not be in need of renewal unless seizure or some other major mechanical failure has occurred.

25 Reassemble the pistons and rods. Make sure that the pistons are fitted the right way round - the clover leaf cut-out on the crown must face the same way as the shell bearing cut-out in the connecting rod. Oil the gudgeon pins before fitting them **(see illustrations)**. When assembled, the piston should pivot freely on the rod.

26 Fit the piston rings using the same technique as for removal. Fit the bottom ring first and work up. When fitting the oil control ring first insert the expander then fit the ring with its gap positioned 180° from the expanders gap. Arrange the gaps of the upper two rings 120° either side of the oil control ring gap. Make sure that No 2 ring is fitted the correct way round **(see illustration)**.

Flywheel/driveplate

Overhaul

27 Examine the clutch mating surface of the flywheel for scoring or cracks. Light grooving or scoring may be ignored. Surface cracks or

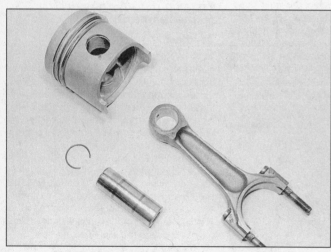

28.22B Piston and connecting rod components

28.25A Pushing the gudgeon pin into the piston

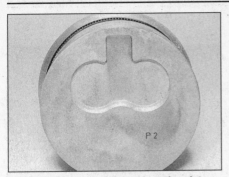

28.25B Clover leaf cut-out on the piston crown

deep grooving can sometimes be removed by specialist machining, provided not too much metal is taken off, otherwise the flywheel must be renewed.

28 Inspect the flywheel/driveplate for damage or cracks and renew it if necessary.

29 Inspect the starter ring gear for damaged or missing teeth. The ring gear can be renewed separately to the flywheel as follows. Drill through the width of the ring gear then split it with a cold chisel and remove it. The new ring gear must be heated then quickly tapped onto the flywheel/driveplate and allowed to cool naturally. The temperature to which the ring gear must be heated is critical - too little heat and the ring gear may not fit or may even jam halfway on. Too much heat and

the temper of the metal may be lost causing it to wear rapidly in use. The correct temperature is normally attached to the new ring gear, however, the average DIY mechanic may prefer to leave the job to a garage or engineering works.

30 The makers recommend that the flywheel/driveplate bolts are renewed at overhaul.

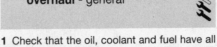

29 Initial start-up after engine overhaul - general

1 Check that the oil, coolant and fuel have all been replenished and that the battery is well charged.

2 On early models fitted with a Roto-Diesel fuel filter unscrew the pump plunger.

3 Switch on the ignition to energise the stop solenoid then actuate the pump on the fuel filter until resistance is felt. Retighten the plunger where necessary.

4 Fully depress the accelerator pedal, turn the ignition key to position "M" and wait for the preheating warning light to go out.

5 Start the engine. Additional cranking may be necessary to bleed the fuel system before the engine starts. On Turbo models, prime the turbo lubrication circuit before start-up, by disconnecting the stop solenoid lead at the fuel pump, and cranking the engine on the starter for three ten-second bursts.

6 Once started keep the engine running at a fast tickover. Check that the oil pressure light goes out, then check for leaks of oil, fuel and coolant.

Pre September 1986 models

7 If all is well, continue to run the engine at 3000 rpm for 10 minutes then switch off the ignition and let the engine cool for at least three and a half hours.

8 Remove the filler cap from the cooling system expansion tank to release any remaining pressure, then refit it.

9 Working on each cylinder head bolt in turn in the correct sequence first loosen the bolt 90° then retighten to the final torque given in the Specifications.

All models

10 If many new parts have been fitted, the engine should be treated as new and run in at reduced speeds and loads for the first 600 miles (1000 km) or so. After this mileage it is beneficial to change the engine oil and oil filter.

11 Have the injection pump timing and idling speed checked and adjusted as described in Chapter 1.

12 After the vehicle has covered 12 000 miles (20 000 km), renew the coolant, as described in Chapter 1. Thereafter renew and check as per maintenance schedule.

2

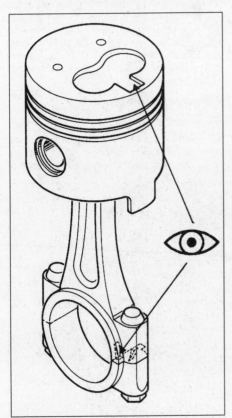

28.25C Correct piston and connecting rod assembly

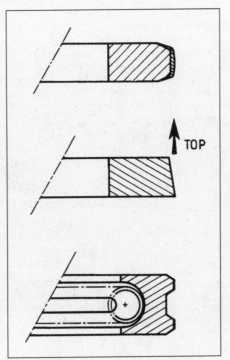

28.26 Piston ring cross sections

Chapter 3
Cooling system

Contents

Degrees of difficulty

| Easy, suitable for novice with little experience | | Fairly easy, suitable for beginner with some experience | | Fairly difficult, suitable for competent DIY mechanic | | Difficult, suitable for experienced DIY mechanic | | Very difficult, suitable for expert DIY or professional | |

Specifications

General

System type	Pressurised, front-mounted radiator, remote expansion tank, coolant pump and thermostat. Electric cooling fan(s)
Thermostat opening temperature:	
Pre late 1992 models	Between 82 and 93°C
Late 1992 models	83°C
Minimal travel	7.5 mm
Radiator cap pressure:	
Except 405 (XUD 9TE) models	1 bar
405 (XUD 9TE) models	1.4 bars
Temperature warning switch operating temperature:	
Except 405 models	110°C
405 models	118°C
Electric cooling fan(s):	
Models up to late 1992 (except Turbo and 405):	
Cut-in temperature:	
1st speed	93°C
2nd speed	97°C
Cut-out temperature:	
1st speed cuts in at	88°C
2nd speed cuts in at	92°C
Early 309 Turbo models:	
Cut-in temperature:	
1st speed	97°C
2nd speed	101°C
Cut-out temperature:	
1st speed cuts in at	92.5°C
2nd speed cuts in at	97.5°C
Early 405 models:	
Cut-in temperature:	
1st speed	93°C
2nd speed	97°C
Cut-out temperature:	
1st speed cuts in at	88°C
2nd speed cuts in at	92°C
All models from late 1992:	
Without air conditioning	92.5/97.5°C (two-stage thermal switch)
With air conditioning:	
Cut-in temperature:	
1st speed	90°C
2nd speed	101°C
Air conditioning cut-off	112°C
Alert	118°C
Post ventilation	112°C (timer operates for 6 minutes, after ignition is switched off)

3

Torque wrench settings

	Nm	lbf ft
Water pump	12	9

1 Description - general

1 The cooling system is pressurised with a front-mounted radiator and a water pump driven by the engine timing belt. The thermostat is located on the flywheel end of the cylinder head and enables the engine to achieve a fast warm-up period by initially restricting the coolant flow within the engine and heater circuits. Thereafter, the coolant flows through the radiator to provide additional cooling. The main engine temperature control is provided by one or two electric cooling fans mounted either in front or behind the radiator, depending on model. A twin action sensor in the radiator activates the fan(s) according to the coolant temperature **(see illustration)**.

2 Essential to the operation of the system is the expansion tank **(see illustration)**. This tank provides a reservoir to allow for expansion and contraction of the coolant with changes in temperature. It also incorporates a filler/pressure relief valve cap.

3 The radiator is of the crossflow type, with plastic or metal side tanks. A temperature warning switch is provided on the water outlet from the cylinder head to warn the driver of excessive temperature.

4 The cooling system on Turbo models have, in addition, coolant feed oil coolers with modified thermostat housings.

2 Cooling system pressure - testing

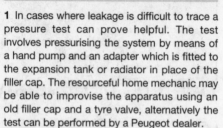

1 In cases where leakage is difficult to trace a pressure test can prove helpful. The test involves pressurising the system by means of a hand pump and an adapter which is fitted to the expansion tank or radiator in place of the filler cap. The resourceful home mechanic may be able to improvise the apparatus using an old filler cap and a tyre valve, alternatively the test can be performed by a Peugeot dealer.

2 Fit the test equipment to the expansion tank or radiator then run the engine to normal operating temperature and switch it off.

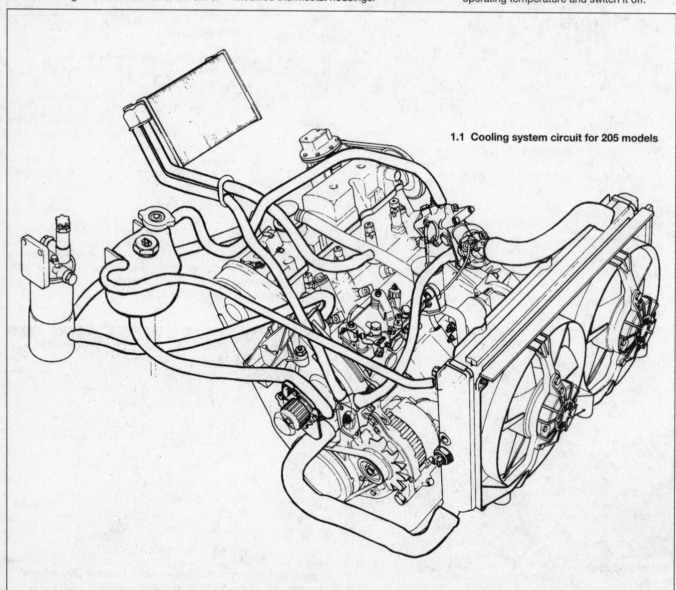

1.1 Cooling system circuit for 205 models

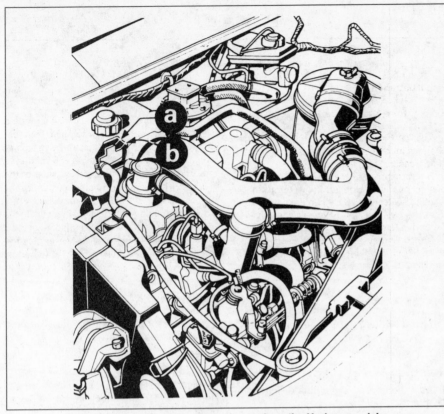

1.2 Cutaway view of the expansion tank on the Horizon models
a Maximum level   *b Minimum level*

3.3 Bottom hose connection to radiator

3 Radiator - removal and refitting

Note: *For other models, refer to the instructions in the relevant main manuals.*

Removal

205 and Horizon models

1 Drain the cooling system as described in Chapter 1.
2 Remove the air cleaner as described in Chapter 4.
3 Loosen the clips and disconnect the top hose, bottom hose, and bypass hose from the radiator **(see illustration)**.
4 Disconnect the wiring from the thermal switch on the right-hand side of the radiator **(see illustration)**.

205 models

5 Remove the radiator grille.
6 Unscrew the upper bolts, the cooling fan frame mounting bolts and the front side nuts so that the front crossmember, complete with bonnet lock and cable, can be secured to the side of the engine compartment **(see illustrations)**.

3 Apply 1.4 bar pressure and check that this pressure is held for at least 10 seconds. If the pressure drops prematurely there is a leak in the cooling system that must be traced and rectified.
4 Besides leaks from hoses, pressure can also be lost through leaks in the radiator and heater matrix. A blown head gasket or a cracked head or block can cause an "invisible" leak, but there are usually other clues to this condition such as poor engine performance, regular misfiring, or combustion gases entering the coolant.
5 After completing the test, allow the engine to cool then remove the test equipment.
6 The condition of the filler cap must not be overlooked. Normally it is tested with similar equipment to that used for the pressure test. The release pressure is given in the Specifications and is also usually stamped on the cap itself. Renew the cap if it is faulty.

3.4 Thermal switch and wiring

3.6A Front crossmember upper bolt - arrowed (205 models)

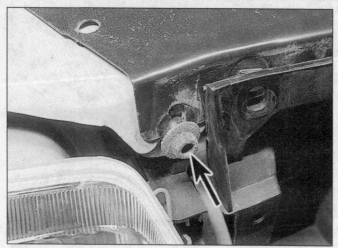

3.6B Front crossmember front side nut - arrowed (205 models)

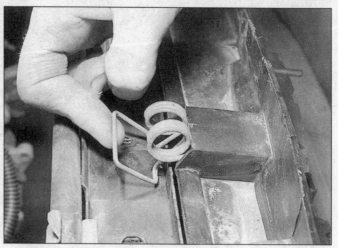

3.7 Releasing the radiator upper spring clips (205 models)

7 Pull up the upper spring clips and move the top of the radiator clear **(see illustration)**.

8 Carefully lift the radiator from the bottom mounting rubbers **(see illustrations)**.

Horizon models

9 Remove the electric cooling fans as described in Section 6.

10 With the upper mounting brackets removed, carefully lift the radiator from the bottom mounting rubbers.

Refitting

Both models

11 Before refitting the radiator, check the condition of the mounting rubbers, and renew as necessary.

12 Refitting is a reversal of removal. Refill the system as described in Chapter 1.

---

4 Thermostat - removal, testing and refitting

Removal

1 Drain the cooling system as described in Chapter 1.

2 Remove the air cleaner, as described in Chapter 4.

3 Loosen the clip and disconnect the top hose from the thermostat housing cover **(see illustration)**.

4 Unscrew the four bolts and remove the thermostat housing cover from the cylinder head water outlet. There is no need to disconnect the fast idle cable. Remove the gasket **(see illustrations)**.

5 Using circlip pliers, extract the circlip from

the cover and lift out the thermostat **(see illustration)**.

6 If necessary pull the rubber seal from the thermostat **(see illustration)**.

Testing

7 To test the thermostat place it in a pan of cold water and check that it is initially closed. Heat the water and check that it begins to open at the temperature given in Specifications. Continue to heat the water and check the fully open temperature and minimum travel. Finally allow the water to cool and check that it fully closes. Discard it if it is faulty.

Refitting

8 Refitting is a reversal of removal, but when inserting the thermostat in the cover, position the vent hole uppermost and fit a new gasket. Refill the system as described in Chapter 1.

3.8A Removing the radiator (205 models)

3.8B Radiator bottom mounting rubber (205 models)

4.3 Top hose connection to thermostat housing cover

4.4A Unscrewing the thermostat housing cover bolts

4.4B Removing the thermostat housing cover gasket

3

4.5 Thermostat and retaining circlip

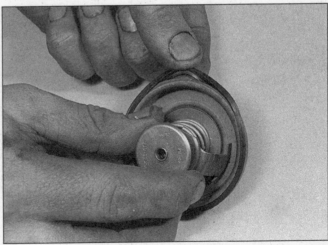

4.6 Removing the rubber seal from the thermostat

5.5A Unscrew the bolts . . .

5.5B . . . and withdraw the water pump

5 Water pump - removal and refitting

Removal

1 Disconnect the battery negative lead.
2 Remove the timing belt as described in Chapter 2.
3 Drain the cooling system as described in Chapter 1.
4 Disconnect the bottom hose from the water pump inlet.
5 Unscrew the bolts and withdraw the water pump from the cylinder block **(see illustrations)**. Remove the gasket.

Refitting

6 Clean the mating faces of the water pump and block.

7 Fit the water pump together with a new gasket, insert the bolts, and tighten them evenly to the specified torque.
8 Reconnect the bottom hose.
9 Refit the timing belt as described in Chapter 2.
10 Reconnect the battery negative lead.
11 Refill the cooling system as described in Chapter 1.

6 Electric cooling fans (205 and Horizon models) - removal and refitting

Note: *For other models, refer to the instructions in the relevant main manuals.*

Removal

1 Disconnect the battery negative lead.

205 models

2 Remove the radiator grille.
3 Disconnect the wiring at the connector.
4 Unscrew the mounting bolts and withdraw the cooling fan frame assembly **(see illustration)**.

Horizon models

5 Unbolt the radiator upper mounting brackets **(see illustration)**.
6 Disconnect the wiring at the connector.
7 Move the top of the cooling fan frame assembly rearwards then lift the locating pegs from the lower mounting rubbers.

Both models

8 If necessary, unscrew the nuts and remove the fan motor(s) from the frame. The fan(s) may also be unbolted from the motor spindle(s), **(see illustration)**.

5.5C Water pump showing impeller vanes

6.4 Cooling fan frame mounting bolts (arrowed)

6.5 Radiator upper mounting bracket (Horizon models)

6.8 Cooling fan and retaining bolt (arrowed)

6.9 Electric cooling fan control relays (205 models)

Refitting

Both models

9 Refitting is a reversal of removal. However, should a fault develop in the electric cooling fans, check the relays, that are located on the left-hand side of the engine compartment **(see illustration)**.

7 Temperature-sensitive switches and senders (all models) - general

According to model and equipment, various temperature-sensitive switches and senders are fitted in the thermostat housing.

When fitting a new switch or sender, it is important to coat its threads with a sealant (Loctite Formseal, or equivalent) to avoid subsequent coolant leaks.

8 Hose clips, modified - general

405 Turbo models

1 From mid-1991 onwards, the hose connections to the radiator and expansion bottle on 405 Turbo models are no longer fitted with metal clips, but have special end fittings with O-rings.
2 To disconnect a new-type clip, turn it anti-clockwise and withdraw it from inside the stub on the engine, radiator or expansion tank.
3 Before refitting a hose, check the condition of the connectors for broken lugs and distorted ends. If any connector is broken or distorted, the complete hose must be renewed. It is not possible to renew a connector separately from the hose. Renew the O-rings if they are damaged or deteriorated.
4 Lubricate the O-ring with a little coolant before locating it in the stub, then insert the hose and turn the clip clockwise to its stop to lock it.

205 models, late 1992

5 For a limited period from late in 1992, a new type of radiator hose clip was fitted to some 205 models with the XUD 7 engine. The new type of clip is shown **(see illustration)**.
6 To disconnect the hose, first extract the spring clip. Peugeot technicians use a special extractor to do this, but it should be possible to pull out the clip using a pair of grips.
7 Ease the hose off the radiator stub, and remove the O-ring.
8 To refit the hose, first locate the spring clip in the notches. To do this, locate part of the clip in one of the notches, then locate the remaining ends in the other notches one at a time.
9 Dip the O-ring in coolant, then locate it in the groove on the end of the hose. The coolant will facilitate fitting the O-ring, do not use any other form of lubrication.
10 Offer the hose to the stub on the radiator with the three lugs correctly aligned, then push on the hose until it clicks into position.
11 Check that the hose is fitted correctly by gently pulling on it.

3

8.5 Early (left) and later (right) coolant hose clips

1 Expansion bottle outlet hose	*3 Large O-ring*	*5 Radiator outlet hose*
2 Radiator outlet hose	*4 Small O-ring*	*6 Expansion bottle outlet hose*

Chapter 4
Fuel and exhaust systems

Contents

Degrees of difficulty

| **Easy,** suitable for novice with little experience | | **Fairly easy,** suitable for beginner with some experience | | **Fairly difficult,** suitable for competent DIY mechanic | ≋ | **Difficult,** suitable for experienced DIY mechanic | ≋ | **Very difficult,** suitable for expert DIY or professional | ≋ |

Specifications

General

System type	Rear-mounted fuel tank, injection pump with integral transfer pump, indirect injection
Firing order	1-3-4-2 (No 1 at flywheel end)
Fuel:	
Type	Commercial diesel fuel for road vehicles (DERV)

Injection pump (Lucas CAV/Roto-Diesel)

Static advance:	
Except 205 and 309 Turbo and 405 models	2.26 ± 0.05 mm BTDC (equivalent to 16° BTDC)
205 and 309 Turbo and 405 models	Value indicated on the pump (refer to text)
Dynamic advance:	
Except XUD 9 pumps with suffix 160A, 205 and	
309 Turbo models	14° BTDC at 800 rpm
XUD 9 pumps with suffix 160A	13.5° BTDC at 800 rpm
205 and 309 Turbo models	12° BTDC at 775 rpm
Idle speed	
Non air conditioned models	800 rpm + 0 - 50
Air conditioned models	850 rpm + 0 - 50
Fast idle speed (405 models)	950 ± 50 rpm
Maximum engine speed (no load):	
Except 405 models	5100 ± 100 rpm
405 models	5150 ± 125 rpm
Rotation	Clockwise from sprocket end

Injection pump (Bosch), (except 405 models)

Static advance:	
1.7 litre models	0.80 ± 0.03 mm BTDC
1.9 litre models	0.50 ± 0.03 mm BTDC
Dynamic advance:	
1.7 litre models	14° BTDC at 800 rpm
1.9 litre models	13.5° BTDC at 800 rpm
Maximum engine speed	5100 ± 100 rpm
Rotation	Clockwise from sprocket end

Injection pump (Bosch), (405 models)

Type	XUD 9A/L	XUD 9Y
Static timing at TDC	1.07 mm	0.77 mm
Dynamic timing (at idle speed)	18° ± 1	12° ± 1
Idling speed:		
Air conditioning off	750 rpm +50 - 0	775 rpm +25
Air conditioning on	800 rpm +50 - 0	775 rpm ±25
Maximum engine speed (no load)	5150 rpm ±125	5100 rpm ±125
Fast idle speed	950 rpm ±50	950 rpm ±50

Type	XUD 9TE/L	XUD 9TE/Y
Static timing at TDC	0.66 mm	0.66 mm
Dynamic timing (at idle speed)	11° ± 1	11° ± 1
Idling speed:		
Air conditioning off	750 rpm +50 - 0	750 rpm +50 - 0
Air conditioning on	800 rpm +50 - 0	800 rpm +50 - 0
Maximum engine speed (no load)	5100 rpm ±80	5100 rpm ±80
Fast idle speed	950 rpm ±50	950 rpm ±50

Injectors

Type	Pintle
Opening pressure (except 405 models):	
Lucas/Roto-Diesel:	
Except 205 and 309 Turbo models	115 ± 5 bar
205 and 309 Turbo models	130 ± 5 bar
Bosch	130 ± 5 bar
Opening pressure (405 models)	
Pink calibration (Lucas)	123 to 128 bars
Pink and green calibration (Lucas)	127 to 132 bars
Silver calibration (Bosch)	130 bars
Blue calibration (Bosch)	175 bars
Yellow calibration	140 ± 3 bars
Yellow and green calibration	145 ± 3 bars

Turbocharger

Make	KKK or Garrett
Type:	
KKK	K14
Garrett	T2
Boost pressure:	
Except 205, 309 and 405 models	0.8 to 0.9 bars at full-load
205 and 309 models	0.85 bars maximum

Torque wrench settings

	Nm	lbf ft
Cylinder head blanking plug	30	22
Heater plug	22	16
Injection pump	18	13
Injection pump (Bosch) blanking plug	20	15
Injection pump sprocket nut	50	37
Injector:		
Bosch	90	66
Roto-Diesel	130	96
Injector pipe union nuts	20	15
Turbocharger mounting bolts	45	33
Turbocharger oil feed pipe unions	20	15

---

1 Description - general

Warning: It is necessary to take certain precautions when working on the fuel system components, particularly the fuel injectors. Before carrying out any operations on the fuel system, refer to the precautions given in "Safety first!" at the *beginning of this manual, and to any additional warning notes at the start of the relevant Sections.*

1 The fuel system consists of a rear-mounted fuel tank, a fuel filter, a fuel injection pump, injectors and associated components **(see illustrations)**. The exhaust system is similar to that used on petrol-engined vehicles.

2 Fuel is drawn from the tank by a vane-type transfer pump incorporated in the delivery head of the injection pump. Before reaching the pump the fuel passes through a fuel filter where foreign matter and water are removed. The injection pump is driven at half crankshaft speed by the timing belt. The high pressure required to inject the fuel into the compressed air in the swirl chambers is achieved by two opposed pistons forced together by rollers running on a cam ring. The fuel passes through a central rotor with a single outlet drilling which aligns with ports leading to the injector pipes and injectors. Fuel metering is

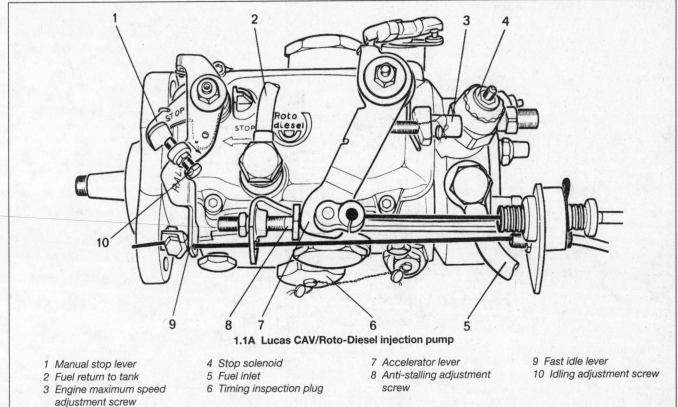

1.1A Lucas CAV/Roto-Diesel injection pump

1 Manual stop lever
2 Fuel return to tank
3 Engine maximum speed adjustment screw

4 Stop solenoid
5 Fuel inlet
6 Timing inspection plug

7 Accelerator lever
8 Anti-stalling adjustment screw

9 Fast idle lever
10 Idling adjustment screw

1.1B Cutaway view of the Lucas CAV/Roto-Diesel injection pump

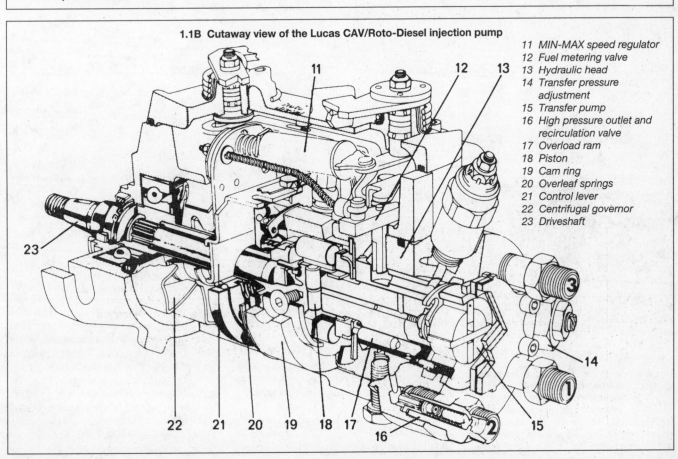

11 MIN-MAX speed regulator
12 Fuel metering valve
13 Hydraulic head
14 Transfer pressure adjustment
15 Transfer pump
16 High pressure outlet and recirculation valve
17 Overload ram
18 Piston
19 Cam ring
20 Overleaf springs
21 Control lever
22 Centrifugal governor
23 Driveshaft

4

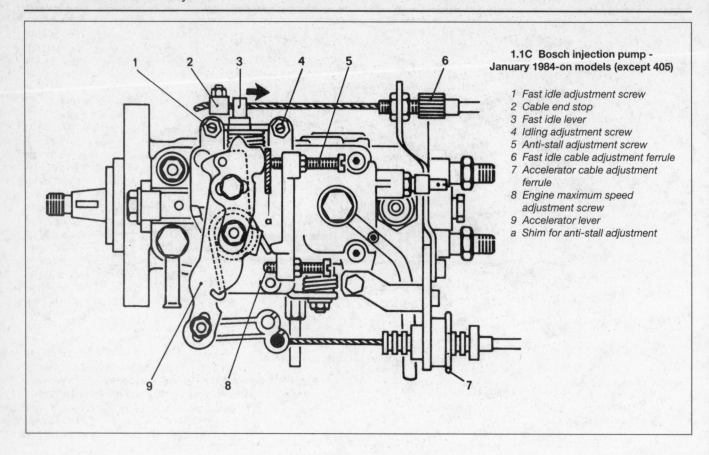

1.1C Bosch injection pump - January 1984-on models (except 405)

1 Fast idle adjustment screw
2 Cable end stop
3 Fast idle lever
4 Idling adjustment screw
5 Anti-stall adjustment screw
6 Fast idle cable adjustment ferrule
7 Accelerator cable adjustment ferrule
8 Engine maximum speed adjustment screw
9 Accelerator lever
a Shim for anti-stall adjustment

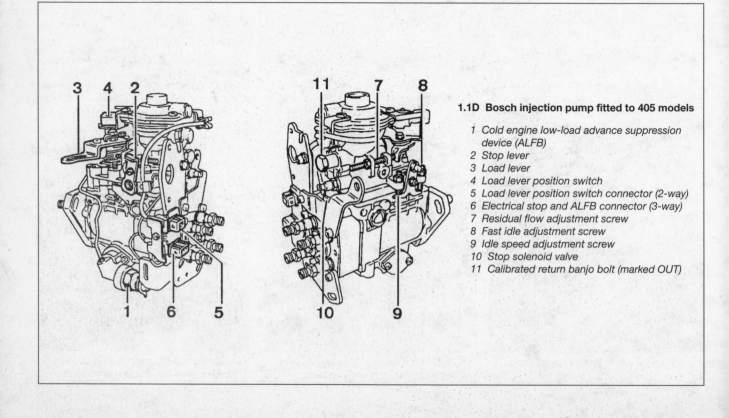

1.1D Bosch injection pump fitted to 405 models

1 Cold engine low-load advance suppression device (ALFB)
2 Stop lever
3 Load lever
4 Load lever position switch
5 Load lever position switch connector (2-way)
6 Electrical stop and ALFB connector (3-way)
7 Residual flow adjustment screw
8 Fast idle adjustment screw
9 Idle speed adjustment screw
10 Stop solenoid valve
11 Calibrated return banjo bolt (marked OUT)

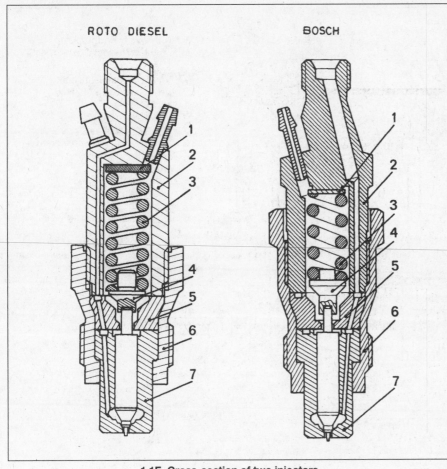

ROTO DIESEL BOSCH

1.1E Cross-section of two injectors

1 Adjustment shim	4 Pushrod
2 Upper body	5 Spacer
3 Spring	

6 Nut	
7 Lower body and needle	

controlled by a centrifugal governor that reacts to accelerator pedal position and engine speed. The governor is linked to the metering valve that moves the rotor sleeve to increase or decrease the amount of fuel transferred to the high pressure chamber. Injection timing is varied by turning the cam ring to suit the prevailing engine speed.

3 There are four precision-made injectors that inject a homogeneous spray of fuel into the swirl chambers located in the cylinder head. The injectors are calibrated to open and close at critical pressures to provide efficient and even combustion. The injector needle is lubricated by fuel that accumulates in the spring chamber and is channelled to the

injection pump return hose by leak-off pipes.

4 Preheater or "glow" plugs are fitted to each swirl chamber to facilitate cold starting. Additionally, a thermostatic sensor in the cooling system operates a fast idle lever to increase the idling speed and supply additional fuel when the engine is cold.

5 A stop solenoid cuts the fuel supply to the injection pump rotor when the ignition is switched off, and there is also a hand-operated stop lever for use in an emergency. The injection pump fitted to Turbo models is similar to that fitted to non-Turbo models, but incorporates an overfuelling device varies the quantity of fuel injected in response to turbo boost pressure **(see illustration)**. Pressure is sensed via a hose connected to the inlet manifold. An electromagnetic timing system advances injection timing when the engine is cold. The system is switched off by a contact activated by movement of the fast idle control lever **(see illustrations)**.

6 Servicing of the injection pump and injectors is very limited for the home mechanic, and any dismantling other than that described in this Chapter must be entrusted to a Peugeot dealer or fuel injection specialist.

7 From late 1989 (205 models) or early 1990 (309 models) the fuel filter is modified. The coolant-heated filter base is no longer fitted. Fuel heating takes place in a heat exchanger on the engine.

2 Turbocharger - description and precautions

4

Description

1 A turbocharger is fitted selected models. It increases engine efficiency by raising the pressure in the inlet manifold above atmospheric pressure. Instead of the air simply being sucked into the cylinders, it is forced in.

2 Energy for the operation of the turbocharger comes from the exhaust gases.

1.5A Overfuelling device (arrowed) on Turbo fuel pump

1.5B Electromagnetic timing device (arrowed) on Turbo fuel pump

1.5C Electromagnetic timing contact (arrowed) on the fast idle control lever

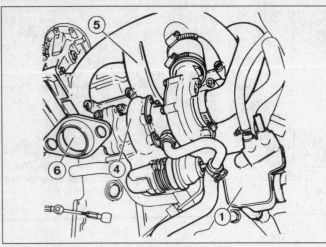

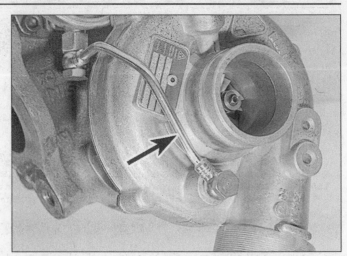

2.2 Fuel preheater (1) and other components on the rear of the XUD 7T engine

4 Turbocharger   5 Inlet manifold   6 Exhaust outlet flange

2.3 View of compressor end of turbocharger, showing wastegate actuator control pipe (arrowed)

The exhaust gas flows through a specially shaped housing (the turbine housing), and in so doing, spins the turbine wheel. The turbine wheel is attached to a shaft, at the end of which is another vaned wheel known as the compressor wheel. The compressor wheel spins in its own housing, and compresses the inducted air on the way to the inlet manifold **(see illustration)**.

3 Boost pressure (the pressure in the inlet manifold) is limited by a wastegate, which diverts the exhaust gas away from the turbine wheel in response to a pressure-sensitive actuator **(see illustration)**.

3.1 Inlet duct connection to front panel tube

4 The turbo shaft is pressure-lubricated by a feed pipe from the main oil gallery. The shaft 'floats' on a cushion of oil. A drain pipe returns the oil to the sump.

Precautions

5 The turbocharger operates at extremely high speeds and temperatures. Certain precautions must be observed, to avoid premature failure of the turbo or injury to the operator.

6 Do not operate the turbo with any parts exposed. Foreign objects falling onto the rotating vanes could cause excessive damage and (if ejected) personal injury.

7 Do not race the engine immediately after start-up, especially if it is cold. Give the oil a few seconds to circulate.

8 Always allow the engine to return to idle speed before switching it off - do not blip the throttle and switch off, as this will leave the turbo spinning without lubrication.

9 Allow the engine to idle for several minutes before switching off after a high-speed run.

10 Observe the recommended intervals for oil and filter changing, and use a reputable oil of the specified quality. Neglect of oil changing, or use of inferior oil, can cause carbon formation on the turbo shaft and subsequent failure.

3 Air cleaner and element - removal and refitting

Removal

1 On 205 and 309 models, disconnect the air inlet duct from the tube on the front panel **(see illustration)**.

2 On 305 models, disconnect the air inlet and outlet ducts from the air cleaner.

3 On Horizon models, disconnect the outlet duct from the air cleaner cover.

4 Unscrew the nut or screw and lift off the cover **(see illustration)**. On some models (i.e. 309 Turbo), the air cleaner cover is secured by spring clips **(see illustration)**. The cover on 405 models can be completely removed by disconnecting the inlet hose **(see illustration)**.

5 Remove the element and wipe clean the inside surfaces of the main body and cover **(see illustrations)**.

6 To remove the main body, on models other than the Horizon, disconnect the crankcase ventilation hose from the oil separator, then unscrew the mounting bolt from the mounting rubbers **(see illustrations)**. If necessary, also disconnect the air duct from the cover. The

3.4A Air cleaner cover retaining screw (205 models)

3.4B One of the spring clips securing the air cleaner assembly cover (405 models)

3.4C Disconnecting the air cleaner inlet hose (405 models)

3.5A Removing the air cleaner element
(205 models)

3.5B Removing the air cleaner element
(405 models)

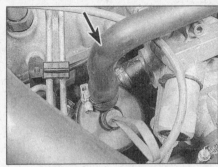

3.6A Disconnect the crankcase ventilation
hose from the oil separator

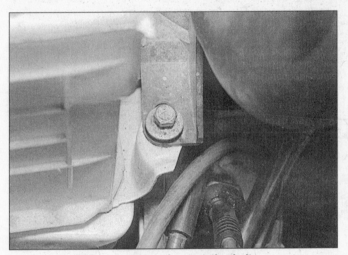

3.6B . . . unscrew the mounting bolt . . .

3.6C . . . and withdraw the air cleaner body from the mounting
rubbers

4

3.6D One of the springs clips securing the air cleaner assembly to
the support tray

3.6E Rubber location grommets in the air cleaner support tray

3.6F Air cleaner support tray mounting nut and bolt

3.7A Disconnect the crankcase ventilation hose from the oil separator . . .

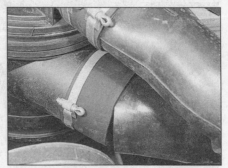

3.7B . . . disconnect the air inlet duct . . .

3.7C . . . release the rubber band . . .

3.7D . . . and lift out the air cleaner. Note the rubber mounting pad - arrowed

3.7E Special spring clip on the air duct (Horizon models)

support tray, on 405 models, may be unbolted if required (see illustrations).

7 On Horizon models, disconnect the crankcase ventilation hose from the oil separator and the inlet duct from the main body. Release the rubber band and lift the main body from its lower mounting rubber pad. If necessary, also disconnect the air duct from the cover and inlet manifold, noting the special clip (see illustrations).

Refitting

8 Refitting is a reversal of removal.

4 Air distribution box (405 non-Turbo models) - removal and refitting

Removal

1 Loosen the clip and disconnect the air inlet hose from the front of the distribution box (see illustration).

2 Loosen the clip and disconnect the crankcase ventilation hose from the oil separator (see illustration).

3 Unscrew and remove the bolts securing the rear of the distribution box to the inlet manifold (see illustration).

4 Lift the air distribution box from the inlet manifold, and withdraw it from the engine compartment (see illustration).

5 Plug the inlet manifold apertures with clean cloth, to prevent dirt ingress (see illustration).

6 Check the condition of the O-rings on the ends of the air distribution box stubs, and if necessary renew them (see illustration).

4.1 Disconnecting the air inlet hose from the front of the distribution box

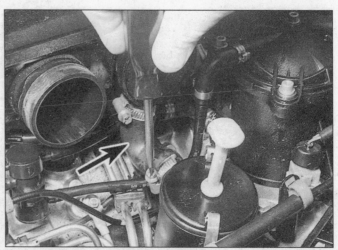

4.2 Disconnecting the crankcase ventilation hose (arrowed), from the oil separator

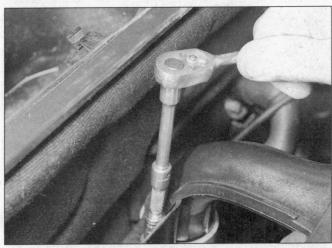

4.3 Removing the air distribution box mounting bolts

4.4 Removing the air distribution box

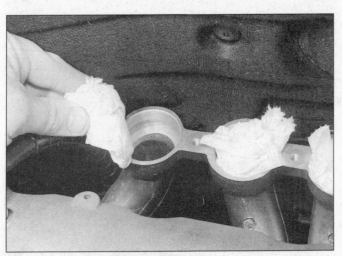

4.5 Plugging the inlet manifold apertures

4.6 Checking the O-rings on the ends of the air distribution box stubs

4

Refitting

7 Refitting is a reversal of the removal procedure.

5.1 The intercooler fitted to Turbo models

5 Intercooler (405 Turbo models) - description, removal and refitting

Description

1 Turbo models are equipped with an intercooler (see illustration). This is an air-to-air heat exchanger, which takes the compressed induction air from the turbocharger, and removes from it some of the heat it gained in being compressed. Removal of this heat increases the efficiency of the engine.

Removal

2 Lift off the rubber surround from the top of the intercooler (see illustration).

3 Slacken the intercooler air inlet hose clip, and disconnect the hose (see illustration).
4 Remove the Allen screws from the rear

5.2 Removing the rubber surround from the top of the intercooler

5.3 Disconnecting the intercooler air inlet hose

5.4A Removing the intercooler rear . . .

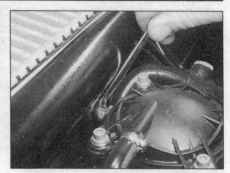

5.4B . . . and front mounting bolts

edge of the intercooler, then unscrew the front mounting bolts **(see illustrations)**.

5 Disconnect the intercooler-to-injection pump hose **(see illustration)**.

6 Unclip the crankcase ventilation system oil trap **(see illustration)**.

7 Lift off the intercooler. Recover the rubber seal between the intercooler outlet and the inlet manifold **(see illustrations)**.

Refitting

8 Clean the intercooler matrix with a soft brush, or by blowing air through it. Make sure that the inlet manifold O-ring seal is in good condition, and renew it if necessary.

9 Refit by reversing the removal operations.

5.5 Disconnecting the intercooler to injection pump hose

5.6 Unclipping the crankcase ventilation system oil trap

5.7A Removing the intercooler

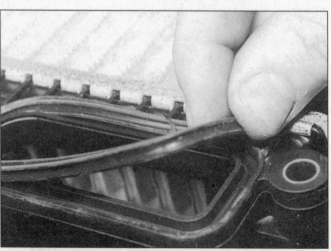

5.7B Removing the rubber seal from the inlet manifold

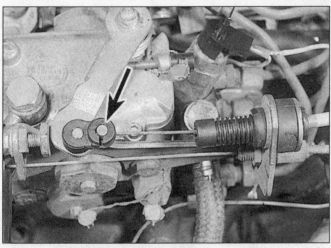

6.7A Accelerator cable connection - arrowed (205 models)

6.7B Accelerator cable connection - arrowed (Horizon models)

6 Injection pump - removal and refitting

Note: *From April 1988, the Lucas CAV/Roto-Diesel pump is fitted with a dust shield to protect the front bearing seals. If an earlier-type pump is removed for any reason, the opportunity should be taken to obtain and fit a dust shield kit.*

Removal

1 Disconnect the battery negative lead.

2 Cover the alternator with a plastic bag as a precaution against spillage of diesel fuel.

3 Remove the air cleaner assembly, as described in Section 3. Disconnect the crankcase ventilation hoses and remove the oil separator, where applicable.

4 Apply the handbrake, then jack up the front right-hand corner of the vehicle until the wheel is just clear of the ground. Support the vehicle on an axle stand and engage 4th or 5th gear. This will enable the engine to be turned easily by turning the right-hand wheel.

5 On Horizon models, remove the centre timing cover section.

6 Pull up the special clip, release the spring clips and withdraw the front timing cover section.

7 Open the accelerator lever on the injection pump and disconnect the cable by passing it through the special slot **(see illustrations)**. Disconnect the cable adjustment ferrule from the bracket.

8 Note the position of the end stop on the fast idle cable then loosen the screw and disconnect the inner cable **(see illustration)**. Unscrew the adjustment locknut and remove the cable and ferrule from the bracket.

9 Loosen the clip and disconnect the fuel supply hose **(see illustration)**. On Turbo models, disconnect the boost pressure hose from the overfuelling device.

10 Disconnect the main fuel return pipe and the injector leak off return pipe from the union tube **(see illustration)**.

11 Disconnect the wire from the stop solenoid **(see illustration)**.

12 Unscrew the union nuts securing the injector pipes to the injection pump **(see illustration)** and injectors. Remove the pipes complete.

6.8 Fast idle cable and end stop - arrowed (Horizon models with early Bosch pumps)

6.9 Fuel supply hose (A) and return pipe (B), (Horizon models with early Bosch pumps)

6.10 Disconnecting the main fuel return pipe (205 models with Lucas CAV/Roto-Diesel pump)

6.11 Stop solenoid and wire (arrowed)

6.12 Injector pipe union nuts on the Lucas CAV/Roto-Diesel injection pump

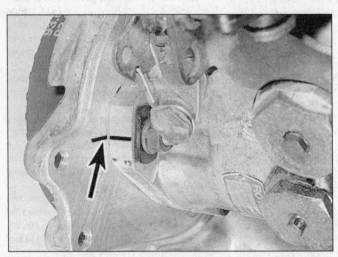

6.15 Mark the injection pump in relation to the mounting bracket (arrowed)

6.16A Injection pump mounting nut and plate (arrowed)

13 Turn the engine by means of the front right-hand wheel or crankshaft pulley bolt until the two bolt holes in the injection pump sprocket are aligned with the corresponding holes in the engine front plate.

14 Insert two M8 bolts through the holes and hand tighten them. The bolts must retain the sprocket while the injection pump is removed thereby making it unnecessary to remove the timing belt.

15 Mark the injection pump in relation to the mounting bracket using a scriber or felt tip pen **(see illustration)**. This will ensure that the correct timing when refitting. If a new pump is being fitted transfer the mark from the old pump to give an approximate setting.

16 Unscrew the three mounting nuts and remove the plates. Unscrew and remove the rear mounting bolt and support the injection pump on a block of wood **(see illustrations)**.

17 On pre-late 1992 models, unscrew the sprocket nut until the taper is released from the sprocket. The nut acts as a puller, together with the plate bolted to the sprocket. From late

1992, the fuel injection pump sprocket bolt no longer incorporates a puller. To free the sprocket from the taper on the injection pump shaft, a flange must be bolted to the sprocket before unscrewing the bolt. The flange can be obtained from an old injection pump sprocket, if available, and used to remove the new sprocket. Alternatively, a flange can be made

up from steel plate. Do not be tempted to free the sprocket by hammering or levering; there is a risk of damaging the injection pump if this is done.

18 Continue to unscrew the sprocket nut and withdraw the injection pump from the mounting bracket **(see illustration)**. Recover the Woodruff key from the shaft groove if it is loose.

6.16B Injection pump mounting bracket (arrowed)

6.18 Removing the injection pump from its mounting bracket

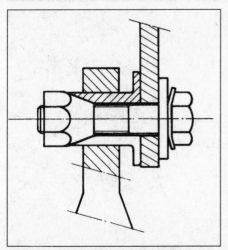

6.26 Cross-section of injection pump rear mounting

Refitting

19 Begin refitting the injection pump by fitting the Woodruff key to the shaft groove (if removed).

20 Unbolt the puller plate from the injection pump sprocket.

21 Insert the injection pump from behind the sprocket, making sure that the shaft key enters the groove in the sprocket. Screw on the nut and hand tighten it.

22 Fit the mounting nuts, together with their plates, and hand tighten the nuts.

23 Tighten the sprocket nut to the specified torque then refit the puller plate and tighten the bolts.

24 Unscrew and remove the two bolts from the injection pump sprocket.

25 If the original injection pump is being refitted, align the scribed marks and tighten the mounting nuts. If fitting a new pump, the timing must be set as described in Sections 7, 8 or 9, as applicable.

26 Refit the rear mounting bolt and special nut, tightening the nut slowly to allow the bush to align itself as shown **(see illustration)**.

27 Refit the injector pipes to the injection pump and tighten the union nuts.

28 Reconnect the wire to the stop solenoid.

29 Refit the fuel supply and return pipes.

30 Refit the fast idle cable and accelerator cable, and adjust them, referring to Sections 12 and 13.

31 Refit the timing cover sections and secure with the spring clips.

32 Lower the vehicle to the ground and apply the handbrake.

33 Remove the plastic bag from the alternator and reconnect the battery negative lead.

34 Where applicable, refit the oil separator and crankcase ventilation hoses.

35 Refit the air cleaner and ducting.

36 Prime the fuel circuit by first switching on the ignition to energise the stop solenoid, then actuating the pump on the fuel filter until resistance is felt. On early models fitted with a Lucas CAV/Roto-Diesel filter the pump plunger must first be unscrewed then retightened after priming.

37 Turn the ignition key to position 'M' and wait for the preheating warning light to go out. Start the engine and adjust the idling speed, referring to Chapter 1.

---

7 Injection pump static timing (Lucas CAV/Roto-Diesel) - checking

Caution: The maximum engine speed and transfer pressure settings, together with timing access plugs, are sealed by the manufacturers at the factory using locking wire and lead seals. Do not disturb the wire if the vehicle is still within the warranty period otherwise the warranty will be invalidated. Also do not attempt the timing procedure unless accurate instrumentation is available.

Pre 1987 models

1 Disconnect the battery negative lead.

2 Cover the alternator with a plastic bag as a precaution against spillage of diesel fuel.

3 Apply the handbrake, then jack up the front right-hand corner of the vehicle until the wheel is just clear of the ground. Support the vehicle on an axle stand and engage 4th or 5th gear. This will enable the engine to be turned easily by turning the right-hand wheel.

4 Disconnect the wire and unscrew the heater plug from cylinder No 4 (timing belt end). Note that the engine is timed with No 4 piston at TDC compression (i.e. No 1 piston at TDC with valves "rocking").

5 Two dial test indicators are now necessary for checking the positions of the No 4 piston and the injection pump. Magnetic type stands will be found helpful or alternatively brackets may be made for fitting to appropriate positions on the engine.

6 Unscrew and remove the blanking plug from the cylinder head next to No 4 injector **(see illustration)**.

7 Turn the engine forwards until pressure is felt in No 4 cylinder indicating that No 4 piston is beginning its compression stroke.

8 Position the dial test indicator over the blanking hole and fit the probe **(see illustration)**.

9 Turn the engine forwards until the maximum lift of piston No 4 is registered on the dial test indicator. Turn the engine slightly back and forth to determine the exact point of maximum lift then zero the indicator.

10 Loosen the lower of the two large side plugs on the side of the injection pump.

4

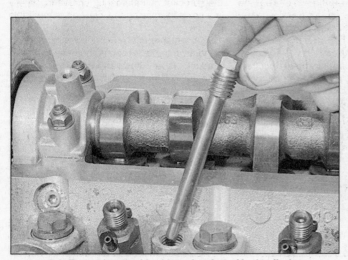

7.6 Removing the blanking plug from No 4 cylinder

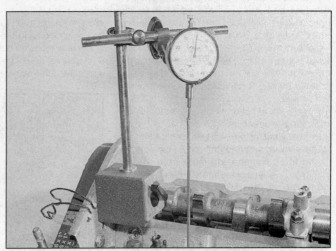

7.8 Setting No 4 piston timing position with a dial test indicator

7.10 Lucas CAV/Roto-Diesel injection pump with the timing plug removed

7.11A Timing the Lucas CAV/Roto-Diesel injection pump with a dial test indicator

Position a small container beneath the plug then remove the plug and catch the escaping fuel in the container **(see illustration)**.

11 Inside the plug aperture there is a probe guide. Insert the probe and connect it to the dial test indicator directly over the hole **(see illustration)**. Note that the end of the probe must be pointed in order to fully engage the groove in the pump rotor **(see illustration)**.

12 Turn the engine backwards approximately 1/8th of a turn or until the No 4 piston has moved 4.0 mm down the cylinder. Now turn the engine slowly forwards while watching the dial test indicator on the injection pump. After the probe has reached the bottom of the timing groove then risen by 0.01 to 0.02 mm, check that the upper dial test indicator reads 2.26 ± 0.05 mm before TDC. If the timing is incorrect continue as follows.

13 Check the zero setting of the upper dial test indicator by repeating the procedure given in paragraph 9.

14 Turn the engine backwards approximately ⅛th of a turn or until No 4 piston has moved 4.0 mm down the cylinder. Now turn the engine slowly forwards until No 4 piston is 2.26 ± 0.05 mm before TDC.

15 Unscrew the union nuts and disconnect the injector pipes from the injection pump. Loosen the injection pump mounting nuts and bolt.

16 Turn the pump body until the probe is at the bottom of the timing groove in the rotor. Zero the dial test indicator. Now turn the pump clockwise (from the injector pipe end) until the probe has risen by 0.01 to 0.02 mm.

17 Tighten the mounting nuts and bolts making sure that there is no movement on the dial test indicator.

18 Recheck the timing as described in paragraph 12.

19 Remove the dial test indicators and refit the plugs. Reconnect the injector pipes and tighten the union nuts.

20 Refit the heater plug and connect the wire.

21 Lower the car to the ground and reconnect the battery negative lead. Remove the plastic bag from the alternator.

22 Prime the fuel system as described in Section 21.

1987-on models

23 From 1987, a modified pump was progressively introduced. The pump can be recognised by the presence of a white plastic disc on its front face. A timing value is engraved on the disc **(see illustration)**. If the disc is blue, this denotes a factory-reconditioned pump. The timing value may also be found on a plastic tag attached to the pump control lever.

24 The pump timing is now carried out at TDC. Only one dial test indicator is needed, but it will be necessary to make up a bent rod

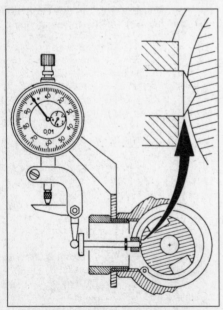

7.11B Checking the timing on the Lucas CAV/Roto-Diesel fuel injection pump

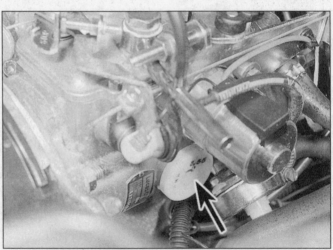

7.23 The white plastic disc (arrowed) fitted to later Lucas injection pumps indicates the static timing setting

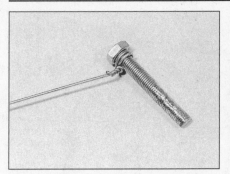

7.24 Home-made TDC setting tool

7.26 Removing the TDC probe plug located near No 4 injector

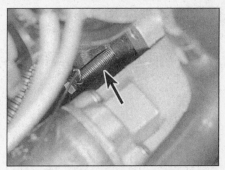

7.27 TDC setting tool (arrowed) inserted into the hole in the block

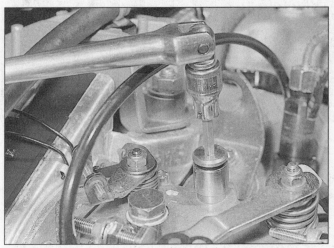

7.28A Removing the inspection plug from the top of the pump

7.28B Dial test indicator positioned over the inspection hole

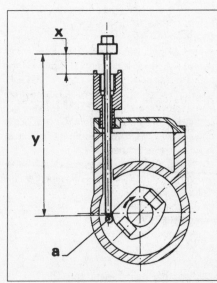

7.29A Timing probe details - later Lucas CAV/Roto-Diesel pump

a Timing piece
x Timing value (engraved on disc)
y 95.5 ± 0.01 mm
    Probe diameter = 7 mm

or similar tool to enter the TDC setting hole. The tool made up in the workshop consisted of an M8 bolt with the threads filed away, attached to a piece of welding rod **(see illustration)**. Alternatively, with the starter motor removed, a twist drill or straight rod can be used. See Chapter 2, Section 25, paragraph 26.

25 Prepare the engine as described in Section 7, paragraphs 1 to 3.

26 Turn the engine to bring No 4 cylinder (timing belt end) to TDC on compression. To establish which cylinder is on compression, remove No 4 cylinder heater (glow) plug or the TDC probe plug located near No 4 injector **(see illustration)**, and feel for pressure. Alternatively, remove the valve cover, and observe when No 1 cylinder valves are `rocking`, (inlet opening and exhaust closing).

27 Insert the TDC setting tool into the hole at the left-hand end of the cylinder block, behind the starter motor location. Turn the engine back and forth slightly until the tool enters the hole in the flywheel. Leave the tool in position **(see illustration)**.

28 Remove the inspection plug from the top of the pump. Position a dial test indicator so that it can read the movement of a probe

inserted into the hole. If a magnetic stand is to be used, the absence of ferrous metal in the vicinity poses a problem; a piece of steel plate can be bolted to the engine mounting or valve cover to carry the stand **(see illustrations)**.

29 Make up a probe to the dimensions shown **(see illustration)**. Insert the probe into the inspection hole so that the tip of the probe rests on the rotor timing piece. Position the dial test indicator to read the movement of the probe **(see illustration)**.

30 Remove the TDC setting tool. Turn the engine approximately a quarter-turn backwards. Zero the dial test indicator.

31 Turn the engine forwards slowly until the TDC setting tool can be re-inserted. Read the dial test indicator; the reading should correspond to the value engraved on the pump disc (± 0.04 mm).

32 If the reading is not as specified, continue as follows.

33 Disconnect the injector pipes from the pump. Slacken the pump mounting nuts and bolts, and swing the pump away from the engine. Zero the dial test indicator.

34 With the engine still at TDC, slowly swing the pump back towards the engine until the dial test indicator displays the value engraved

4

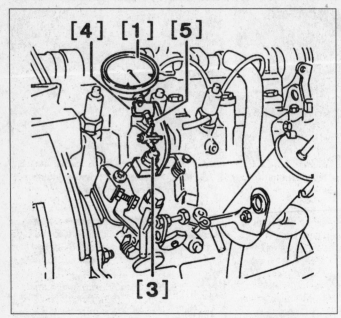

7.29B Checking the static timing on the Lucas injection pump
1 Dial test indicator   3 Probe   4 Fixture   5 Finger

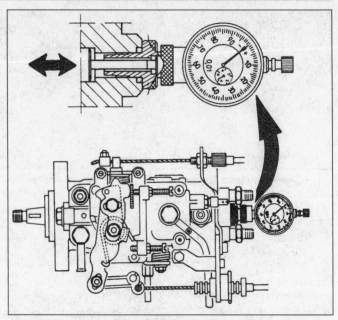

8.12 Checking the timing on the Bosch fuel injection pump

on the pump disc. In this position, tighten the pump mountings. Remove the TDC setting tool, and recheck the timing as just described.

35 When the timing is correct, reconnect the injector pipes, remove the dial test indicator and TDC setting tool, and refit the inspection plug.

36 Refit any other disturbed components, remove the plastic bag from the alternator, and lower the vehicle to the ground.

8   Injection pump static timing (Bosch), (except 405 models) - checking

Caution: Some of the injection pump settings and access plugs may be sealed by the manufacturers at the factory using locking wire and lead seals. Do not disturb the wire if the vehicle is still within the warranty period otherwise the warranty will be invalidated. Also do not attempt the timing procedure unless accurate instrumentation is available.

1 Disconnect the battery negative lead.

2 Cover the alternator with a plastic bag as a precaution against spillage of diesel fuel.

3 Apply the handbrake, then jack up the front right-hand corner of the vehicle until the wheel is just clear of the ground. Support the vehicle on an axle stand and engage 4th or 5th gear. This will enable the engine to be turned easily by turning the right-hand wheel.

4 Disconnect the wire and unscrew the heater plug from cylinder No 4 (timing belt end). Note that the engine is timed with No 4 piston at TDC compression (i.e. No 1 piston at TDC with valves "rocking").

5 Two dial test indicators are now necessary for checking the positions of the No 4 piston and the injection pump. Magnetic type stands will be found helpful or alternatively brackets may be made for fitting to appropriate positions on the engine.

6 Unscrew and remove the blanking plug from the cylinder head next to No 4 injector.

7 Turn the engine forwards until pressure is felt in No 4 cylinder, indicating that No 4 piston is beginning its compression stroke.

8 Position the dial test indicator over the blanking hole and fit the probe.

9 Turn the engine forwards until the maximum lift of piston No 4 is registered on the dial test indicator. Turn the engine slightly to and fro to determine the exact point of maximum lift then zero the indicator.

10 Unscrew the union nuts and disconnect the injector pipes for cylinders 1 and 2 from the injection pump.

11 Unscrew the blanking plug from the end of the injection pump between the injector pipe connections. Be prepared for the loss of some fuel.

12 Insert the probe and connect it to the dial test indicator positioned directly over the hole. The fixture used by Peugeot technicians is shown **(see illustration)**.

13 Turn the engine backwards approximately 1/8th of a turn or until the No 4 piston has moved 4.0 mm down the cylinder.

14 Zero the dial test indicator on the injection pump.

15 Turn the engine slowly forwards until the dial test indicator on the injection pump reads 0.30 mm. Then check that the upper dial test indicator reads 0.80 ± 0.03 mm before TDC for 1.7 litre models or 0.50 ± 0.03 mm before

TDC for 1.9 litre models. If the timing is incorrect continue as follows.

16 Check the zero setting of the upper dial test indicator by repeating the procedure given in paragraph 9.

17 Turn the engine backwards approximately ⅛th of a turn or until the No 4 piston had moved 4.0 mm down the cylinder. Now turn the engine slowly forwards until the upper dial test indicator reads 0.80 ± 0.03 mm before TDC for 1.7 litre models or 0.50 ± 0.03 mm before TDC for 1.9 litre models.

18 Unscrew the union nuts and disconnect the remaining injector pipes from the injection pump. Loosen the injection pump mounting nuts and bolt.

19 Turn the pump body anti-clockwise (from the injector pipe end) and check that the dial test indicator is zeroed. Now turn the pump body slowly clockwise until the dial test indicator reads 0.30 mm.

20 Tighten the mounting nuts and bolts, making sure that there is no movement on the dial test indicator.

21 Recheck the timing as described in paragraphs 13 to 15.

22 Remove the dial test indicators and refit the plugs. Reconnect the injector pipes and tighten the union nuts.

23 Refit the heater plug and connect the wire.

24 Lower the car to the ground and reconnect the battery negative lead. Remove the plastic bag from the alternator.

25 Prime the fuel system as described in Section 21.

9.3A Release the clip . . .

9.3B . . . and remove the front timing cover

9.4A Disconnecting the crankcase
ventilation hose

9 Injection pump static timing (Bosch), (405 models) - checking

Caution: Some of the injection pump settings and access plugs may be sealed by the manufacturers at the factory using locking wire and lead seals. Do not disturb the wire if the vehicle is still within the warranty period otherwise the warranty will be invalidated. Also do not attempt the timing procedure unless accurate instrumentation is available.

1 Remove the air cleaner, as described in Section 3. If preferred, unscrew and remove the TDC probe plug located near No 4 injector instead of removing the heater plug (refer to Section 7, paragraph 26).
2 Remove the intercooler (Turbo models) or air distribution box (non-Turbo models).
3 Unclip and remove the front timing cover (see illustrations).
4 Note the location of the injector pipes, then unscrew the union nuts and disconnect them from the injection pump and injectors. This is necessary to give free movement of the injection pump. Be prepared for the loss of some fuel. To give additional working room,

disconnect the crankcase ventilation hose from the valve cover, and disconnect the fuel return hoses and valve. Fit covers to the pipe adapter apertures, to prevent dust and dirt entering the fuel system (see illustrations).

> **HAYNES HINT**
> *Cut the fingertips from an old pair of rubber gloves and secure them over the pipe apertures with elastic bands.*

5 Unscrew the blanking plug from the end of the injection pump between the injector pipe connections (see illustration).

9.4B Disconnecting the fuel return
hoses . . .

9.4C . . . and valve

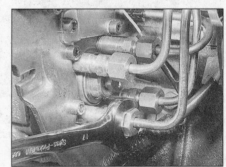

9.4D Unscrew the union nuts . . .

9.4E . . . and disconnect the injector pipes

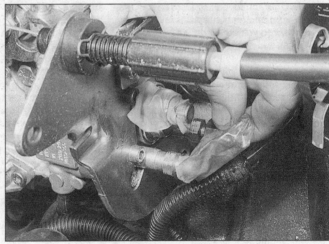

9.4F Fitting covers to the pipe adapters

4

9.5 Removing the blanking plug

9.6A Fit the adapter . . .

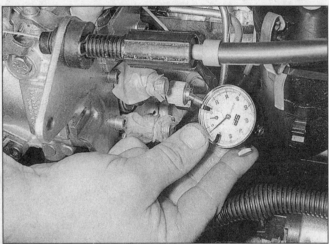

9.6B . . . and the dial test indicator

9.7 Inserting the TDC timing rod

6 Fit a dial test indicator (DTI) to the end of the injection pump, and load it by 2 or 3 mm **(see illustrations)**. Depending on the size of the DTI, it may be found helpful to tie back the engine oil separator with a plastic cable-tie.

7 Turn the engine forwards until pressure is felt in No 4 cylinder, indicating that No 4 piston is commencing its compression stroke. Continue turning the engine in its normal direction until a 8 mm diameter rod can be inserted through the timing hole behind the starter motor into the flywheel. At this point, No 4 piston is at TDC on compression. The ideal tool for doing this is a length of metal rod bent to pass behind the starter motor **(see illustration)**. Alternatively, the home-made TDC setting tool described earlier in Section 7, paragraph 24, may be used.

8 Remove the TDC setting tool, and turn the crankshaft anti-clockwise until the injection pump plunger is at its bottom dead centre (BDC) position, indicated by the reading on the DTI ceasing to fall. Zero the dial test indicator at this position.

9 Turn the crankshaft slowly in its normal direction of rotation, until No 4 piston reaches TDC and the setting tool can be inserted into the flywheel.

10 Check that the reading on the DTI corresponds to the static timing plunger movement given in the Specifications for the relevant engine.

11 If adjustment is necessary, first loosen the injection pump mounting bolts, and turn the complete pump away from the engine to its fully retarded position **(see illustration)**.

12 Turn the injection pump slowly in the opposite direction until the correct static timing plunger movement is registered on the DTI.

13 Tighten the injection pump mounting bolts to the specified torque, then re-check the static timing.

14 Remove the timing rod and the dial test indicator.

15 Refit the blanking plug to the end of the injection pump, and tighten securely.

16 Refit the injector pipes and tighten the union nuts.

17 Refit the front timing cover.

18 Refit the air distribution box (non-Turbo models) or intercooler (Turbo models).

19 Refit and tighten the TDC probe plug or heater (glow) plug, as applicable.

20 Remove the plastic bag from the alternator, and reconnect the battery negative lead.

21 Lower the vehicle to the ground.

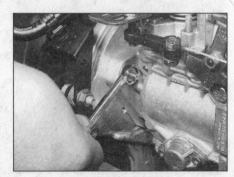

9.11 Loosening the injection pump mounting bolts

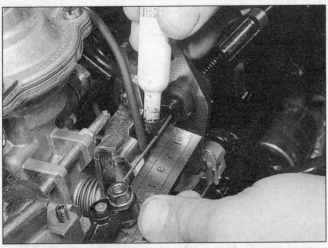

10.1 Marking the accelerator inner cable 11.0 mm from the end of the outer cable

10.3 Load lever position switch

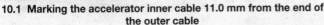

10 Load lever switch, Bosch fuel injection pump (405 models) - adjustment

11 Injection pump dynamic timing (all models) - checking

12 Fast idle control - removal, refitting and adjustment

1 Mark the accelerator inner cable 11.0 mm from the end of the outer cable **(see illustration)**.

2 Move the load lever until the mark on the inner cable coincides with the end of the outer cable, and hold the lever in this position.

3 Loosen the switch mounting screws, then turn the switch until the internal contacts click open **(see illustration)**.

4 Tighten the mounting screws with the switch in this position, then release the lever.

5 Move the lever again, and check that the switch contacts operate when the mark on the inner cable reaches the end of the outer cable.

Dynamic timing is given in the Specifications for certain models. However, the specialist equipment necessary to check the timing is quite expensive, and will not normally be available to the home mechanic. Also, the setting-up procedure varies according to the type of equipment used, so it is important to refer to the equipment maker's instructions when connecting the equipment to the engine. Note that most dynamic checking testers are only accurate to approximately ± 2°.

Dynamic timing should only be used within the limitations of the checking equipment. If the timing appears incorrect, then it must only be adjusted using the static timing method.

Removal

1 Remove the air cleaner and ducting, as necessary.

2 Drain the cooling system as described in Chapter 1.

3 Loosen the clamp screw or nut and remove the end fitting from the inner cable **(see illustrations)**.

4 Unscrew the locknut and remove the adjustment ferrule and outer cable from the bracket on the injection pump **(see illustration)**.

5 Unscrew the thermostatic sensor from the thermostat housing cover and recover the washer.

12.3A Fast idle inner cable and end fitting (arrowed) on the early Bosch injection pump

12.3B Fast idle inner cable and end fitting (arrowed) on the later Bosch injection pump

12.4 Fast idle cable adjustment ferrule on the Lucas CAV/Roto-Diesel injection pump

13.1A Accelerator cable on the Lucas CAV/Roto-Diesel injection pump

Refitting

6 Fit the new thermostatic sensor and washer and tighten it.

7 Insert the cable and ferrule in the bracket and screw on the locknut finger tight.

8 Insert the cable end through the lever and fit end fitting loosely.

Adjustment

9 With the engine cold, push the fast idle lever or the knurled adjuster (pre January 1984, Bosch injection pumps) fully towards the flywheel end of the engine. Then tighten the clamp screw or nut with the end fitting touching the lever or adjuster.

10 Adjust the ferrule to ensure that the fast idle lever is touching its stop then tighten the locknuts.

11 Measure the exposed length of the inner cable.

12 Refill the cooling system as described in Chapter 1, and run the engine to normal operating temperature.

13 With the engine hot, check that the length of the inner cable has increased by at least 6.0 mm indicating that the thermostatic sensor is functioning correctly.

14 On pre January 1984, Bosch injection pumps, check that there is a gap of 1.0 mm, between the cable end fitting and the of the adjuster. If not, adjust the ferrule.

15 Check that the engine speed increases when the fast idle lever or adjuster is pushed towards the flywheel end of the engine. On the early Bosch pump the speed should be 200 ± 50 rpm and on other models the fast idling speed should be 950 ± 50 rpm. Turn the knurled adjuster or lever stop, as necessary.

16 Switch off the engine.

13 Accelerator cable - removal, refitting and adjustment

Removal

1 Open the accelerator lever on the injection pump and disconnect the inner cable by passing it through the special slot (see illustrations).

2 Disconnect the cable adjustment ferrule and outer cable from the bracket (see illustration).

3 Working inside the vehicle, remove the lower facia panel where necessary then release the inner cable end fitting from the top of the accelerator pedal.

4 Pull the spring shock absorber from the bulkhead and withdraw the accelerator cable from inside the engine compartment.

13.1B Accelerator cable attachment on the Bosch injection pump

13.2 Accelerator cable adjustment ferrule on the Bosch injection pump

13.6 Spring clip for adjusting accelerator cable (arrowed)

Refitting

5 Refitting is a reversal of removal, but adjust the cable as follows.

Adjustment

6 Have an assistant fully depress the accelerator pedal then check that the accelerator lever on the injection pump is touching the maximum speed adjustment screw. If not, pull the spring clip from the adjustment ferrule, reposition the ferrule and fit the spring clip in the groove next to the metal washer **(see illustration)**. With the accelerator pedal fully released check that the accelerator lever is touching the anti-stall (deceleration) adjustment screw. On the early Bosch pump, the engine must not be hot, otherwise the lever will be touching the fast idle knurled adjuster.

14 Injection pump anti-stall (Lucas CAV/Roto-Diesel) - adjustment

Note: *This adjustment requires the use of a tachometer - refer to Chapter 1, Section 17, for alternative methods.*

1 Run the engine to normal operating temperature then switch it off.
2 Insert a 3.0 mm shim or feeler blade between the accelerator lever and the anti-stall adjustment screw.
3 Turn the stop lever clockwise until it is clear of the hole in the fast idle lever then insert a 3.0 mm dowel rod or twist drill.
4 Start the engine and allow it to idle. The engine speed should be 900 ± 50 rpm.
5 If adjustment is necessary loosen the locknut, turn the anti-stall adjustment screw as required, then tighten the locknut **(see illustration)**.
6 Remove the feeler blade and twist drill and adjust the idling speed as described in Chapter 1.
7 Turn the accelerator lever to increase the engine speed to 3000 rpm then quickly release the lever. If the deceleration is too fast and the engine stalls turn the anti-stall adjustment screw ¼ turn anti-clockwise (viewed from flywheel end of engine). If the deceleration is too slow, resulting in poor engine braking, turn the screw ¼ turn clockwise.
8 Retighten the locknut after making an adjustment then recheck the idling speed as described in Chapter 1.
9 With the engine idling check the operation of the manual stop control by turning the stop lever clockwise. The engine must stop instantly.
10 Switch off the ignition switch.

15 Injection pump anti-stall (Bosch, January 1984-on) - adjustment

Note: *This adjustment requires the use of a tachometer - refer to Chapter 1, Section 17, for alternative methods.*

1 Run the engine to normal operating temperature. Note the exact idling speed then switch off the engine.
2 Insert a 1.0 mm shim or feeler blade between the accelerator lever and the anti-stall adjustment screw.
3 Start the engine and allow it to idle. The engine speed should exceed the normal idling speed by 50 rpm.
4 If adjustment is necessary loosen the locknut and turn the anti-stall adjustment screw as required. Retighten the locknut.
5 Remove the feeler blade and allow the engine to idle.
6 Move the fast idle lever fully towards the flywheel end of the engine and check that the engine speed increases to 950 ± 50 rpm. If necessary loosen the locknut and turn the stop adjusting screw as required, then retighten the locknut.
7 With the engine idling, check the operation of the manual stop control by turning the stop lever. The engine must stop instantly.
8 Switch off the ignition switch.

16 Maximum engine speed - checking and adjustment

Caution: On Lucas CAV/Roto-Diesel injection pumps the maximum speed setting is sealed by the manufacturers at the factory using locking wire and a lead seal. Do not disturb the wire if the vehicle is still within the warranty period otherwise the warranty will be invalidated. This adjustment requires the use of a tachometer - refer to Chapter 1, Section 17, for alternative methods.

Checking

1 Run the engine to normal operating temperature.
2 Have an assistant fully depress the accelerator pedal and check that the maximum engine speed is as given in the Specifications. Do not keep the engine at maximum speed for more than two or three seconds.

Adjustment

3 If adjustment is necessary stop the engine then loosen the locknut, turn the maximum engine speed adjustment screw as necessary, and retighten the locknut **(see illustration)**.

4

14.5 Anti-stall adjustment on the Lucas CAV/Roto-Diesel injection pump showing feeler blades (1) and twist drill (2)

16.3 Maximum engine speed adjustment screw on the Lucas CAV/Roto-Diesel injection pump

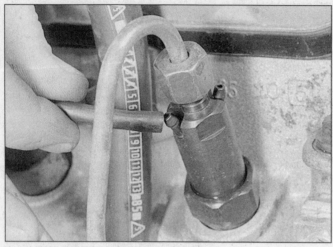

17.3 Disconnect the leak off pipes from the injectors

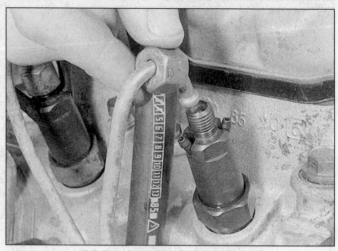

17.5 Disconnecting the injector pipes

17.6A Removing an injector

17.6B An injector

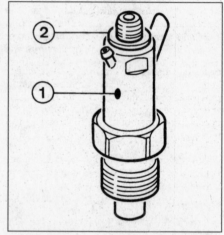

17.6C Injector markings from late 1992
1 Calibration paint mark (see Specifications)
2 Green ring

4 Repeat the procedure in paragraph 2 to check the adjustment.
5 Switch off the ignition switch.

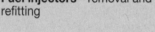

17 Fuel injectors - removal and refitting

⚠ *Warning: Exercise extreme caution when working on the fuel injectors. Never expose the hands or any part of the body to injector spray, as the high working pressure can cause the fuel to penetrate the skin,*

with possibly fatal results. You are strongly advised to have any work that involves testing the injectors under pressure, carried out by a dealer or fuel injection specialist.

Removal

1 Remove the air cleaner and ducting, referring to Section 3.
2 Clean around the injectors and injector pipe union nuts.
3 Pull the leak off pipes from the injectors **(see illustration)**.
4 Loosen the injector pipe union nuts at the injection pump.
5 Unscrew the union nuts and disconnect the

pipes from the injectors **(see illustration)**. If required the injector pipes may be completely removed.
6 Unscrew the injectors and remove them from the cylinder head **(see illustrations)**.
7 Recover the copper washers, fire-seal washers, and sleeves from the cylinder head **(see illustrations)**.

17.7A Removing an injector copper washer . . .

17.7B . . . fire-seal washer . . .

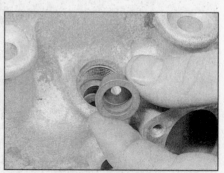

17.7C . . . and sleeve

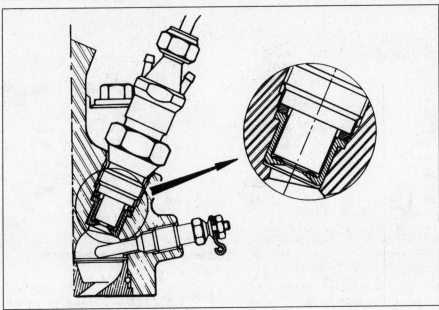

17.13 Cross-section of cylinder head showing location of injector and heater plug
Note fire-seal washer position in inset

18 Preheater system -
description and testing

Description

1 Each swirl chamber has a preheater plug (commonly called a glow plug) screwed into it. The plugs are electrically operated before, during and immediately after starting a cold engine. Preheating is not required on a hot engine.

2 On all engines, the glow plugs are operated for approximately 7 seconds before starting the engine.

3 A post-heating system on some later engines keeps the glow plugs operating for up to 3 minutes after the engine has been started, provided that the load lever switch is closed and that the engine temperature is below 60°C. This reduces noise and smoke in the period after a cold start.

4 A thermoswitch located behind the fuel filter housing monitors the temperature. The thermoswitch is identified by having a mauve plastic ring.

Testing

5 If the system malfunctions, testing is ultimately by substitution of known good units, but some preliminary checks may be made as follows.

6 Disconnect the main supply cable from the relevant heater plug terminal **(see illustration)**.

7 Connect a voltmeter between the supply cable and earth making sure that the cable is kept clear of the engine and bodywork. Have an assistant switch on the preheater and check that there is a 12 volt supply for several seconds before the system cuts out. Typically there should be a 7 second supply at an ambient temperature of 20°C (68°F), but this will increase with colder temperatures and

8 If an injector sleeve is tight in the cylinder head, it can be removed using the following procedure. First block the injector sleeve hole with grease, to prevent debris entering the combustion chamber. Cut a thread in the sleeve using a tap, then screw in a stud having a matching thread. Using a thick washer in contact with the cylinder head, tighten a nut onto the washer, and pull out the sleeve.

Refitting

9 Obtain new copper washers and fire-seal washers.

10 Take care not to drop the injectors or allow the needles at their tips to become damaged. The injectors are precision-made to fine limits and must not be handled roughly, in

particular do not mount them in a bench vice.

11 Accurate testing and calibration of the injectors must be left to a specialist.

12 Begin refitting by inserting the sleeves. New injector sleeves may be inserted in the cylinder head by using an old injector as a drift. Do not fit the sealing washer or fire ring until the new sleeve is fully installed.

13 Fit the fire-seal washers (convex face uppermost), and copper washers **(see illustration)**.

14 Insert the injectors and tighten them to the specified torque **(see illustration)**.

15 Refit the injector pipes and tighten the union nuts to the specified torque.

16 Reconnect the leak off pipes **(see illustration)**.

17 Refit the air cleaner and ducting.

4

17.14 Tightening an injector

17.16 A leak off pipe connected between two injectors

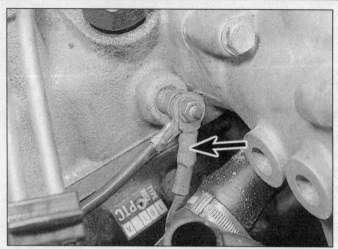

18.6 Heater plug terminal and main supply cable - arrowed (205 models)

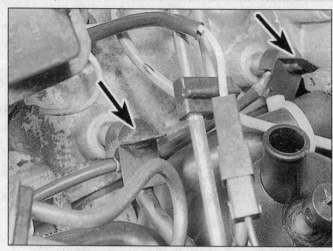

19.3 Plastic clips (arrowed) on heater plug terminals

decrease with higher temperatures. If there is no supply, the relay or associated wiring is at fault. Switch off the ignition.

8 Connect an ammeter between the battery positive terminal and the heater plug inter-connecting wire. Check that the current draw after 20 seconds is 12 amps per working plug, i.e. 48 amps if all four plugs are working.

9 If one or more heater plugs appear to be not drawing the expected current disconnect the inter-connecting wire and check them individually or use an ohmmeter to check them for continuity and equal resistance.

10 Re-connect the main supply cable after completing the tests.

19 Heater plugs and relay - removal and refitting

Heater plugs

Removal

1 Check that the ignition switch is off.
2 Remove the air cleaner and ducting, referring to Section 3, if necessary.
3 Prise the plastic clips from the heater plugs (see illustration).
4 Unscrew the nuts from the heater plug terminals. Remove the main supply cable from the relevant heater plug then remove the inter-connecting wire from all the plugs (see illustration).
5 Unscrew the heater plugs and remove them from the cylinder head (see illustrations).

Refitting

6 Refitting is a reversal of removal; tighten the plugs to the specified torque (see illustration).

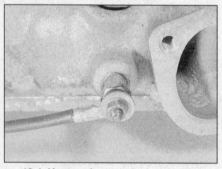

19.4 Heater plug terminal and inter-connecting wire

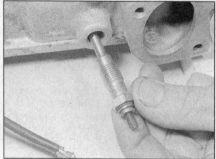

19.5A Removing a heater plug

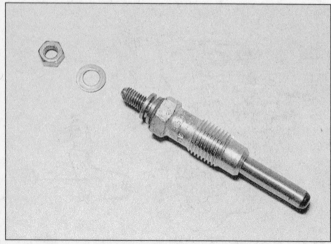

19.5B Heater plug and terminal nut

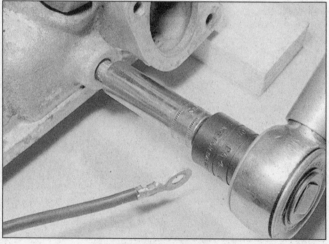

19.6 Tightening a heater plug

19.7 Heater plug control unit on 205 models

Relay

Removal

7 The relay is located on the left-hand side of the engine compartment near the battery **(see illustration)**.

8 First disconnect the battery negative lead.

Unbolt the relay from the side panel and disconnect the wiring.

Refitting

9 Refitting is a reversal of removal.

20 Stop solenoid - description, removal and refitting

Description

1 The stop solenoid is located on the end of the injection pump by the injector pipes **(see illustrations)**. Its purpose is to cut the fuel supply when the ignition is switched off. If an open circuit occurs in the supply wiring it will be impossible to start the engine as the fuel will not reach the injectors.

Removal

2 With the ignition switched off unscrew the

nut and disconnect the wire **(see illustration)**.

3 Before removing the stop solenoid, clean the surrounding area, to prevent dust and dirt entering the fuel system.

4 Unscrew and remove the stop solenoid and recover the washer or O-ring. On the Bosch pump, the fast idle cable support plate may be removed first **(see illustration)**.

5 After removing the solenoid, recover the plunger piston and spring if they have remained in the injection pump.

Refitting

6 Operate the hand-priming pump several times, to discharge any debris from the threads in the pump casing.

7 Fit a new O-ring to the solenoid.

8 Refitting is a reversal of the removal procedure. Tighten the solenoid to the specified torque.

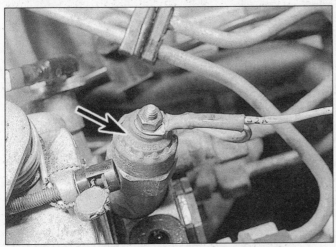

20.1A Stop solenoid (arrowed) on the Lucas CAV/Roto-Diesel pump

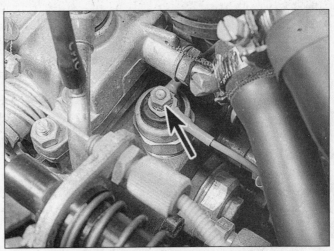

20.1B Stop solenoid (arrowed) on the early Bosch pump

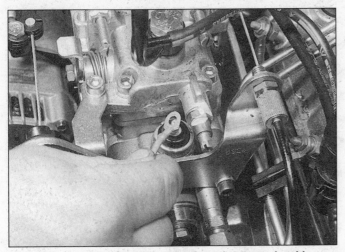

20.2 Disconnecting the wiring from the stop solenoid

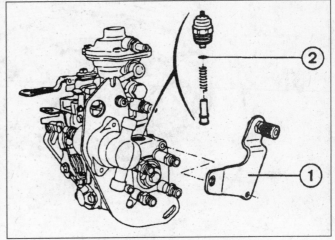

20.4 Stop solenoid removal
1 Fast idle cable support plate   2 O-ring

21 Fuel injection system - priming

Pre 1993 models

1 After disconnecting part of the fuel injection system or running out of fuel it is necessary to carry out the priming procedure before starting the engine.

2 Loosen the bleed screw on the fuel filter head two or three turns. On the Lucas CAV/Roto-Diesel filter a plastic drain tube may be fitted to the bleed screw and a small container positioned to catch the fuel.

3 Actuate the plunger until fuel free from air bubbles flows from the bleed screw. On some Lucas CAV/Roto-Diesel filter heads the plunger must first be unscrewed **(see illustration)**, and with this type the plunger may become detached from the internal piston. If this happens, unscrew the housing and press the piston back onto the plunger. Refit the housing and operate the plunger slowly.

4 Tighten the bleed screw.

5 Turn on the ignition so that the stop solenoid is energised then activate the plunger until resistance is felt.

6 Where applicable on Lucas CAV/Roto-Diesel filters retighten the plunger.

7 Turn the ignition switch to position "M" and wait for the preheater warning light to go out.

8 Fully depress the accelerator pedal and start the engine. Additional cranking may be necessary to finally bleed the fuel system before the engine starts.

1993-on models

9 Priming of the system is carried out by switching on the ignition and repeatedly

21.3 Lucas CAV/Roto-Diesel fuel filter plunger

squeezing the hand-priming bulb, located on the right hand side of the engine compartment, until increased resistance is felt. There is no need to open any bleed screws.

10 Purging of air from the high pressure side of the injection pump and the injectors is carried out when the engine is turned by the starter motor. This process may be accelerated by slightly loosening each pipe union in turn at the injector end, until fuel emerges as the engine is being turned. Note that the fuel may spurt out under considerable pressure when doing this; wrap a rag around the slackened union and keep well away to avoid personal injury. Tighten the unions on completion, and mop up any spilt fuel.

22 Fuel gauge sender unit (405 models) - checking

Note: *For other models, refer to the relevant main manual.*

1 If the fuel gauge sender unit is suspected of being faulty, check that it is fitted correctly,

since it is possible for the operating arm movement to be restricted.

2 For vehicles from service code 1238 (VIN No 70237064), the sender unit must be positioned in line with the right-hand mark instead of the centre mark **(see illustration)**.

3 A more thorough check of the sender unit may be made by removing it from the fuel tank. Check that the arm moves correctly over its full travel by inverting it and allowing the arm to move of its own accord. Do not move the arm forcibly by hand. Note that the arm incorporates a silicone damper, and it may take up to 10 minutes to move over its full travel.

4 Hold the sender unit upright, and allow the float arm to drop to its lowest position. The float should now be level with the bottom of the sender unit.

5 Connect an ohmmeter between terminals 1 and 2 on the sender unit, and check that the resistance is 280 ± 10 ohms.

6 Now connect the ohmmeter between terminals 1 and 3, and check that the resistance is 9 ± 2 ohms.

7 Connect the wiring plug to the sender unit, and position it upright. With the ignition switched on, the fuel gauge should read empty, and the low-level warning light should be on.

8 Now position the sender unit upside-down, and leave it for 10 minutes until the arm has moved to its "full" position. The fuel gauge should now read "full".

9 Disconnect the sender unit from the wiring, and connect the ohmmeter between terminals 1 and 2. The resistance should be 3 ± 3 ohms.

10 If the sender unit does not perform as described above, it should be renewed.

11 To refit the sender unit in the fuel tank, first make sure that the seal is located in the fuel tank aperture correctly.

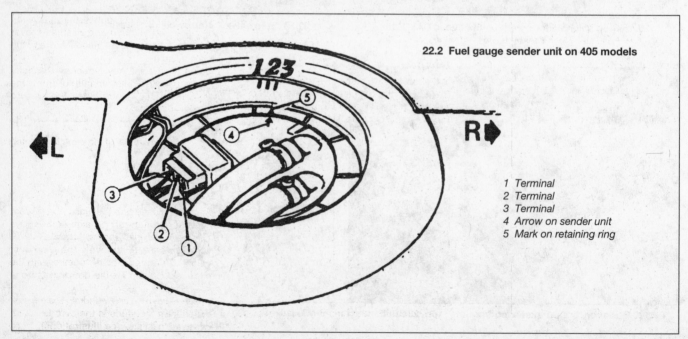

22.2 Fuel gauge sender unit on 405 models

1 Terminal
2 Terminal
3 Terminal
4 Arrow on sender unit
5 Mark on retaining ring

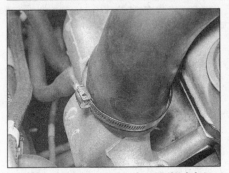

23.2A Air duct connection to the inlet manifold (205 models)

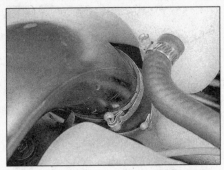

23.2B Air duct connection to the inlet manifold (Horizon models)

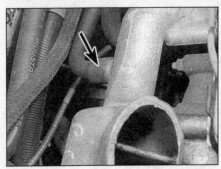

23.3 Brake vacuum pump outlet hose connection to the inlet manifold (arrowed)

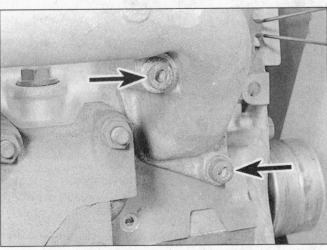

23.5A Inlet manifold bolts (arrowed)

23.5B Removing the inlet manifold (engine removed from car)

12 Lower the sender unit into the fuel tank, with the arrow in line with the right-hand mark on the fuel tank.

13 Apply a little soap to the threads of the retaining ring and the sender unit face, then screw down the ring onto the sender unit by hand as far as possible. Tighten the ring down further until the arrow on the ring is in line with, or just past, the arrow on the sender unit. Peugeot technicians use a special tool to carry out this final tightening; careful use of a screwdriver will, however, do just as well.

23 Manifolds - removal and refitting

Inlet

Removal

1 Disconnect the battery negative lead.
2 Remove the air cleaner, as described in Section 3. Also disconnect the air duct from the inlet manifold (**see illustrations**).

3 Remove the brake vacuum pump from the inlet manifold, as described in Chapter 7. Also disconnect the pump outlet hose from the manifold (**see illustration**).
4 On Horizon models, unbolt the expansion tank from the bulkhead and position it over the engine. There is no need to drain the cooling system.
5 Using a hexagon key, unscrew the bolts and remove the inlet manifold from the cylinder head (**see illustrations**). There are no gaskets.

Refitting

6 Refitting is a reversal of removal, but tighten the bolts evenly.

Exhaust

Removal

7 Apply the handbrake then jack up the front of the car and support on axle stands (see "*Jacking and vehicle support*").
8 Unscrew and remove the exhaust manifold-to-downpipe bolts, together with the springs and collars. Tie the downpipe to one side.
9 Unscrew the nuts and withdraw the exhaust manifold from the studs in the cylinder head. Recover the gaskets (**see illustrations**).

4

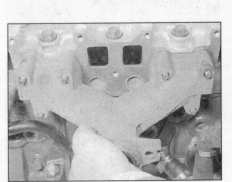

23.9A Removing the exhaust manifold

23.9B Exhaust manifold gasket

23.11 Tightening the exhaust manifold nuts

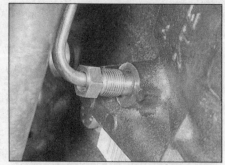

24.4A Turbo oil feed pipe union in block

24.4B Turbo oil return hose connection to block

10 Where applicable, unbolt the resonator from the manifold and remove the gasket.

Refitting

11 Refitting is a reversal of removal, but clean the mating faces and fit new gaskets. Tighten the nuts evenly **(see illustration).**

24 Turbocharger - removal, inspection and refitting

24.4C Oil feed pipe bracket

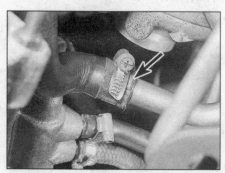

24.4D Oil return hose connection to turbo pipe (arrowed)

> ⚠ **Warning:** *Refer to the precautions in Section 2, before starting any work on the turbocharger.*

Removal

1 Disconnect the battery earth lead.
2 Raise and support the vehicle. Remove the engine undertray.
3 Remove the exhaust system. Recover the two dowels that locate the exhaust downpipe on the turbo outlet flange.
4 Be prepared for some oil spillage. Disconnect the turbo oil feed pipe and return hose from the cylinder block. Also unbolt the bracket that secures the feed pipe. Disconnect the return hose from the pipe on the turbo, and remove it **(see illustrations).**

5 Unbolt and remove the engine bottom mounting-to-crossmember link **(see illustration).** The engine will move forwards slightly when this is done.
6 Lower the vehicle. Where applicable, remove the vacuum pump, its drivebelt and hoses (Chapter 7).
7 Remove the trunking that joins the air cleaner to the inlet manifold, and the associated crankcase ventilation hoses **(see illustration).**
8 Remove the small hose that joins the inlet manifold to the injection pump.
9 Slacken the hose clips on the turbo-to-inlet manifold hoses.

10 Remove the seven bolts that secure the inlet manifold, using a 6 mm Allen key. The bolts are very tight, and access is not easy. The middle bolt hole is slotted, so if wished, the middle bolt can just be slackened.
11 Remove the inlet manifold. The gasket is shared with the exhaust manifold, so it will stay in place **(see illustration).**
12 Remove the short hose from the turbo outlet **(see illustration).**
13 Disconnect the oil feed pipe from the top of the turbo. Remove the pipe. Note the strainer in the pipe **(see illustrations).**
14 Remove the turbo-to-manifold bolt that is accessible from above **(see illustration).**

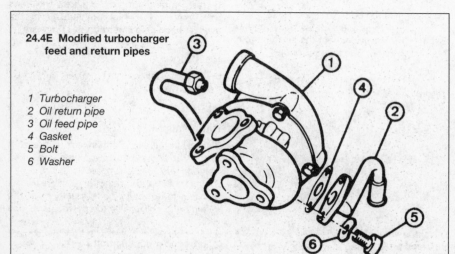

24.4E Modified turbocharger feed and return pipes

1 Turbocharger
2 Oil return pipe
3 Oil feed pipe
4 Gasket
5 Bolt
6 Washer

24.5 Engine bottom mounting-to-crossmember link

24.7 Removing the air inlet trunking

24.11 Removing the inlet manifold

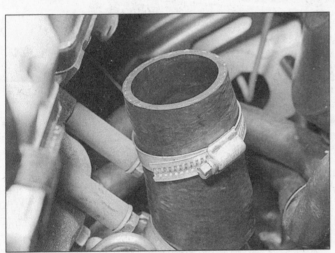

24.12 Turbo outlet hose

24.13A Turbo oil feed pipe union

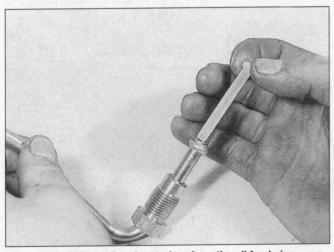

24.13B Removing the strainer from the oil feed pipe

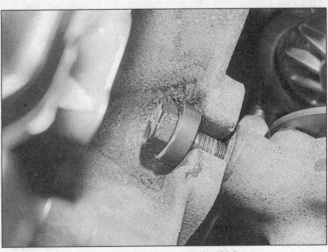

24.14 Turbo top mounting bolt

4

15 Raise and support the vehicle again. Remove the two other turbo-to-manifold bolts **(see illustration)**. Lower the vehicle.

16 Unbolt and remove the heat shield from the bulkhead **(see illustration)**.

17 Manipulate the turbocharger and lift it out from above, exhaust end first **(see illustration)**. It is a tight fit, but it can be done. It may help to have an assistant pull the engine forwards slightly.

18 If it is wished to renew the manifold gasket, the exhaust manifold must now be removed.

Inspection

19 With the turbocharger removed, inspect the housing for cracks or other visible damage.

20 Spin the turbine or the compressor wheel to verify that the shaft is intact, and to feel for excessive shake or roughness. Some play is normal - in use, the shaft is 'floating' on a film of oil. Check that the wheel vanes are undamaged.

21 On the KKK turbo, the wastegate and actuator are integral, and cannot be checked or renewed separately.

22 If the exhaust or induction passages are oil-contaminated, the turbo shaft oil seals have probably failed.

23 No DIY repair of the turbo is possible. A new unit may be available on an exchange basis.

Refitting

24 Refit by reversing the removal operations, noting the following points:

  a) *If a new turbocharger is being fitted, change the engine oil and filter. Also renew the strainer in the oil feed pipe.*

  b) *Do not fully tighten the oil feed pipe unions until both ends of the pipe are in place.*

24.15 Turbo bottom mounting bolts (arrowed)

24.16 Removing the heat shield

  c) *Before starting the engine, prime the turbo lubrication circuit by disconnecting the stop solenoid lead at the fuel pump and cranking the engine on the starter for three ten-second bursts* **(see illustration)**.

25 After initial start-up, do not race the engine. Inspect the turbo and its lubrication pipes for oil leaks. Stop the engine and check the oil level.

26 A new turbo should be run-in like any other major mechanical unit.

25 Emission control systems - general

1 Certain engines are equipped with systems designed to reduce the emission of harmful by-products of the combustion process into the atmosphere.

2 The following systems may be fitted, according to model.

Crankcase emission control system

3 A crankcase ventilation system is fitted to all models.

4 Oil fumes and piston blow-by gases (combustion gases that have passed by the piston rings) are drawn from the crankcase and the camshaft cover through the oil filler tube, into the air inlet tract. The oil filler tube contains an oil separator. The gases are then drawn into the engine with the inlet air, and burnt.

Exhaust emission control system

5 To minimise the level of exhaust gas pollutants released into the atmosphere, a catalytic converter is fitted in the exhaust system of some models.

6 The catalytic converter consists of a canister containing a fine mesh impregnated with a catalyst material, over which the exhaust gases pass. The catalyst speeds up the oxidation of carbon monoxide, unburnt hydrocarbons and soot, effectively reducing the quantity of harmful products reaching the atmosphere.

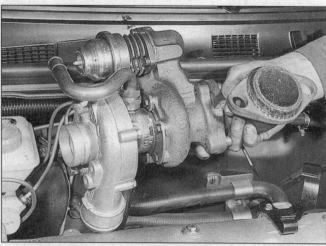

24.17 Removing the turbocharger

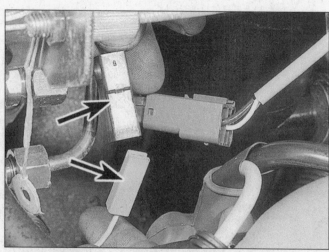

24.24 Stop solenoid lead connectors (arrowed)

Chapter 5
Engine electrical systems

Contents

Degrees of difficulty

Easy, suitable for novice with little experience	**Fairly easy,** suitable for beginner with some experience	**Fairly difficult,** suitable for competent DIY mechanic	**Difficult,** suitable for experienced DIY mechanic	**Very difficult,** suitable for expert DIY or professional

Specifications

General
System type . . . . 12 volt, negative earth, with alternator and pre-engaged starter motor
Battery:
  Type . . . . 60 Ah

Alternator
Type . . . . 3-phase, 750 watt
Regulated voltage (warm) . . . . 13.8 to 14.5 volts

Starter motor
Make . . . . Bosch or Mitsubishi/Melco
Minimum brush length . . . . 12.7 mm

Torque wrench settings

	Nm	lbf ft
Alternator pivot bolt	39	29
Alternator top mounting bolt and locknut	20	15
Starter motor	34	25

1 Description - general

The electrical system is of 12 volt negative earth type. The main components are a 12 volt battery, an alternator with integral voltage regulator, and a pre-engaged starter motor (with reduction gears on some models). The starter motor incorporates a one-way clutch on its pinion shaft to prevent the engine driving the motor when it starts.

It is important to disconnect the battery leads before charging the battery, removing the alternator, or working on wiring circuits that are permanently live. Additionally the alternator wiring must be disconnected before using electric arc welding equipment.

2 Alternator - general, removal and refitting

Models with air conditioning

General

1 On early models with air conditioning (up to mid-1992), the threaded part of the alternator mounting bolt which carries the tensioner roller has an M8 x 125 left-hand thread (i.e. it unscrews clockwise).

2 From mid-1992, the alternator mounting bolts and tensioner roller are modified. The thickness of the bolt head is increased to 12.0 mm from 6.0 mm, and the threaded part of the bolt that holds the tensioner roller is changed to M12 x 125 right-hand thread (i.e. it unscrews anti-clockwise, as normal). The tensioner roller bearing diameter is also increased.

3 On earlier models, one or more washers were fitted between the bolt and the roller, to correctly align the roller; on later models, the

2.6 Alternator wires (arrowed)

2.7A Alternator pivot bolt

arrangement varies according to model, as follows. On 405 models, there are no washers fitted; on the 205 and 309, one washer only is fitted.

4 Old and new type parts are only interchangeable as complete assemblies. In the case of the 205, if it is wished to fit new type parts to an earlier model, it will also be necessary to fit new coolant hoses. Refer to a Peugeot dealer for further information.

All models

Removal

5 Disconnect the battery negative lead.
6 Disconnect the wiring from the back of the alternator **(see illustration)**.
7 Loosen the pivot and adjustment bolts. Then swivel the alternator towards the engine and slip the drivebelt from the pulleys. On later models, a tension adjustment bolt is provided and this must be slackened, so that the alternator will swivel inwards **(see illustrations)**.

8 Remove the adjustment bolt(s) and withdraw the alternator from the engine. Note that it is not necessary to remove the pivot bolt, as the alternator housing is slotted.

Refitting

9 Refitting is a reversal of removal. Tension the drivebelt so that there is approximately 6.0 mm deflection under moderate thumb pressure midway between the pulleys.

3 Starter motor - removal and refitting

Removal

1 Disconnect the battery negative lead.
2 Remove the air cleaner and ducting (Chapter 4).
3 Unscrew the nut and disconnect the large cable from the solenoid. Also disconnect the small trigger wire **(see illustrations)**.

4 Using a hexagon key, unscrew the three mounting bolts.
5 Withdraw the starter motor from the transmission housing **(see illustration)**.

Refitting

6 Refitting is a reversal of removal, but tighten the bolts evenly to the specified torque.

4 Starter motor overhaul - general

If the starter motor is thought to be suspect, it should be removed from the vehicle and taken to an auto-electrician for testing. Most auto-electricians will be able to supply and fit brushes at a reasonable cost. However, check on the cost of repairs before continuing as it may prove more economical to obtain a new or exchange motor.

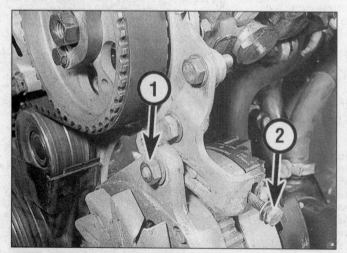

2.7B Alternator adjustment locknut (1) and adjustment bolt (2)

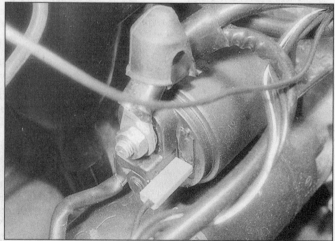

3.3A Starter motor solenoid wiring (Bosch)

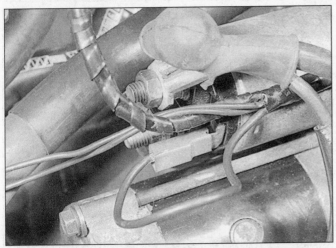

3.3B Starter motor solenoid wiring (Mitsubishi/Melco)

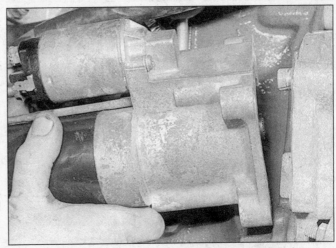

3.5 Removing the starter motor (Mitsubishi/Melco)

5 Drivebelt, alternator - removal and refitting

Except 405 models, with power steering or air conditioning

Removal

1 To remove the belt, loosen the pivot bolt and adjustment locknut.
2 Unscrew the adjustment bolt to release the tension. The drivebelt can now be removed from the pulleys.

Refitting

3 Refitting is a reversal of removal.

405 models, with power steering or air conditioning

Removal

4 Apply the handbrake, then jack up the front of the vehicle and support it on axle stands (see "*Jacking and vehicle support*"). Remove the front right-hand wheel.
5 Remove the front right-hand splash shield for access to the timing end of the engine.
6 To remove the drivebelt, loosen the two bolts (one located within the tensioner roller,

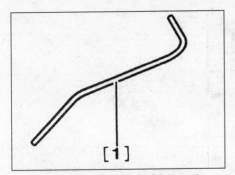

5.15 Peugeot tool (1) for holding the automatic tensioner roller

and the other on the bracket), then tighten the adjustment bolt to its stop to release the tension.
7 Slip the drivebelt off the pulleys and roller.

Refitting

8 Check that the tensioner roller turns freely, without any tight spots, but also without excessive play.
9 Locate the drivebelt on the pulleys and around the tensioner roller, making sure that it is correctly engaged with the grooves in the pulleys.
10 To adjust the drivebelt, turn the adjustment bolt as necessary to move the bracket up or down until the tension is correct.
11 Peugeot technicians use a special tool to check the tension. Without this tool, adjust the drivebelt so that it deflects by approximately 6.0 mm (0.25 in) midway between the power steering pump and alternator pulleys, under firm finger or thumb pressure.
12 With the drivebelt tensioned correctly, tighten the tensioner roller securing bolts.
13 Rotate the engine four revolutions in a clockwise direction, then check the adjustment again.
14 After making the adjustment, refit the splash shield and front wheel, then lower the vehicle to the ground.

405 models, with power steering and air conditioning

Removal

15 Before starting work, note that a rod is necessary to hold the automatic tension roller in its released position. The special Peugeot tool is shown **(see illustration)**, but a length of metal rod will do just as well.
16 Apply the handbrake, then jack up the front of the vehicle and support it on axle stands (see "*Jacking and vehicle support*"). Remove the front right-hand wheel.
17 Remove the front right-hand splash shield

for access to the timing end of the engine.
18 To remove the drivebelt, first loosen the two tensioner bolts (one located within the manual tensioner roller, and the other on the bracket). Note that access to the upper bolt is through a hole in the cover.
19 Turn the manual adjustment bolt on the bracket until it is possible to insert the metal rod to hold the automatic tension roller.
20 Tighten the manual adjustment bolt to its stop, then slip the drivebelt from the pulleys and rollers.

Refitting

21 .Check that the tensioner rollers turn freely, without any tight spots, but also without excessive play.
22 Locate the drivebelt on the pulleys and around the tensioner rollers, making sure that it is correctly engaged with the grooves in the pulleys.
23 The drivebelt is automatically adjusted by the spring-tensioned roller, however it is also necessary to make an initial manual adjustment. Once the initial manual adjustment has been made, the automatic adjustment roller will keep the drivebelt correctly tensioned for the duration of its life. First tighten the manual adjustment bolt until it is just possible to remove the metal rod from the automatic tension roller.
24 Tighten the two bolts on the manual tensioner bracket.
25 Refit the front right-hand splash shield.
26 Refit the wheel, and lower the vehicle to the ground.

6 Wiring diagrams - general

Typical wiring diagrams appear on the following pages. Not all items shown are fitted to all models.

5

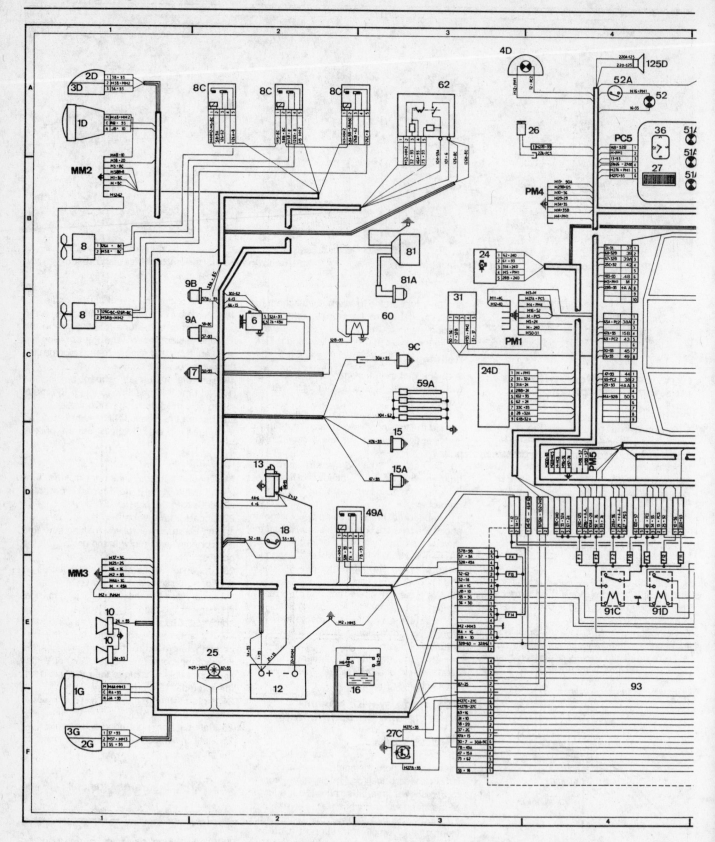

Wiring diagram 1: 305 models up to 1985

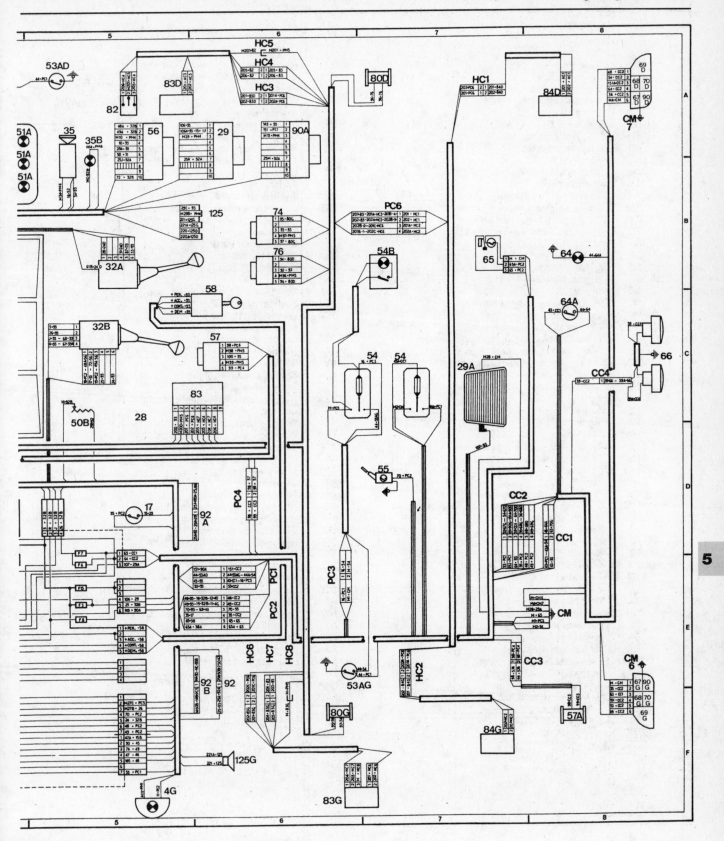

Wiring diagram 1: 305 models up to 1985 (continued)

1D	Headlamp, RH	27	Heating/ventilation switch or rheostat
1G	Headlamp, LH	27A	Rheostat resistor or heating/ventilation fan resistor
2D	Direction indicator, front RH	27B	Rear heating/ventilation switch
2G	Direction indicator, front LH	27C	Air conditioning control unit
3D	Sidelamp, RH	29	Heated rear window switch
3G	Sidelamp, LH	29A	Heated rear window
4D	Indicator repeater, RH	30	Windscreen wiper/windscreen washer switch
4G	Indicator repeater, LH	30A	Rear window wiper/washer switch
5	Starter relay	31	Direction indicator flasher unit
5A	Neutral safety relay	32	Lighting – windscreen wiper/windscreen washer switch
6	Alternator		
7	Sender unit, oil pressure	32A	Windscreen wiper/windscreen washer switch
7A	Sensor, engine oil level	32B	Lighting/direction indicator/horn control switch
7B	Control unit, engine oil level	33	Headlights flasher relay
7C	Checking diode, engine oil level	34	Sidelamps
8	Motor, engine cooling fan	35	Cigar lighter, front
8A	Disengaging fan relay	35A	Cigar lighter, rear
8B	Air conditioning electric fan	35B	Illumination, cigar lighter
8C	Electric fan relay	36	Clock
8D	Diodes	37	Direction indicator repeater light
8	Motor, engine cooling fan	38	Fuel gauge
8F	Resistor, cooling fan motor	38A	Warning light, low fuel level
9	Temperature switch, fan motor	39	Main beam warning light
9A	Temp. switch, fan clutch, cooling system	39A	Dip beam warning light
9B	Temp. switch, fan clutch, lube system	40	Hazard warning light
9C	Sender unit, oil temperature gauge	41	Rev counter
10	Horn	42	Sidelamp warning light
11	Headlight relay	43	Brake safety warning light
12	Battery	43A	Brake safety warning light checking diode
12A	Battery cutout	44	Coolant temperature gauge
13	Starter motor	44A	Warning lamp, minimum coolant level
14	Brake pads	45	Warning light, low oil pressure
15	Sender unit, coolant temperature	45A	Warning light, high oil temperature
15A	Switch, coolant temperature	45B	Warning light, oil pressure and temp.
15B	Coolant temp, warning light switch or coolant temp. warning light	46	Choke warning light
		47	Oil and water warning light
15C	Resistor, coolant temp. gauge	48	Preheater warning light
15D	Checking diode, coolant temp. warning light	49	Charge/discharge warning light
15E	Switch, coolant level	50	Instrument panel lighting
16	Brake fluid reservoir	50A	Gear change gate light
17	Stop switch	50B	Rheostat, gear change gate light
18	Reversing light switch	50C	Switch lighting
19	Starter safety cut-out	51	Heater lighting
21	Regulator	51A	Console lighting
24	Windscreen wiper	51B	Console lighting rheostat
24A	Windscreen wiper relay	52	Glove compartment light
24B	Windscreen wiper timer	52A	Glove compartment light switch
24C	Rear window wiper	53	Front door switch
24D	Windscreen wiper unit	53A	Rear door switch
25	Windscreen washer pump	53AD	Courtesy switch, RH front door
25A	Rear window washer pump	53AG	Courtesy switch, LH front foor
26	Heating/ventilation fan, front	54	Interior lamp
26A	Rear heating/ventilation fan	54A	Light under facia panel
26B	Heating/ventilation fan switch	54B	Map reading light
26C	Air conditioning blower	54C	Illumination, courtesy mirror
26D	Relay, air conditioning blower	55	Handbrake switch

Key to wiring diagram 1 for 305 models up to 1985

56	Hazard warning light switch
57	Sunroof switch
57A	Sunroof motor
57E	Locking relay, sunroof
58	Steering lock
58B	Ignition switch light
59	Preheat – starter switch
59A	Preheater plugs
60	Pump cut-out motor or solenoid valve
61	Preheater warning light switch
62	Preheater relay
63	Direction indicator and horn control
64	Boot or rear compartment lighting
64A	Boot lid or tailgate switch
65	Fuel gauge tank with or without low fuel warning
65A	External tank unit resistor
65B	Rheostat, fuel gauge
66	Number plate light
67	Reverse lamps
67D	Reverse lamp, RH
67G	Reverse lamp, LH
68	Stop-lamp
68B	Stop/tail lamp (twin filament)
68BD	Stop/tail lamp, RH
68BG	Stop/tail lamp, LH
69	Rear direction indicator
69D	Direction indicator, rear, RH
69G	Direction indicator, rear, LH
70	Tail lamp
71	Tailgate switch
72	Door mounted light
73	Left hand rear window winder switch
73A	Locking relay, LH rear window winder
74	Window winder switch, LH front
74A	Locking relay, LH front window winder
75	Interlock, rear window winder
76	Window winder switch, RH front
76A	Locking relay, RH front window winder
76D	Switch, RH electric window, front, RH
76G	Switch, LH electric window, front, RH
77	Window winder switch, RH rear
77A	Locking relay, RH rear window winder
78	Left-hand window winder rear switch
79	Right-hand window winder rear switch
80	Window winder motor
80A	Window winder relay
80D	Motor, electric window, front, RH
80G	Motor, electric window, front, LH
81	Diagnostic socket
81A	TDC sensor, diagnostic socket
82	Door lock switch
83	Control box, central door locking
83A	Actuator, door lock
83B	Actuator, fuel filler flap
83C	Actuator, tailgate lock
83D	Actuator, door lock, front, RH

83G	Actuator, door lock, front, LH
83AD	Actuator, door lock, rear, RH
83AG	Actuator, door lock, rear, LH
86	Fuel pump
86A	Primary fuel pump
87	Solenoid valve
87A	Solenoid valve control switch
90	Rear foglights
90A	Rear foglight switch
90B	Rear foglight warning light
91	Relay
91B	Tachymetric relay
91C	Accessory relay
91D	Heated rear window relay
92 to 92F	Multi-plug/connectors
93	Connector board
93A	Fuse box No 1
93B	Fuse box No 2
94	Conductive tailgate stay
95	Brake servo vacuum switch
96	Brake pedal travel switch
97	Headlight washer/wiper switch
98	Headlight washer pump
99	Headlight wiper motor
99A	Headlight wiper relay
100	Pressure drop indicator
101	Tachograph
102	Flasher light
102A	Flasher light switch
103	Centre interior light
103A	Centre interior light switch
104	Feed warning light
104A	Feed warning light switch
105	Air fan
105A	Air fan switch
106	Warning bell
106A	Warning bell switch
107	Electrical plug
107A	Socket, towing attachment
108	Compressor clutch
108A	Compressor clutch switch
108B	Relay, compressor clutch
109	Thermostat
109A	Protection diode, thermostat
110	Constant pressure unit
111	Idling speed compensation solenoid valve
111A	Air conditioning shut-off pressure switch
118	Control pressure regulator
119	Additional air control
120	Sensor plate switch
121	Cold starting injector
122	Thermal time switch
123	Speed regulator switch
123A	Speed regulator electronic unit
123B	Speed regulator servo
123C	Speed regulator safety switch

5

Key to wiring diagram 1 for 305 models up to 1985 (continued)

123D	Speed regulator disengagement switch		172	Control unit, knock detector
123E	Speed regulator pick-up		172A	Knock detector
123F	Speed regulator fuse		173	Warning light, LED, knock detector
123G	Safety relay speed regulator		174	Relay, capsule venting
123H	Vacuum capsule		175	Electronic relay
123I	Safety relay		180	Relay, fuel injection system
123J	Main switch, speed regulator		181	Calculator, fuel injection system
125	Radio connection		182	Airflow sensor
125D	Radio speaker, front RH		183	Injector
125G	Radio speaker, front LH		184	Throttle switch unit
125AD	Radio speaker, rear RH		185	Temperature sensor, engine
125AG	Radio speaker, rear LH		190	Sensor, fuel pressure
125E	Connector, radio speaker		191	Sensor, turbocharger excess pressure
129	Speed sensor		192	Gauge, turbocharger pressure
142	Tachymetric relay, fuel cut-off on over-run		195	100 mbar switch – turbo full load control, turbo injection intercooler
142A	Relay, fuel injection cut-off on over-run		196	Switch advance curve selector
142B	Control unit, for delay of fuel injection cut-off		197	Resistor, full load circuit, turbo injection intercooler
150	Warning light, economy		200	Control unit, voice synthesizer
150A	Vacuum pick-up		200A	Filter
151	Switch, water detector		201	Test button, voice synthesizer
151A	Warning light, water detector switch		210	Trip computer
152	Connector, front foglamps		211	Display control
152A	Switch, front foglamps		212	Fuel flow sensor
152B	Relay, front foglamps		213	Digital display
153	Sensor, oil pressure		+ AA	Supply to accessories
153A	Oil pressure gauge		F	Fuse
165D	Long range driving lamp, RH		M	Earth
165G	Long range driving lamp, LH		+ P	Supply from battery
170	Relay ignition system			
171	Calculator, ignition advance			

Not all items fitted to all models

Key to wiring diagram 1 for 305 models up to 1985 (continued)

1	Cigar lighter, front	126	Audible warning (key in the ignition/steering lock with the driver's door open)
3	Cigar lighter, rear		
5	Distributor, ignition	127	Audible warning, excessive speed
9	Idling actuator (idling solenoid)	128	Audible warning, (lights on, door open or 'STOP' warning lamp on)
10	Alternator		
11	Transistor, heater blower control (power transistor)	129	Condenser, radio interference
13	Strut (earth connection)	130	TDC sensor
14	Ammeter (battery charge)	131	Altitude sensor
20	Radio aerial, electric	132	Knock detector
25	Horn	133	Sensor, engine speed
25A	Horn, low note	134	Sensor, absolute pressure
25B	Horn, high note	135	Sensor, potentiometer (econoscope vacuum)
27	Connector, towing attachment	136	Sensor, demisting the rear glass
28	Dimmer, dipped beams	137	Pressure sensor, inlet manifold
30	Radio	138	Pressure sensor
35	Actuator, fuel output (VP15)	140	Speed sensor, speedometer cable
40	Radio balance control, front	141	Speed sensor, trip computer
41	Radio balance control, front/rear	142	Sensor, oil pressure
45	Battery	143	Sensor, No 1 cylinder
46	Control unit, positive supply	144	Sensor, diesel injector needle lifted
47	Diodes unit	145	Direction indicator flasher unit
48	Unit, electric pump group (EPG)	146	Antilock sensor, LH front wheel
49	Unit, fuse board group (FBG)	147	Antilock sensor, RH front wheel
50	Ignition coil	148	Antilock sensor, LH rear wheel
53	Control box, exhaust emission, for pilot carburettor	149	Antilock sensor, RH rear wheel
		150	Air temperature sensor, (air conditioning)
54	Emission control unit (ignition advance modulator)	15	Load sensor (Diesel)
		155	Pilot carburettor
55	Emission control unit (idle retard)	160	Battery isolator
56	Control unit, automatic transmission (idle speed)	165	Instrument panel
		167	Connector, emission control setting
57	Alarm unit, theft protection	169	Switch, starter/preheater
58	Control unit, injection	170	Switch, luggage compartment lamp
60	Control unit, air conditioning	171	Switch, enrichment (LPG)
61	Electronic unit, brake antilock	172	Switch, air filter clogging warning lamp
65	Control unit, screen wiper	173	Switch, number plate
66	Control box, power steering	175	Switch, door lock
75	Control unit, ignition, or pick-up amplifier module	176	Switch, vacuum (LPG)
		177	Switch, LH front lock (door open detector)
76	Detector unit, bulb failure	178	Switch, RH front lock (door open detector)
80	Cruise control unit	179	Switch, LH rear lock (door open detector)
85	Indicator unit, oil level	180	Switch, RH rear lock (door open detector)
86	Indicator unit, coolant level	181	Switch, luggage compartment lock (lid open detector)
90	Control unit, central door locking		
95	Infra red signal receiver (PLIP)	182	Switch, bonnet lock (bonnet open detector)
96	Control unit, knock detector	185	Switch, stop-lamps
97	Thermostat unit (passenger compartment)	186	Switch, brake pedal travel
98	Electronic control unit for differential locking	190	Switch, handbrake
		195	Switch, low pressure (Freon)
110	Control unit, preheater	196	Switch, mean pressure (Freon)
111	Control unit, fuel cut-off on overrun	200	Thermal switch (Freon)
112	Control unit, fuel flow (trip computer)	205	Switch, glovebox lamp
113	Electronic control unit, advance	210	Switch, seat belt
114	Control box, coolant temperature, air conditioning	211	Switch, display (trip computer)
		215	Switch, starter inhibitor
115	Preheater plug	216	Switch, reverse lamp
120	Terminal connector		
121	Buzzer (P4, warning, coolant temperature, oil pressure, charge warning light)		
122	Buzzer, direction indicator (P4)		
125	Audible warning, seat belt		

5

Key to wiring diagrams 2 and 3 for 305 models from 1985

217	Switch, reverse lamp/starter inhibitor	306	Checking diode, brake warning light
220	Switch, heating/ventilation fan	307	Diode, air conditioning control
221	Switch, heating/ventilation fan (rear)	308	Diode, lighting dimmer
225	Switch, choke warning light	309	Diode, electric fan
229	Switch, ignition/steering lock	310	Diode, compressor
230	Door switch, LH front	311	Diode, roof lamp
231	Door switch, RH front	312	Diode, speech synthesizer
232	Door switch, LH rear	313	Flow sensor
233	Door switch, RH rear	314	Diode, boot locking
234	Control switch, audible warning (ignition key 'in')	328	Solenoid valve, turbo-charge regulator
235	Switch, brake fluid pressure drop	329	Solenoid valve, cruise control deceleration
236	Switch, brake fluid level	330	Solenoid valve, air conditioning
237	Switch, coolant level	331	Solenoid valve, EGR (pilot carburettor)
238	Switch, water sensing, fuel system	332	Solenoid valve, opening the carburettor throttle valve
239	Switch, washer bottle level	333	Solenoid valve, injection cut-off on over-run
240	Limit switch, sunroof	334	Solenoid, emission control advance modulator
241	Switch on accelerator pedal (idle speed)	335	Solenoid, exhaust emission
242	Switch, idle speed	336	Solenoid, carburettor breather
243	Switch, power take-off (P4)	337	Main solenoid, brake anti-lock
247	Switch, rear differential lock	338	Control solenoid, brake anti-lock
248	Switch, front differential lock	340	Solenoid, pump stop
249	Switch, windscreen wiper lockout (P4)	343	Solenoid valve, air intake
250	Disengaging switch, cruise control (brake)	344	Solenoid, turbine fan
250A	Disengaging switch, cruise control (clutch)	345	Solenoid valve, fast idle stabiliser
251	Throttle switch (idling + full load)	346	Solenoid, canister
252	Level switch, brake anti-lock	347	Solenoid, cruise control
253	Switch, driver's passive seat belt	348	Advance solenoid, diesel
254	Switch, passenger's passive seat belt	349	Solenoid valve, temperature control
260	Control, lighting/direction indicators/horn	350	Switches, illumination
261	Control, lighting/screen wiper/screen wash	351	Illumination, instrument panel
262	Control, lighting/screen wiper/direction indicator/horn	355	Illumination, heating/ventilation control
263	Control, screen wiper/wash	360	Illumination, console
264	Control, lighting/horn	361	Courtesy lamp
265	Control, direction indicator/horn	364	Illumination, cigar lighter
266	Switch, cruise control	365	Illumination, luggage compartment (or tailgate)
267	Switch, cruise control/direction indicator	375	Illumination, glovebox
268	Switch, flasher unit	380	Illumination, engine compartment
269	Switch, lighting/blackout (P4)	385	Illumination, number plate LH
270	Switch, windscreen wiper (P4)	386	Illumination, number plate RH
275	Control, driver's seat position	390	Illumination, ignition switch/steering lock
276	Control, rear view mirror LH	395	Floor illumination, driver's side
277	Control, rear view mirror RH	396	Floor illumination, passenger's side
280	Supplementary air device (cold start)	397	Sill illumination, driver's side
281	Corrector, fuel reheating	398	Sill illumination, passenger side
285	Capacitor, coil positive	400	Illumination, gear selector lever
286	Capacitor, direction indicator flasher unit	410	Clutch, compressor
290	Tachometer	420	Idling cut-off, carburettor
295	Compressor	425	Map reading lamp
296	Compressor, air horn	440	Sidelamp LH
300	Starter motor	441	Sidelamp RH
301	Vapour relief valve (LPG)	445	Tail lamp cluster LH
302	Diode, relay protection	446	Tail lamp cluster RH
303	Diode, rear foglamps	452	Marker lamp, LH rear
304	Protection diode, electronic control unit	453	Marker lamp, RH rear
305	Checking diode, coolant temperature warning light	455	Door marker lamp LH

Key to wiring diagrams 2 and 3 for 305 models from 1985 (continued)

456	Door marker lamp RH
457	Front foglamp RH
458	Front foglamp LH
459	Fuse holder (front foglamps)
460	Rear foglamp LH
461	Rear foglamp RH
462	Reverse lamp
463	Stop-lamp
464	Reverse lamp + foglamp (rear)
465	Suppression filter, tachometer
466	Fuse holder (+ accessories, brake anti-lock)
467	Fuse holder (for warning light, brake anti-lock)
468	Fuse holder (power circuit, brake anti-lock)
469	Fuse holder, LAMBDA sensor heater
470	Fuses (fusebox)
471	Fuse holder (radio)
472	Fuse holder (locks)
473	Fuse holder (dipped beams)
474	Fuse holder (speech synthesizer)
475	Fuse holder (carburettor heater)
476	Fuse holder (cruise control)
477	Fuse holder (supply pump)
477A	Fuse holder (injection and ignition control unit supply)
478	Flashing lamps, priority
479	Fuse holder (pump, brake anti-lock)
480	Direction indicator lamp, LH front
481	Direction indicator lamp, RH front
482	Direction indicator lamp, LH rear
483	Direction indicator lamp, RH rear
484	Sidelamp/direction indicator, LH front
485	Sidelamp/direction indicator, RH front
486	Suppression filter, speech synthesizer
487	Fuse holder (control unit, fuel output VP15)
488	Fuse holder (control unit, advance regulator VP15)
489	Fuse holder, cooling fan group (CFG)
490	Impulse generator (speed)
491	Rotating lamp
500	Loudspeaker, LH front
501	Loudspeaker, RH front
502	Loudspeaker, LH rear
503	Loudspeaker, RH rear
505	Hour meter (P4)
510	Switch, front foglamps
511	Switch, rear foglamps
512	Switch, auxiliary driving lamp
513	Switch, siren
514	Switch, rotating lamp
515	Switch, rheostat, instrument panel illumination
516	Switch, parking lights
517	Switch, general (military P4)
518	Test switch, oil, coolant or charging fault (P4)
519	Switch, horn (P4)
520	Switch, window winder (driver's)
521	Switch, window winder (passenger's)
521A	Switch, passenger's window winder

522	Switch, window winder, LH rear
523	Switch, window winder, RH rear
524	Switch, window winder, LH rear (in rear compartment)
525	Switch, window winder, RH rear (in rear compartment)
526	Child safety switch, rear window winders
527	Switch, main/dip beams
530	Switch, sunroof
532	Switch, heated rear window
535	Switch, driver's seat heating
536	Switch, passenger's seat heating
540	Switch, preheater
545	Switch, central roof lamp
548	Test switch, brake wear warning light
549	Diagnostic switch, diesel
550	Switch, rear screen wiper
552	Switch, headlamp wiper
555	Switch, fuel supply warning light
556	Switch, police horn
557	Switch, rotating lamp
558	Switch, air fan
560	Switch, warning bell
565	Switch, pressure drop
566	Switch, air conditioning control
567	Switch, cruise control
570	Switch, hazard warning
571	Test switch
572	Switch, lamps (police)
574	Injectors
575	Cold start injector
576	Information display, injection control box
580	Fuel tank unit
590	Map reading lamp
591	Indicator, coolant temperature
592	Gauge, turbocharger pressure
593	Fuel gauge
594	Gauge, engine oil temperature
595	Gauge, engine oil pressure
598	Electronic control unit, ignition
600	Motor, screen wiper
601	Motor, window wiper, rear
605	Wiper motor, headlamp LH
606	Wiper motor, headlamp RH
607	Motor, heater control flap
610	Motor, sunroof
615	Motor, LH front window winder
616	Motor, RH front window winder
617	Motor, LH rear window winder
618	Motor, RH rear window winder
620	Motor, heating/ventilation fan
625	Actuator, LH front door lock
626	Actuator, RH front door lock
627	Actuator, LH rear door lock
628	Actuator, RH rear door lock
629	Actuator, luggage compartment lock
630	Motor, fuel filler flap lock

5

Key to wiring diagrams 2 and 3 for 305 models from 1985 (continued)

631	Motor, driver's passive seat belt
632	Motor, passenger's passive seat belt
635	Motor, engine cooling fan
636	Motor, air conditioning fan
640	Clock
645	Pressure switch, brake servo
646	Pressure switch, power steering
647	Pressure switch, air conditioning cut-out
650	Oil pressure switch
651	Vacuum-pressure switch
652	Pressure switch, turbocharger cut-out
653	Full throttle enrichment switch
654	Advance curve selection switch
660	Trip computer
660A	Keyboard, trip computer
660B	Display, trip computer
668	PTC (positive temperature coefficient resistance)
669	Potentiometer, throttle
669A	Potentiometer, accelerator pedal (Diesel)
670	Headlamp LH
671	Headlamp RH
672	Headlamp blackout (P4)
673	Driving lamp LH
674	Driving lamp RH
675	Brake pads, LH front
676	Brake pads, RH front
677	Brake pads, LH rear
678	Brake pads, RH rear
679	Vacuum pump, cruise control
680	Washer pump, front
681	Washer pump, rear
682	Washer pump, headlamp
683	Fuel supply pump
684	Scavenge pump
685	Coolant heater matrix
686	Hydaulic pump, brake anti-lock
688	Interior lamp, front
689	Interior lamp, rear
690	Interior lamp, centre
691	Interior lamp, LH front
692	Interior lamp, RH front
693	Interior lamp, LH rear
694	Interior lamp, RH rear
697	PLIP
700	Pressure switch
705	Connector board
706	Services connector board
710	Battery supply socket
720	Diagnostic socket
721	Test socket (injection)
723	Front foglamp LH
724	Front foglamp RH
727	Lambda sensor heating relay
728	Relay, passive seat belt (non motorised)
729	Relay, emission control
730	Relay, starter motor
731	Relay, preheater
732	Relay, fan clutch
733	Relay, electric fan motor
734	Relay, hour meter (P4)
735	Relay, main beams
736	Relay, auxiliary driving lamps
737	Relay, dipped beams
738	Relay, heating/ventilation fan, fast speed
740	Relay, coil
741	Relay, coil resistance
742	Relay, cold start control
743	Relay, compressor
744	Tachymetric relay or pump control relay
745	Relay, air horn compressor
746	Tachymetric relay (cut-off on over-run)
747	Relay, CLT
748	Relay, ECU, exhaust emission
749	Relay, cold cut-off
750	Relay, front foglamps
751	Relay, rear foglamps
752	Relay, compressor cut-out (105°)
753	Relay, pump, brake anti-lock
754	Relay, power circuit, brake anti-lock
755	Relay, headlamp wiper
756	Relay, headlamp wiper timer
757	Relay, advance curve selection
758	Relay, brake warning lamp (anti-lock brake system)
760	Relay, heated rear window
761	Relay, rear electric window
762	Relay, front electric window
763	Relay, sunroof
764	Relay, sunroof tilt + central locking
765	Relay, front screen wiper
766	Relay, rear window wiper
767	Relay, warning light occultation (P4)
770	Relay, accessories
771	Relay, visual warning
772	Relay, two-speed (mixture control)
773	Relay, carburettor heater
775	Relay, starter motor isolator
776	Relay, cruise control disengagement
777	Relay, pilot carburettor supply
778	Relay, scavenge pump
779	PTC resistance control relay
780	Relay, lighting dimmer
781	Relay, excessive speed
782	Relay, ignition supply
783	Relay, injection supply
784	Relay, trip computer/cruise control/speech synthesizer information
785	Relay, brake warning (Australia)
786	Resistor, coil
787	Resistor, heating/ventilation fan
788	Resistor, two-speed cooling fan
789	Resistor, lighting dimmer
790	Heater, diesel fuel
791	Heater, carburettor
793	Resistor, preheater (P4)
794	Resistor, injection matching
795	Rheostat, instrument illumination
800	Regulator, voltage
801	Regulator, control pressure
810	Side repeater flasher LH
811	Side repeater flasher RH
812	Rheostat, temperature display
814	Rear view mirror LH
815	Rear view mirror RH
817	Heater seat, front LH
818	Heater seat, front RH
820	Bell
821	Diagnostic test socket
829	Servo, power steering
830	Servo, cruise control
832	Sensor, evaporator
833	Sensor, blown air
834	Sensor, interior air temperature
835	Sensor, oil level
836	Sensor, fuel flow (trip computer)
837	Sensor, coolant level
838	Sensor, mixture regulator
840	Sensor, high temperature
841	Siren
845	Speech synthesizer
846	Sensor, body temperature (exhaust)
847	Sensor, passenger compartment temperature regulation
848	Lambda sensor

Key to wiring diagrams 2 and 3 for 305 models from 1985 (continued)

849 Sensor, external air temperature
850 Thermal switch, cooling fan (coolant)
852 Thermal switch, transmission oil
853 Thermal switch, 18°C (coolant temperature)
855 Thermal switch, coolant
861 Thermal switch, 40°C (coolant temperature)
862 Thermal switch, 60°C (coolant temperature)
865 Thermostat, electronic (air conditioning)
870 Thermal time switch (cold start opening)
871 Temperature switch 15 degrees (air temperature)
880 Tachograph
885 Timer switch, seat belt
886 Timer switch, interior lamp
887 Timer switch, headlamp wash
888 Sender unit, oil temperature gauge
889 Temperature sender unit, injection
890 Sender unit, coolant temperature gauge
891 Temperature sender unit, electronic
      (heating/ventilation)
892 Sender unit, engine oil temperature
893 Timer switch, rear screen wiper
893A Timer switch, windscreen wiper
894 Temperature sender unit, controlling cooling fan
      motors by ECU (liquid cooling)
895 Sender unit, exhaust emission
896 Thermal resistor, inlet air temperature
897 Tester, anti-lock
898 Sender unit, oil pressure
899 Test unit, variable power steering
929 Proportioning valve, cruise control
930 Fan, electromagnetic clutch
935 Fan, heating/ventilation
936 Fan, heating/ventilation, rear
945 Heater rear window
950 Fan
955 Ram, driver's seat
960 Fan, air conditioning
965 Cold start flap
970 Voltmeter
+ AA Supply from accessories terminal
+ AC Supply from ignition switch

Not all items fitted to all models

BL Screened cable
+ D Supply from starter motor
L1   Warning lamp, seat belt
L2   Warning lamps, direction indicator
L3   Warning lamp, low fuel level
L4   Warning lamp, main beams
L5   Warning lamp, hazard warning
L6   Warning lamp, side/tail lamps 'on'
L7   Warning lamp, no battery charge
L8   Warning lamp, preheater
L9   Warning lamp, choke control
L10 Warning lamp, oil pressure
L11 Warning lamp, oil and coolant
L12 Warning lamp, coolant temperature
L13 Warning lamp, brake safety
L14 Warning lamp, rear fog lamps
L15 Warning lamp, fuel supply
L16 Warning lamp, 'stop'
L17 Warning lamp, brake fluid/stop-lamps
L18 Warning lamp, sidelamp failure
L19 Warning lamp, tail lamp failure
L20 Warning lamp, screenwash level
L21 Warning lamp, coolant level
L22 Warning lamp, engine oil level
L23 Warning lamp, brake pad wear
L24 Manual test switch, instrument panel
L25 Warning lamp, oil temperature
L26 Warning lamp 'door open'
L27 Warning lamp, tail lamp or rear foglamp failure
L30 Warning lamp, rear differential lock
L31 Warning lamp, front differential lock
L32 Warning lamp, knock detector
L33 Warning lamp, diagnosis
L34 Warning lamp, water in fuel
L35 Warning lamp, dipped beams
L36 Warning lamp, trailer direction indicator
L37 Warning light, power take-off (P4)
L39 Warning lamp, catalytic converter
L39 Warning lamp, brake anitlock alert
M Earth connections
+ P Supply from battery

5

Colour code (where used)

AZ	Sky Blue	NR	Black
BA	White	OR	Orange
BE	Blue	RG	Red
GR	Slate	RS	Pink
JN	Yellow	VE	Green
MR	Brown	VI	Purple

Guidance for use

The vehicle is divided into 4 sections. Section codes are given before the component code

M	Engine	H	Passenger compartment
P	Facia	C	Luggage area

For connections between harnesses, the Section codes, followed by C, are used to indicate where the connection is eg MC indicates a connector
between the engine and facia harnesses which is located in the engine compartment
For earthing points the Section code is followed by M
eg CM indicates an earthing point in the luggage area

Key to wiring diagrams 2 and 3 for 305 models from 1985 (continued)

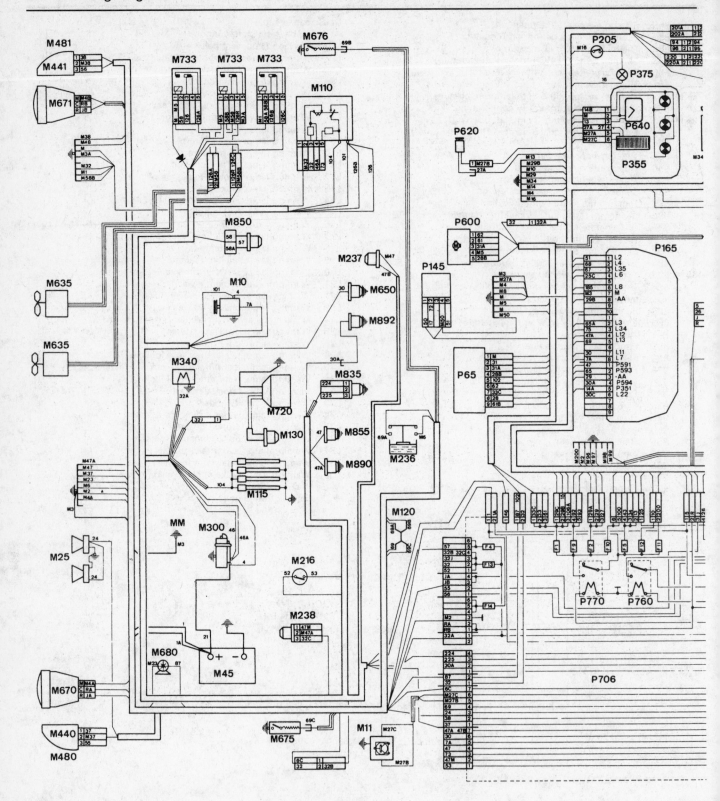

Wiring diagram 2: 305 models from 1985

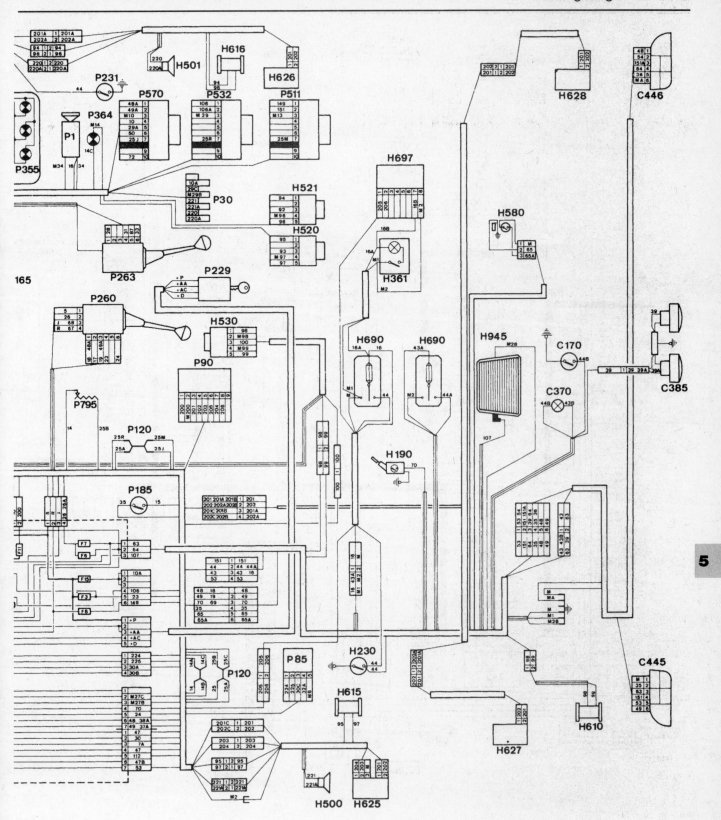

5

Wiring diagram 2: 305 models from 1985 (continued)

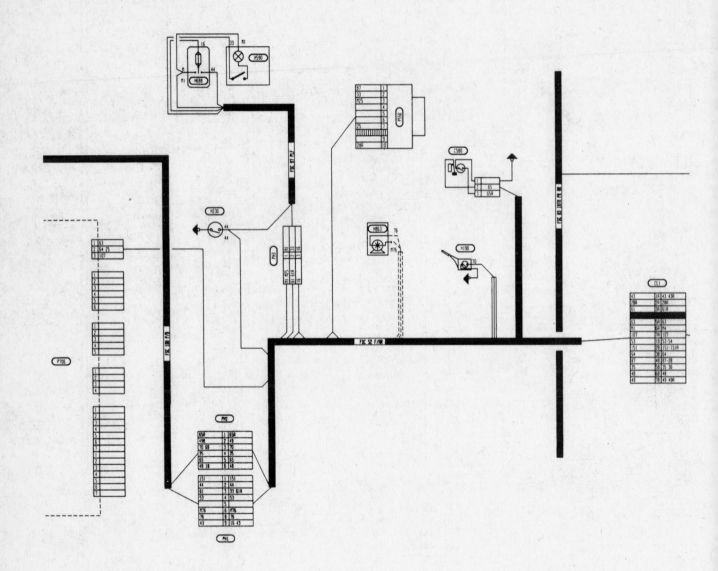

Wiring diagram 3: Supplementary wiring diagram for 305 Estate models from 1986

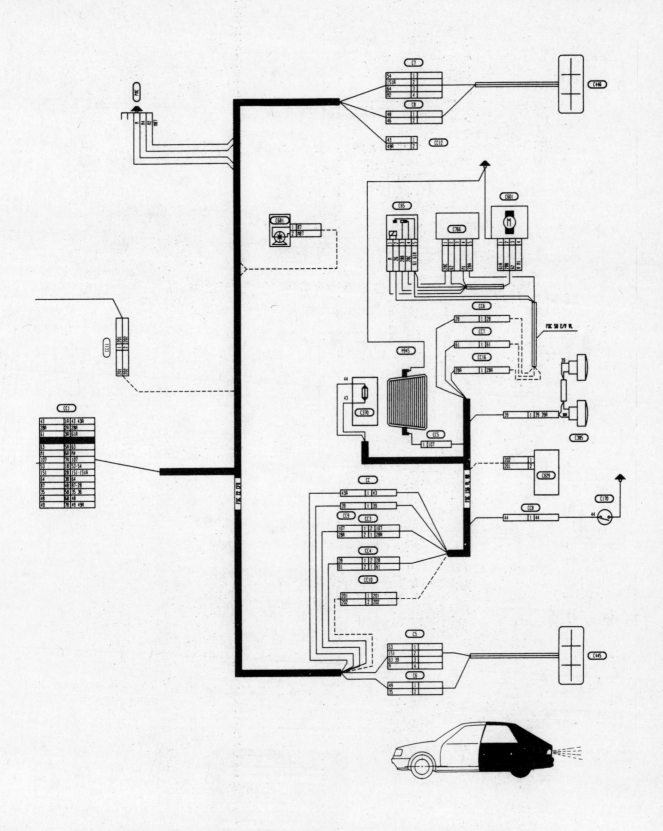

Wiring diagram 3: Supplementary wiring diagram for 305 Estate models from 1986 (continued)

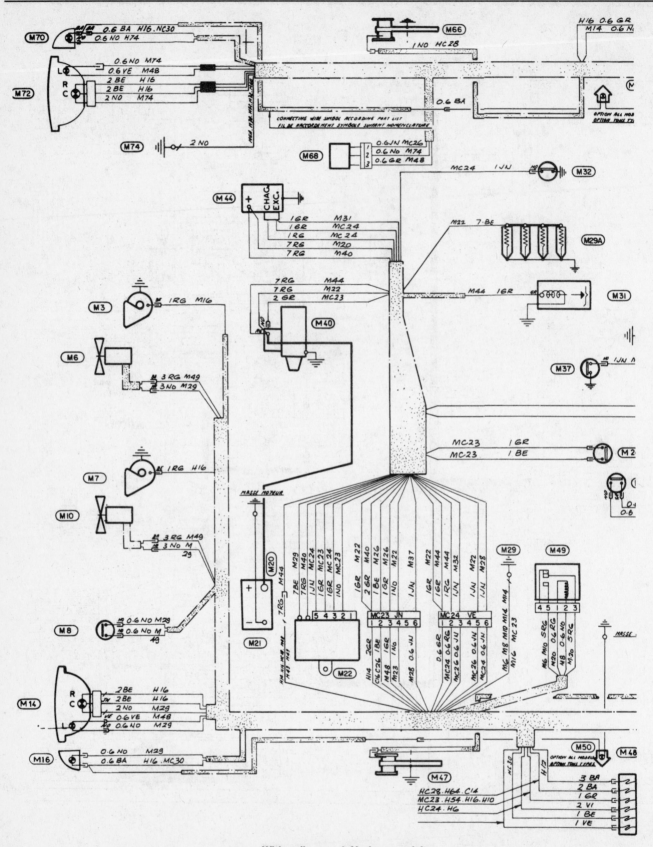

Wiring diagram 4: Horizon models

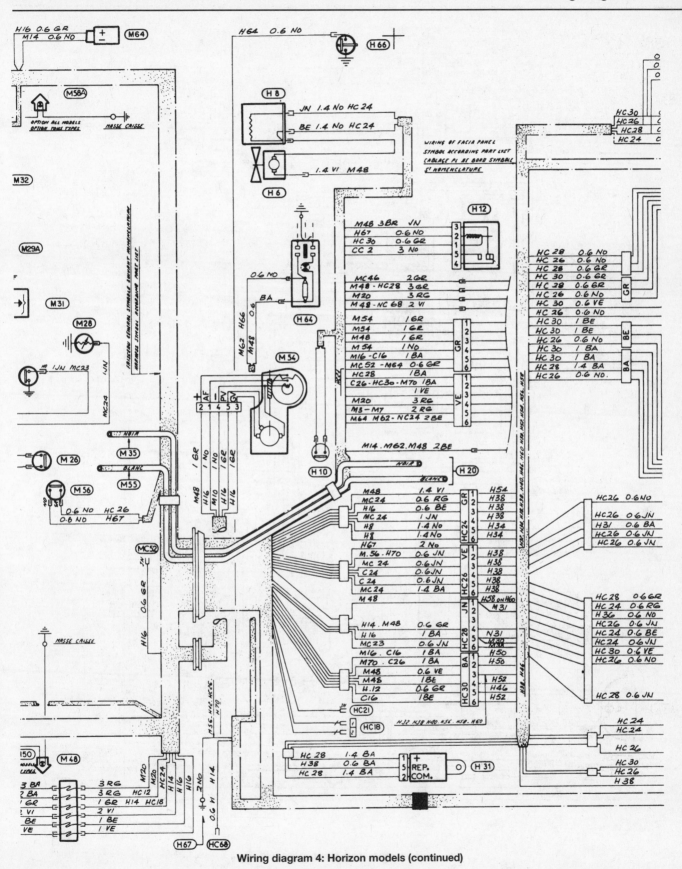

Wiring diagram 4: Horizon models (continued)

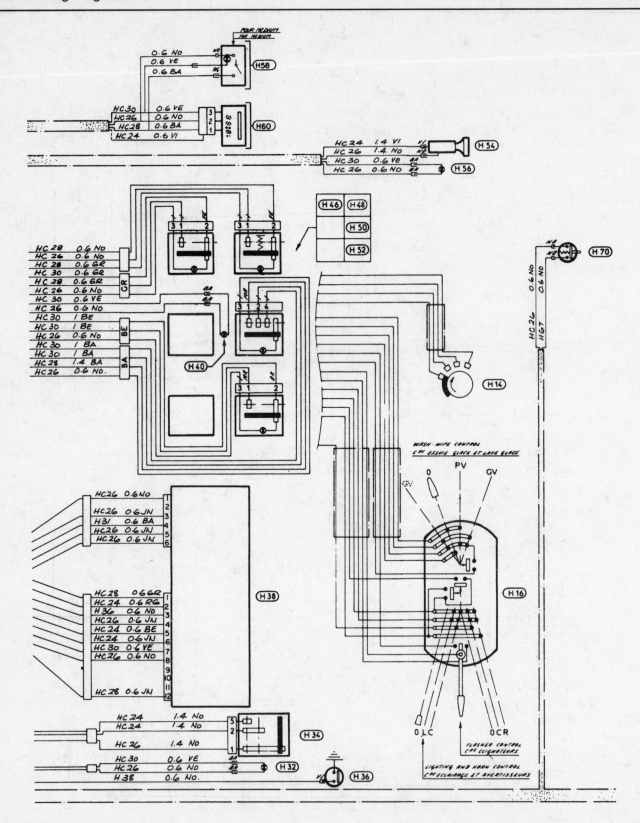

Wiring diagram 4: Horizon models (continued)

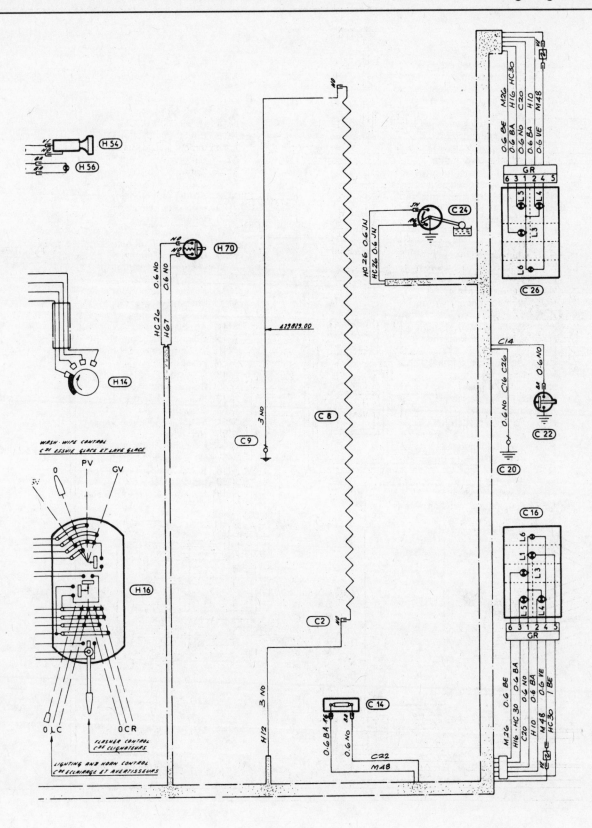

Wiring diagram 4: Horizon models (continued)

C8	Heated rear window	M3	Horn RH
C9	Earth on body	M6	Cooling fan motor
C14	Illumination, luggage compt	M7	Horn LH
C16	Rear lamp cluster LH	M10	Cooling fan motor
C20	Earth on body	M10	Earth on body
C22	Switch, luggage compt lamp	M14	Headlamp LH
C24	Fuel tank gauge unit	M16	Direction indicator LH
C26	Rear lamp cluster RH	M19	Indicator repeater LH
H6	Heater blower motor	M21	Battery
H8	Resistor, heater motor	M22	Control unit, preheaters
H10	Switch, stop-lamps	M26	Switch, reverse lamps
H12	Relay, heated rear window	M28	Sender unit, coolant temperature
H14	Ignition/starter switch	M29A	Preheater plugs
H16	Combination switch	M30	Ignition coil
H20	Heater control	M31	Injection pump
H31	Flasher unit, direction indicators	M32	Sender unit, oil pressure
H32	Illumination, heater controls	M34	Connector, engine oil pressure
H34	Switch, heater blower motor	M35	Vacuum connection
H36	Switch, choke control	M36	Horn, high note
H38	Instrument panel	M37	Sender unit, coolant temp
H40	Illumination, push-push	M30	Starter motor
H46	Switch, heated rear window	M42	Horn, low note
H50	Switch, hazard warning	M44	Alternator
H52	Switch, rear foglamps	M45	Diagnostic socket
H54	Cigar lighter	M47	Wear indicator, LH brake
H56	Illumination, ashtray	M48	Fusebox
H58	Clock, analogue	M49	Relay, cooling fan
H60	Clock, digital	M50	Control unit, ignition
H62	Courtesy switch LH	M50	Indicator repeater LH
H64	Interior lamp	M53	Capacitor
H66	Courtesy switch RH	M54	Motor, windscreen wiper
H67	Earth on body	M55	Heater valve
H70	Switch, handbrake	M56	Indicator, brake fluid level
L1	Foglamps, rear	M57	Wear indicator, RH brake
L2	Reverse lamps	M58	Pump, windscreen washer
L4	Stop/tail lamps	M58A	Indicator repeater
L5	Direction indicators	M68	Detector, water in diesel fuel
L6	Illumination, number plate		

Colour code
BA	White
BE	Blue
GR	Slate
JN	Yellow
MR	Brown
NO	Black
RG	Red
VE	Green
VI	Purple

Key to wiring diagram 4 for Horizon models

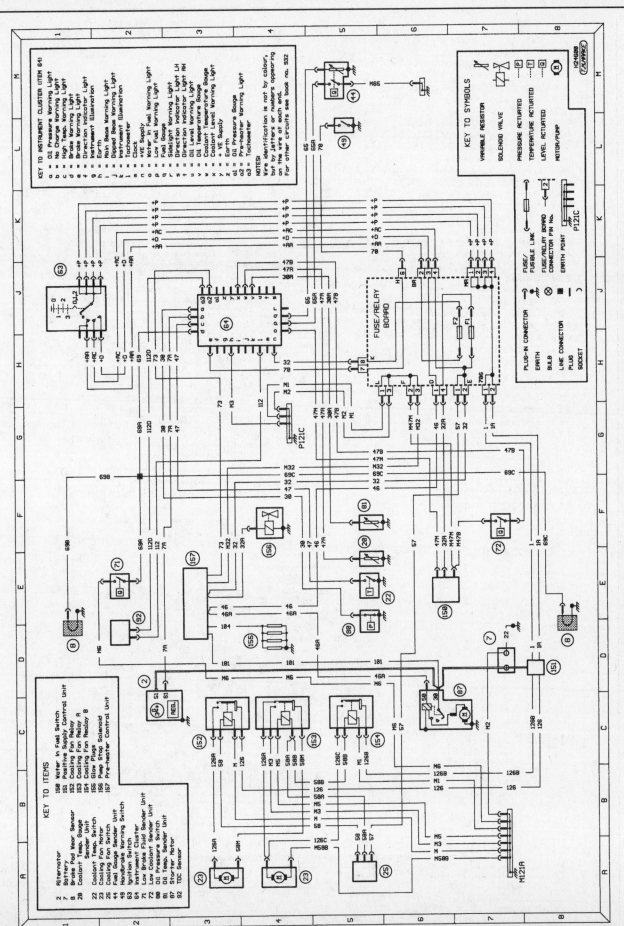

Wiring diagram 5: Typical starting, charging, cooling fan, warning lights and gauges - 205 models

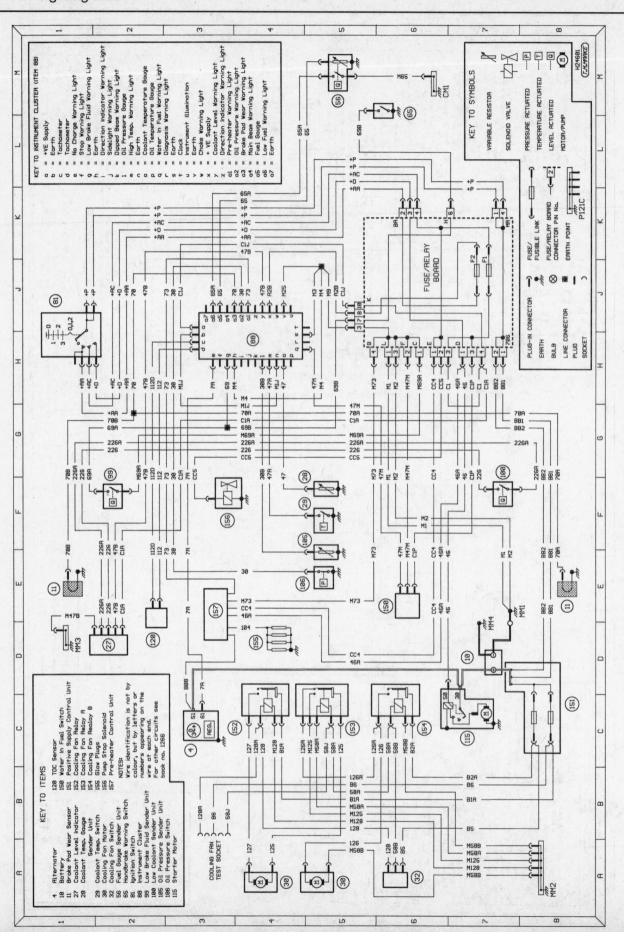

Wiring diagram 6: Typical starting, charging, cooling fan, warning lights and gauges - 309 models

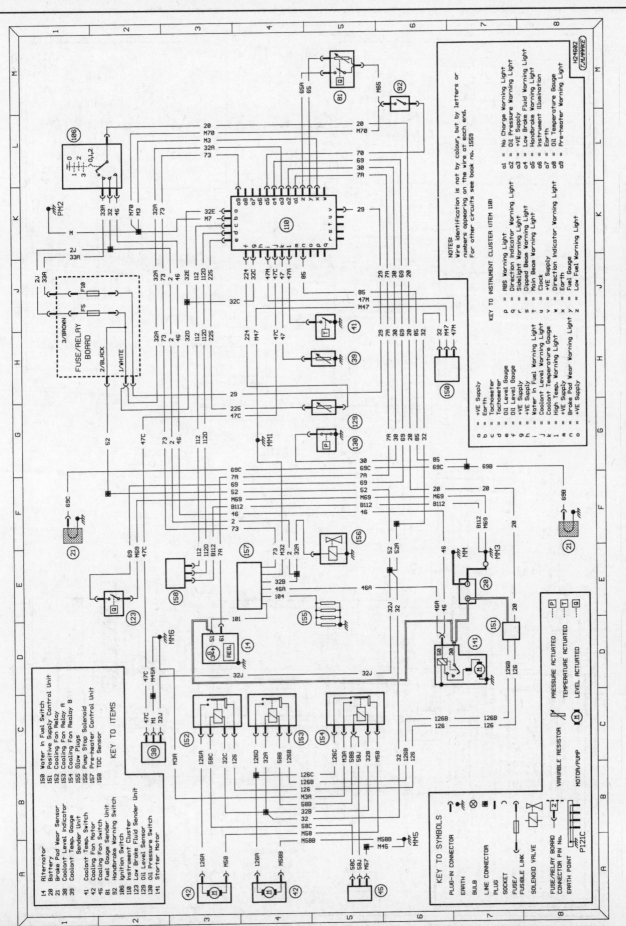

Wiring diagram 7: Typical starting, charging, cooling fan, warning lights and gauges - 405 models to 1992

5

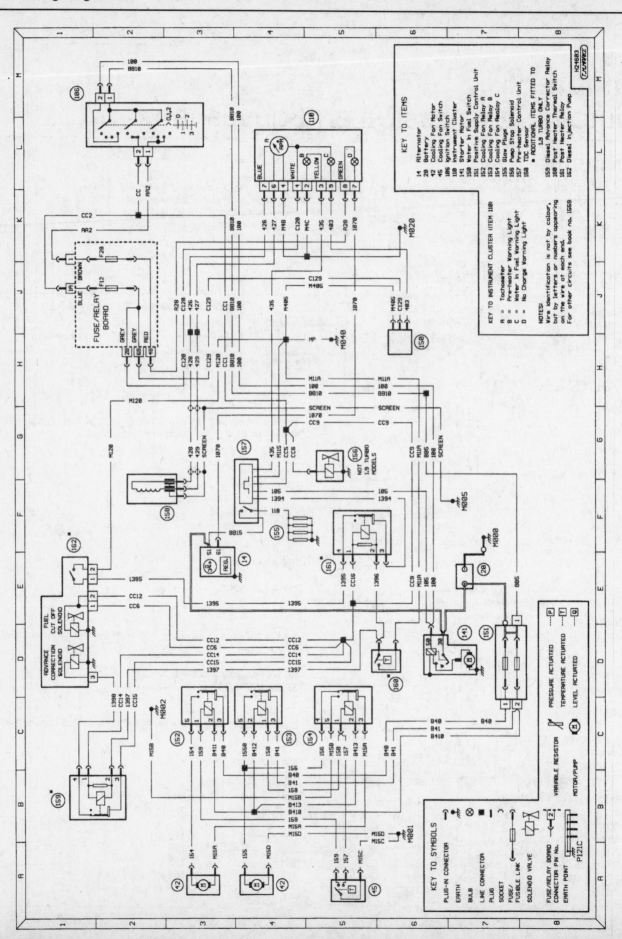

Wiring diagram 8: Typical starting, charging, cooling fan, warning lights and gauges – 405 models from 1992

Chapter 6
Clutch, transmission and driveshafts

Contents

Degrees of difficulty

Easy, suitable for novice with little experience		Fairly easy, suitable for beginner with some experience		Fairly difficult, suitable for competent DIY mechanic		Difficult, suitable for experienced DIY mechanic		Very difficult, suitable for expert DIY or professional	

Specifications

Clutch

Type . . . . Single dry plate with diaphragm spring. Hydraulically operated on Horizon models, cable operated on other models.

Friction plate diameter:
   Except 205, 309 and 405 Turbo models . . . . 200 mm
   205, 309 and 405 Turbo models . . . . 215 mm
Lining thickness . . . . 7.7 ± 0.3 mm
Release bearing type . . . . Sealed ball
Pedal free play . . . . Not applicable
Pedal travel:
   205 and 309 models . . . . 140.0 mm
   305 models . . . . 135.0 mm
   Horizon models . . . . Not adjustable
   405 models:
      XUD9A/L and XUD9TE/L engines . . . . 162.0 ± 12 mm
      XUD9A and XUD7TE engines . . . . 145.0 mm

Transmission

Type . . . . Four or five forward speeds and one reverse, synchromesh on all forward gears

Code:
   Pre 1989 models . . . . BE 1/4 (four speed) or BE 1/5 (five speed)
   1989-on models . . . . BE 3/4 (four speed) or BE 3/5 (five speed)

Driveshafts

Type . . . . Solid shaft with inner tri-axe joints and outer six-ball constant velocity joints

Grease capacity:
   Inner (tri-axe) joint . . . . 150 grams
   Outer (CV) joint . . . . 100 grams

Torque wrench settings

	Nm	lbf ft
Clutch pressure plate	50	37
Driveshaft nut:		
205 models	260	192
305 models	250	185
309 models	265	196
Horizon models	195	144

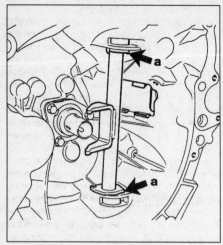

**1.1 Clutch release pivot shaft -
BE3 transmission**
a Bearings

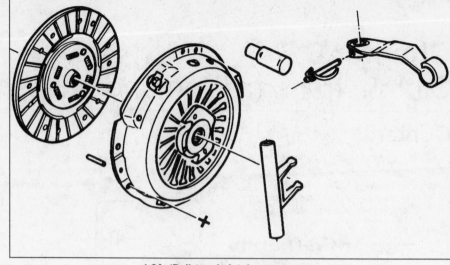

1.2A 'Pull-type' clutch components

1 Description - general

All models

1 Clutch components are virtually identical to those used in petrol-engined models. Access to the clutch is made by removing the transmission. Instead of the clutch release fork pivoting on a ball stud as in the BE1 transmission, in the later BE3 transmission, a pivot shaft is used **(see illustration)**.

Clutch (XUD 9TE engine with BE3/5 transmission)

2 The above engine/transmission combination is fitted with a 'pull-type' clutch **(see illustration)**. At the transmission end of the clutch cable, the inner cable is attached to a fixed mounting bracket, and the outer cable acts against the release fork lever **(see illustration)**. Depressing the clutch pedal pulls the outer cable towards the fixed end of the inner cable, and this in turn rotates the release fork by acting on the lever at the fork's upper end, above the bellhousing. The release fork lifts the release bearing, which is attached to the diaphragm spring fingers, away from the friction plate, and thus releases the clamping force of the diaphragm spring.

3 The internal arrangement of the pressure plate assembly differs from the 'push-type' clutch, in that the diaphragm spring pivots at its outer periphery on the cover **(see illustration)**.

4 Note that the release bearing forms part of the clutch cover assembly, and therefore cannot be renewed separately as is the case with the conventional 'push-type' clutch.

5 After removing the transmission as described later in Section 4, the clutch replacement procedure is as described in the relevant main manual.

6 The BE3/4 and BE3/5 transmissions progressively replaced the BE1/4 and BE1/5 transmissions, from the beginning of 1989. The main difference is in the gearshift components. The driver will notice that reverse gear is now in the same plane as 2nd and 4th, opposite 5th, where applicable. Also the lifting collar below the gear knob for selecting reverse gear is now obsolete.

7 Overhaul procedures will be found in the relevant main manual.

8 The oil filler/level plug for the BE3 transmission is in the end cover; it is accessible through the left-hand wheel arch.

All models

9 Procedures for the BE1 type transmission can be found in the appropriate main manual. However on 205 models fitted with a four-speed transmission, differences compared with a five-speed transmission are described in Section 5.

10 The driveshafts are solid with inner 'tri-axe' joints and outer constant velocity joints.

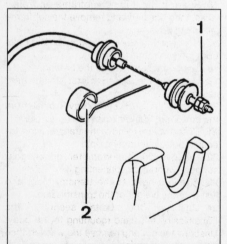

1.2B Clutch cable locknuts (1) and release lever (2)

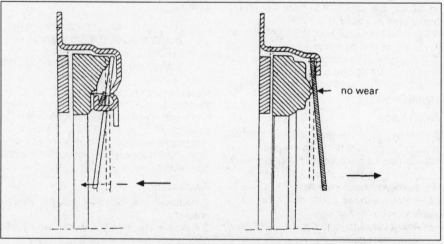

1.3 Comparison of 'push-type' and 'pull-type' clutch mechanisms

no wear

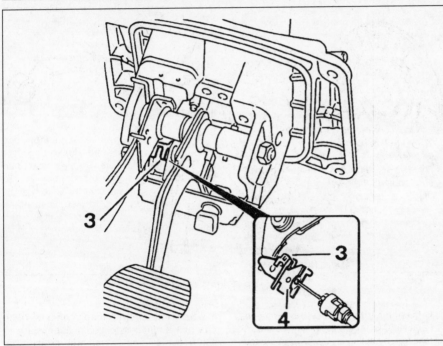

2.5 Cable connection to the clutch pedal
3 Clip   4 Plastic holder

2   Clutch cable (XUD9TE engine with BE3/5 transmission) - removal, refitting and adjustment

Removal

1 Remove the air cleaner and associated air hoses.
2 Remove the battery and battery support bracket.
3 Loosen the adjustment nuts on the end of the inner cable.
4 Release the inner cable from the bracket on the transmission, and also disconnect the outer cable from the release lever.
5 Working inside the vehicle, press on the clip to detach the inner cable from the plastic holder **(see illustration)**.
6 Prise out the rubber boot from the bulkhead in the engine compartment.
7 Pull on the outer cable to detach the bush from the pedal bracket cable stop.
8 Withdraw the cable from within the engine compartment.

Refitting

9 Refitting is a reversal of the removal procedure, but note the following points:
a) Turn the rubber boot inside-out before refitting the cable, then locate it on the bulkhead when the cable is in position.
b) Make sure that the bush on the cable stop is locked in the groove.
c) Adjust the clutch pedal travel, using the adjustment nuts on the end of the inner cable, to the dimension given in the Specifications.

3   Transmission removal (BE1 transmissions) - general

1 The procedure is basically the same as described in the relevant main manual, except the following.
2 Where necessary, the air cleaner and air duct must be removed first.
3 On all models remove the starter motor.
4 On Horizon models, where applicable, remove the power steering pump and secure it to one side, without disconnecting the hoses.
5 After tightening the mounting bolt on Horizon models, lock it by bending over the lock tab.

4   Transmission (BE3/5 with XUD9TE engine) - removal and refitting

Note: *A 'pull-type' clutch is fitted to the XUD9TE engine. Although the basic removal and refitting procedure is the same as described for other models, the following paragraphs describe the complete procedure, including the special procedures for the `pull-type' clutch.*

Removal

1 Remove the battery and its support bracket.
2 Remove the air cleaner and the air inlet hose.
3 Identify all wiring and hoses attached to the transmission, then disconnect them.

4 Disconnect the clutch cable.
5 Unscrew and remove the starter mounting bolts, and pull the starter motor away from the transmission without removing it completely.
6 Withdraw the retaining pin, and remove the clutch release lever from the top of the release fork shaft (where necessary, unscrew the bolt first). The lever must be removed to allow the fork shaft to rotate freely, and disengage from the release bearing as the transmission is pulled away from the engine. Make an alignment mark across the centre of the clutch release fork shaft using a scriber, paint or similar, and mark its relative position on the transmission housing. Unscrew the retaining bolts, and remove the clutch cable bracket from the top of the transmission housing.
7 Unscrew the bolts securing the anti-roll bar links to the front suspension lower arms on both sides.
8 Apply the handbrake, then jack up the front of the vehicle and support on axle stands (see *"Jacking and vehicle support"*). Remove both front wheels.
9 Position a container beneath the transmission, then unscrew the drain plug and drain the transmission oil. Clean the drain plug, and refit it when the oil has drained.
10 Remove the splash shield from the left-hand side, below the transmission.
11 Disconnect the front suspension lower balljoints on both sides.
12 Unscrew the bolt from the engine rear mounting.
13 Unscrew and remove the right-hand driveshaft nut.
14 Loosen (but do not remove) the nuts securing the right-hand driveshaft intermediate shaft bearing to the bracket at the rear of the engine. Turn the bolts through 90°, then pull the right-hand driveshaft together with its intermediate shaft from the transmission (refer to the relevant petrol-engined manual for more details if necessary).
15 Pull the left-hand driveshaft from transmission.
16 Support the engine subframe on trolley jacks, then unscrew and remove the subframe mounting bolts.
17 Unscrew the steering gear mounting bolts from the subframe.
18 Lower the subframe to the ground.
19 Unscrew the speedometer driven gear securing bolt.
20 Unbolt the bellhousing cover plate from the bottom of the transmission.
21 Unscrew and remove the transmission-to-engine bottom mounting bolt.
22 Remove the speedometer driven gear support, without disconnecting it.
23 Attach a hoist to the transmission, and just take the weight of the transmission.
24 Unscrew the bolts securing the transmission left-hand mounting to the body. Unscrew the nut and remove the washer, then remove the mounting.
25 Unbolt the mounting bracket from the top of the transmission.

6

26 The engine must now be supported while the transmission is being removed. To do this, either position a trolley jack with interposed piece of wood beneath the sump, or preferably support the engine with a hoist from above.

27 Unscrew and remove the remaining bolts securing the transmission to the engine. Note the correct fitted positions of each bolt (and any relevant brackets) as they are removed, to use as a reference on refitting. Make a final check that all necessary components have been disconnected, and that they are positioned clear of the transmission, so that they will not hinder the removal procedure.

28 With the bolts removed, move the trolley jack and transmission to the left, to free it from its locating dowels.

29 Once the transmission is free, lower the jack and manoeuvre the unit out from under the car. If they are loose, remove the locating dowels from the transmission or engine, and keep them in a safe place.

30 Make a second alignment mark on the transmission housing, marking the position of the release fork mark after removal, noting the angle at which the release fork is positioned. This mark can then be used to position the release fork before installation, to ensure that the fork correctly engages with the clutch release bearing as the transmission is installed.

Refitting

31 Check the differential output oil seals in the sides of the transmission, and renew them if necessary. The space between the oil seal lips should be lightly greased before the transmission is refitted and the driveshafts inserted.

32 The transmission is refitted by a reversal of the removal procedure, remembering the following points:

a) Apply a little high-melting-point grease to the splines of the transmission input shaft, release bearing guide sleeve, and the tips of the release fork arms. Do not apply too much, otherwise there is a possibility of the grease contaminating the clutch friction plate.

b) Ensure that the locating dowels are correctly positioned prior to installation.

c) Before refitting the transmission, position the clutch release bearing so that its 'HAUT' mark is at the top, and the BAS mark is at the bottom (if these marks are not present, the bearing will have a top-facing arrow). Align the release fork shaft mark with the second mark made on the transmission housing. This will ensure that the release fork and bearing will engage correctly as the transmission is refitted to the engine. The release fork arms should be positioned at 60° to the bellhousing face of the transmission. Check that the notches in the bearing face towards the front of the vehicle. If the bearing and fork are correctly engaged when the transmission is refitted, the mark on the shaft should be aligned with the original mark made on the transmission housing. Ensure that the release fork and bearing are correctly engaged before bolting the transmission onto the engine.

d) Apply thread-locking fluid to the engine/transmission left-hand mounting stud threads before refitting it to the transmission. Tighten the stud to the specified torque.

e) Tighten all nuts and bolts to the specified torque (where given).

f) On completion, refill the transmission with the specified type and quantity of lubricant.

5 Transmission - dismantling and reassembly

Dismantling

1 The four-speed and five-speed transmissions differ only in respect of the 5th gear and its associated components.

2 To remove the components the input and output shafts must be locked before unscrewing the end nuts. The best way to do this is to engage a gear then immobilise the input shaft using an old clutch disc to which a metal bar has been welded **(see illustration)**. It is unwise to attempt to grip the input shaft splines with any other tool as damage may be caused.

3 With the input and output shaft nuts slackened continue as described for the five-speed transmission.

Reassembly

4 When reassembling the transmission use the same method described in paragraph 2 to tighten the shaft nuts. Remember to stake the nuts after tightening them.

6 Driveshaft renewal (Horizon models) - general

1 The procedure is similar to that for petrol engine models, with the following exceptions.

2 The right hand driveshaft is supported by an intermediate bearing incorporated in the lower torque link mounting bracket. When removing the driveshaft unscrew the nuts and withdraw the bearing cap and retaining clips **(see illustration)**. Clean the bearing and seating before refitting the cap and tightening the nuts.

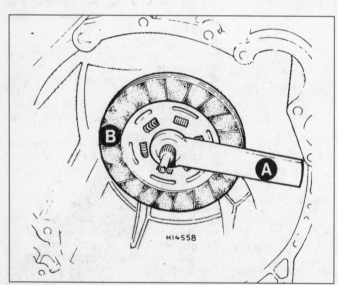

5.2 Tool for locking the transmission input shaft
Lever (A) welded to old clutch disc (driven plate) (B)

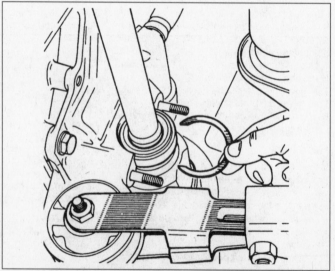

6.2 Removing the retaining clips from the right-hand driveshaft intermediate bearing on Horizon models

3 When inserting the right hand driveshaft through the final drive oil seal, it is important to protect the oil seal from the driveshaft splines. This is no problem when a new oil seal is being fitted, as a split protector is provided, as described in Section 8. A piece of thin plastic works just as effectively, if it is first greased, to prevent it from being pushed into the final drive housing.

4 If both driveshafts are being removed on models manufactured before July 1984, remove the left hand driveshaft first. Then support the left hand differential side gear using a dowel, preferably wooden. If this precaution is not taken, the side gears may become misaligned when the right hand driveshaft is removed.

7 Driveshaft rubber bellows - removal and refitting

Removal

1 With the driveshaft removed (refer to the relevant manual for petrol-engined models for removal procedure) loosen the clips on the outer rubber bellows. If plastic straps are fitted cut them free with snips **(see illustration)**.
2 Prise the bellows large diameter from the outer joint housing **(see illustration)**, then tap the centre hub outwards using a soft metal drift to release it from the retaining circlip. Slide the outer joint complete from the driveshaft splines.
3 Extract the circlip from the groove in the driveshaft **(see illustration)**.

7.1 Plastic straps on the outer rubber bellows

4 Prise off the rubber bellows. If necessary remove the plastic seating from the recess in the driveshaft **(see illustrations)**.
5 Loosen the clips on the inner rubber bellows. If plastic straps are fitted cut them free.

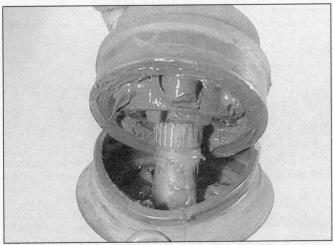

7.2 Removing the rubber bellows from the outer joint housing

7.3 Driveshaft outer joint retaining circlip (arrowed)

6

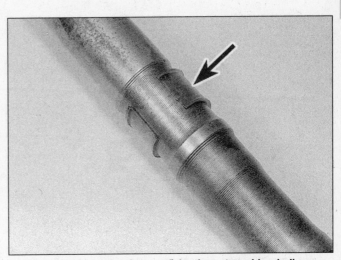

7.4A Removing the outer rubber bellows from the driveshaft

7.4B Plastic seating (arrowed) for the outer rubber bellows

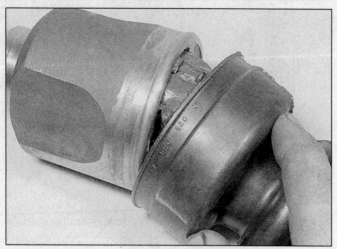

7.6 Removing the inner rubber bellows

7.7 Separating the driveshaft and rollers from the inner joint housing

7.8 Left-hand driveshaft with rollers retained with adhesive tape

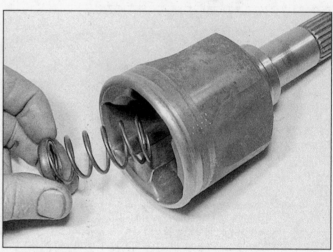

7.9 Removing the pressure pad and spring from the inner joint housing

7.11 Injecting grease into the inner joint housing

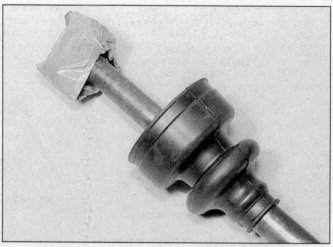

7.12 Inner rubber bellows located on the driveshaft

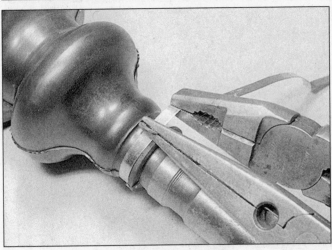

7.15A Tighten the metal clip. . .

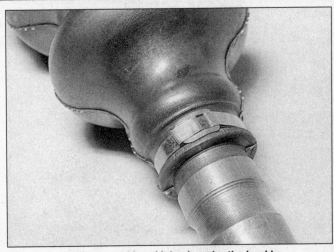

7.15B . . . and bend it back under the buckle

6 Prise the bellows large diameter from the inner joint housing and slide the rubber bellows off the outer end of the driveshaft **(see illustration)**.

7 Mark the driveshaft and inner joint housing in relation to each other then separate them, keeping the rollers engaged with their respective spigots **(see illustration)**.

8 Clean away the grease then retain the rollers using adhesive tape **(see illustration)**.

9 Remove the pressure pad and spring from inside the inner joint housing **(see illustration)**.

Refitting

10 Clean away the grease then begin reassembly by inserting the pressure pad and spring into the inner joint housing with the housing mounted upright in a soft-jawed vice.

11 Inject half the required amount of grease into the inner joint housing **(see illustration)**.

12 Locate the new inner rubber bellows halfway along the driveshaft **(see illustration)**.

13 Remove the adhesive tape and insert the driveshaft into the housing.

14 Inject the remaining amount of grease in the joint.

15 Keeping the driveshaft pressed against the internal spring, refit the rubber bellows and tighten the clips. Metal type clips can be tightened using two pliers, by holding the buckle and pulling the clip through. Cut off the excess and bend the clip back under the buckle **(see illustrations)**.

16 Fit the plastic seating in the driveshaft recess and refit the new rubber bellows small diameter on it.

17 Refit the circlip in the driveshaft groove.

18 Inject the required amount of grease in the outer joint then insert the driveshaft, engage the splines, and press in until the circlip snaps into the groove.

19 Ease the rubber bellows onto the outer joint, and fit the two clips, tightening them as previously described.

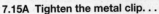

8 Driveshaft oil seals - removal and refitting

Removal

1 Jack up the front of the vehicle and support on axle stands (see "*Jacking and vehicle support*"). Apply the handbrake.

2 Unscrew the drain plug(s) and drain the transmission oil into a container. On completion refit and tighten the plug(s).

3 Disconnect the front track control arms from the stub axle carriers **(see illustration)**.

4 Have an assistant pull the left-hand wheel outwards while the left-hand driveshaft is levered from the differential side gear. Hold the strut/carrier outwards with a block of wood.

5 On models manufactured before July 1984, the left-hand differential side gear must be supported using a dowel, preferably wooden. If this precaution is not taken, the side gears may become misaligned when the right-hand driveshaft is removed.

6 On Horizon models, unscrew the nuts and withdraw the bearing cap and retaining clip

retaining the right hand driveshaft intermediate bearing.

7 On models other than the Horizon, loosen the two nuts retaining the right-hand driveshaft intermediate bearing in the bracket bolted to the rear of the cylinder block and turn the bolt heads through 90° to release the bearing.

8 Have an assistant pull the right-hand wheel outwards while the right-hand driveshaft is removed from the differential side gear. Hold the strut out with a block of wood.

9 Using a screwdriver lever the oil seals from the transmission **(see illustration)**.

Refitting

10 Clean the oil seal seatings in the transmission.

11 Press the new left-hand oil seal squarely into the transmission until flush using a block of wood.

12 The new right-hand oil seal is supplied with a protector to be used when fitting the driveshaft. First remove the protector and press the oil seal squarely into the transmission until flush using a block of wood. Refit the protector having applied a little grease to the seal lips **(see illustrations)**.

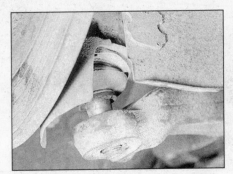

8.3 Disconnecting a front track control arm

8.9 Levering a driveshaft oil seal from the transmission

6

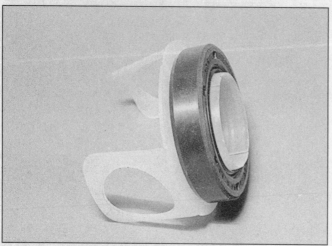

8.12A The right-hand driveshaft oil seal is supplied with a protector

8.12B Right-hand driveshaft oil seal installed ready for driveshaft refitting

8.13 Refitting the right-hand driveshaft

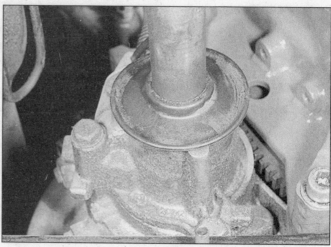

8.15 Right-hand driveshaft rubber dust seal

13 Insert the right-hand driveshaft while guiding the intermediate bearing in the bracket **(see illustration)**.

14 Pull out the protector and discard it. The protector is split so that it will pass over the driveshaft.

15 Slide the rubber dust seal next to the oil seal, where applicable **(see illustration)**.

16 Refit and tighten the intermediate bearing bolts.

17 Apply a little grease to the left-hand oil seal lips then insert the left-hand driveshaft **(see illustration)**.

18 Reconnect the front track control arms to the stub axle carriers.

19 Lower the vehicle to the ground and refill the transmission with oil as described in Chapter 1.

8.17 Refitting the left-hand driveshaft

Chapter 7
Braking systems

Contents

Degrees of difficulty

Easy, suitable for novice with little experience	**Fairly easy,** suitable for beginner with some experience	**Fairly difficult,** suitable for competent DIY mechanic	**Difficult,** suitable for experienced DIY mechanic	**Very difficult,** suitable for expert DIY or professional

7

Specifications

General
System type .... Front disc brakes, rear drum brakes, servo assistance by vacuum pump (exhauster) belt driven from camshaft.

Vacuum pump
Oil capacity .... 40 cc

Torque wrench settings

	Nm	lbf ft
Vacuum pump (later belt-driven type):		
Drivebelt top and bottom adjusting bolts	20	15
Pump support bolt	20	15
Pivot bracket pivot bolt	40	30
Vacuum pump diaphragm nut/screw (early models)	9	7

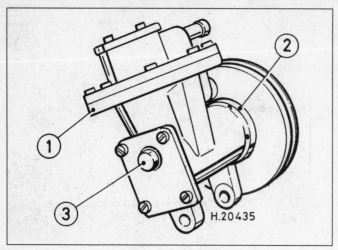

1.1 Early vacuum pump

1 Type number location   3 Oil filler/level plug
2 Alignment marks for
   checking oil level

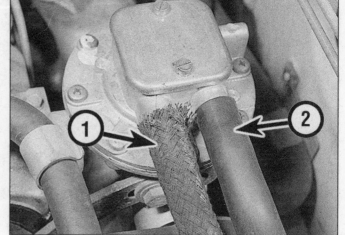

2.2 Vacuum (1) and discharge (2) hoses on the vacuum pump

1 Description - general

The braking system is identical to petrol engined models, except for the addition of a vacuum pump. Since there is no throttle valve in the diesel engine, there is insufficient vacuum in the inlet manifold to operate the brake servo unit. The vacuum pump provides the necessary vacuum **(see illustration)**.

It is mounted on the inlet manifold and belt driven from a pulley on the end of the camshaft. The discharge hose is connected to the inlet manifold.

2 Vacuum pump (except camshaft driven pumps) - removal and refitting

Removal

1 Remove the air cleaner and ducting.
2 Disconnect the inlet and discharge hoses **(see illustration)**.
3 Loosen the pivot and adjustment link bolts and nuts, swivel the vacuum pump upwards and slip the drivebelt from the pulleys.
4 Remove the pivot, adjustment bolts and withdraw the vacuum pump from the inlet manifold.

Refitting

5 Refitting is a reversal of removal. However before tightening the pivot and adjustment bolts, swivel the pump away from the engine until the deflection of the drivebelt, midway between the pulleys is approximately 5.0 mm, under firm finger or thumb pressure.
6 Check and if necessary, top-up the pump oil level, as described in Chapter 1.

3 Vacuum pump (camshaft-driven) - removal and refitting

Note: *Camshaft driven vacuum pumps, were introduced during early 1992.*

Removal

1 When applicable, remove the intercooler as described in Chapter 4.
2 Loosen the clip and disconnect the vacuum hose from the vacuum pump **(see illustration)**.
3 Unscrew the mounting bolts and remove the brake vacuum pump from the end of the cylinder head **(see illustrations)**.

3.2 Disconnecting the vacuum hose from the vacuum pump

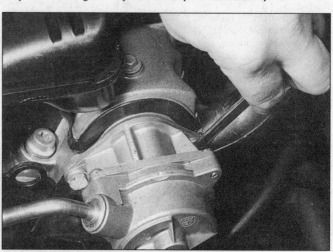

3.3A Unscrew the mounting bolts . . .

3.3B . . . and remove the vacuum pump

3.4A Removing the large O-ring . . .

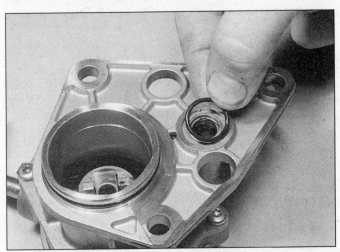

3.4B . . . and small O-ring from the grooves in the pump

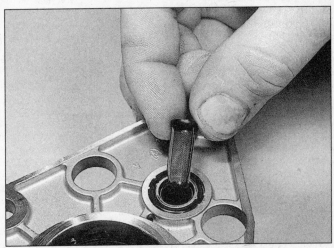

3.5 Removing the vacuum pump oil filter

4 Extract the two O-rings from the grooves in the pump **(see illustrations)**.

5 Using a small screwdriver, extract the filter from the oil lubrication channel in the vacuum pump **(see illustration)**.

Refitting

6 Before refitting the pump, clean the O-ring grooves, and also clean the mating surfaces of the pump and cylinder head. Clean the filter, or if necessary renew it.

7 Locate the filter in the oil lubrication channel.

8 Fit new O-rings in the grooves on the pump, and lightly oil them.

9 Locate the pump on the end of the cylinder head, making sure that the dog engages correctly with the end of the camshaft.

10 Insert and tighten the mounting bolts.

11 Connect the vacuum hose, and tighten the clip.

12 When applicable, refit the intercooler as described in Chapter 4.

13 Start the engine, and check that the brake pedal operates correctly, with assistance from the vacuum pump. Check around the pump for signs of oil leakage.

---

4 Vacuum pump - testing and overhaul

Testing

1 A vacuum gauge is required to test the vacuum pump. Connect the gauge to the inlet port on the pump, using a T-piece and two lengths of hose as shown **(see illustration)**. The push valve is necessary to accurately time the test period.

2 Start the engine and let it idle, then close the push valve and check that a minimum of 500 mm Hg is recorded after 1 minute. Stop the engine.

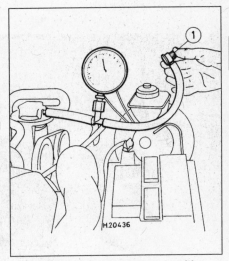

4.1 Testing the vacuum pump with a vacuum gauge
1 Push valve

7

3 If the correct result is not obtained, either the drivebelt is slipping or the vacuum pump is faulty.

Overhaul

4 To renew the valves, extract the two screws and lift off the cover and gasket, followed by the springs, valves and seals. Fit the new valves, together with new seals and a new cover gasket. Tighten the two screws.

5 To renew the diaphragm, first mark the cover in relation to the main body. Remove the screws and lift of the cover. Unscrew the nut or screw and remove the diaphragm and support plates from the piston. Prise the O-ring from the recess in the piston, where fitted **(see illustration)**.

6 Turn the pulley so that the piston is at the top of the stroke. Then attempt to move the top of the piston from side to side. If wear is evident, renew the complete vacuum pump.

7 Clean the components and begin reassembly by fitting a new piston O-ring, where applicable.

8 Fit the new diaphragm and support plates on the piston, making sure the curved edges of the plates are next to the diaphragm. Where applicable, the smaller of the two plates should be fitted on top of the diaphragm.

4.5 Exploded view of the vacuum pump

1 *Cover screws*
2 *Inlet valve spring*
3 *Outlet valve springs*
4 *Cover*
5 *Gasket*
6 *Inlet valve*
7 *Outlet valves*
8 *Seals*
9 *Diaphragm cover*
10 *Nut*
11 *Diaphragm*
12 *Support plates*
13 *Screw*
14 *O-ring*
15 *Piston*

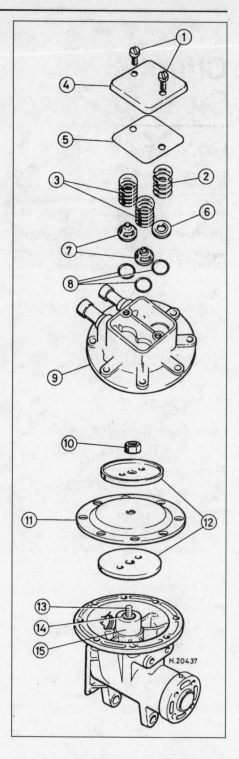

9 Apply locking fluid to the threads of the nut or screw, then fit and tighten to the specified torque.

10 Refit the cover and tighten the screws progressively.

11 Check and if necessary top-up the oil level with reference to Chapter 1.

Chapter 8
Steering, wheels and tyres

Contents

Refer to the Note at the beginning of each Section concerning the fitment of the power steering pump.

Degrees of difficulty

Easy, suitable for novice with little experience		Fairly easy, suitable for beginner with some experience		Fairly difficult, suitable for competent DIY mechanic	Difficult, suitable for experienced DIY mechanic	Very difficult, suitable for expert DIY or professional

Specifications

Power assisted steering
Fluid capacity . . . . 0.65 litre
Fluid type/specifications . . . . Dexron ATF (automatic transmission fluid)

Front wheel alignment
Toe-in:
    205 models . . . . 2.5± 1mm
    305 models . . . . 4.0± 1mm
    309 models . . . . 2.0± 1mm
    Horizon models . . . . 0± 1mm per wheel
Camber:
    205 models . . . . 0° 30'± 30'
    305 models . . . . 0° 25'± 30'
    309 models . . . . 0°± 30'
    Horizon models . . . . 0°± 30'
Castor:
    205 models . . . . 1° 40'± 30'
    305 models . . . . 1° 45'± 30'
    309 models . . . . 0° 30'± 30'
    Horizon models . . . . 2°± 30'
Steering axis inclination:
    205 models . . . . 8° 50'± 30'
    305 models . . . . 9° 20'± 30'
    309 models . . . . 9° 30'± 30'
    Horizon models . . . . 12°± 45'

Wheels and tyres
Note: *For tyre pressures, refer to Chapter 1*
Wheel sizes:
    205 models . . . . 450 B13 FH 435 or 500 B13 FH 428
    305 models . . . . 500 B14 FH 425
    309 models:
        Non Turbo . . . . 500 B13 FH 420
        Turbo:
            Steel 5.5J14 FH4-24
            Alloy 5.5J14 CH4-24
    405 models:
        Steel . . . . 5J14 FH4-25 or 5.5J14 FH4-24
        Alloy . . . . 5.5J14 CH4-25 or 5.5J14 CH4-24
    Horizon models . . . . 4 1/2 J x 13 or 5J x 13

8

Wheels and tyres (continued)

Tyre sizes:

205 models (except GRD)	145 SR 13
205 GRD models	165/70 SR 13
305 models	155 R 14 S
309 models:	
Non Turbo	165/70 SR 13
Turbo	175/65 R14H
405 models:	
Non-Turbo	165/70 R14T or 175/70 R14T
Turbo	185/65 R14H
Horizon models	155 SR 13

Torque wrench settings

	Nm	lbf ft
Power steering:		
Pump union	23	17
Steering gear mounting	35	26
Tie-rod to rack	55	41
Track rod end	35	26

---

1 Description - general

The procedures are identical to those on petrol engine models, except for the addition of power steering on 305, 309 and Horizon models.

On the diesel engine the power steering pump is belt driven by a pulley on the end of the camshaft (see illustrations). The location of the injection pump prevents it's location at the timing end of the engine (as on petrol engined models).

On 405 models, the power steering pump can be located, either on top of the transmission, the front lower side of the engine or on the front upper side of the engine (see illustration).

2 Power steering system - draining and refilling

Draining

1 Disconnect the battery leads, negative lead first.
2 Where necessary, remove the air cleaner and ducting.
3 On 305 and Horizon models, unscrew the union nut and disconnect the high pressure pipe from the steering gear valve. Then drain the fluid into a container.
4 On 309 models, loosen the clips and disconnect both hoses from the fluid cooler (see illustration). Then drain the fluid into a container.
5 To ensure complete draining, turn the steering slowly, from lock to lock, at least three times.
6 Reconnect the pipe or hoses and tighten the nut or clips.

Refilling

7 Remove the reservoir cap and refill to approximately 25 mm below the rim.
8 With the engine stopped, turn the steering slowly, from lock to lock several times. Top-up with fluid to the lower cold mark on the filler cap dipstick. Refer to Chapter 1, if necessary.
9 Run the engine at idling speed and continue to turn the steering slowly, from lock to lock several times. Top-up the fluid as the level drops.
10 Switch off the engine and top-up the fluid to the lower cold level mark. Refit the cap.

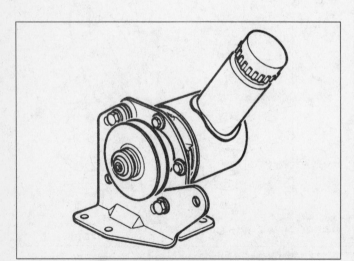

1.2A Early type power steering pump

1.2B Later type power steering pump

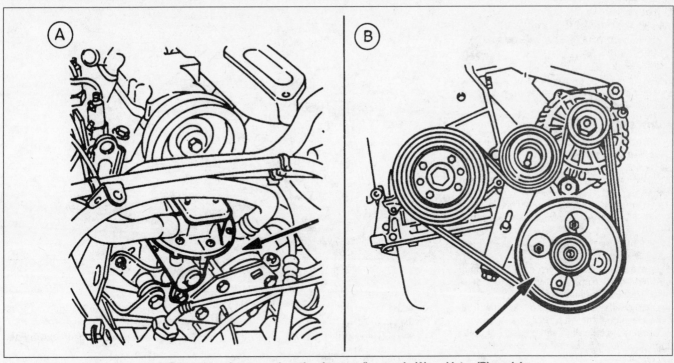

1.3 Power steering pump location (arrowed) on early (A) and later (B) models

3 Power steering pump (except 405 models) - removal and refitting

Removal

1 Remove the air cleaner and ducting, as described in Chapter 4.

2 Disconnect both battery leads (negative lead first), unbolt the mounting clamp and remove the battery.

3 Loosen the power steering pump mounting and adjustment bolts, as applicable, move the pump upwards and slip the drivebelt from the pulleys.

4 Drain the power steering fluid, as described in Section 2.

5 Using two spanners, unscrew the high pressure union nut on the pump, while holding the union stationary. Disconnect the high pressure pipe.

6 Loosen the clip and disconnect the low pressure return hose.

7 Unscrew the mounting bolts and remove the pump from the bracket on the transmission.

Refitting

8 Refitting is a reversal of removal. However, tension the drivebelt as described in Chapter 1. On 309 models, position the high pressure hose up to 20° rearwards **(see illustration)**, before tightening the union nut. Fill the system with fresh fluid, as described in Chapter 1.

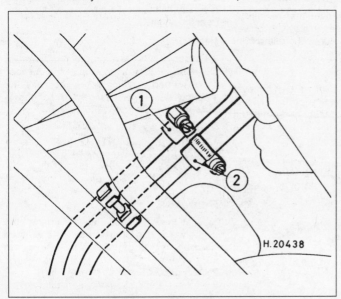

2.4 Fluid cooler hoses (1 and 2) on 309 models

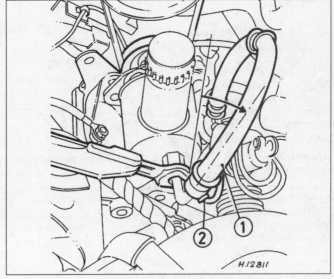

3.8 High pressure (1) and low pressure (2) hoses on the 309 power steering pump
Note angle of high pressure hose

8

4 Power steering pump (early 405 models) - removal and refitting

Note: *This procedure applies to the power steering pump, that is located on top of the transmission.*

Removal

1 Drain the steering fluid by unscrewing the union nut at the steering gear valve. Refer to Section 2.
2 Disconnect the leads, and remove the battery.
3 Unbolt the fuel filter assembly and move it out of the way, being careful not to strain the hoses.
4 Unscrew the bolts and remove the battery support.
5 Loosen the clip, and disconnect the fluid supply hose from the top of the power steering pump **(see illustration)**.
6 Unscrew the union nut, and disconnect the pressure pipe from the power steering pump.
7 Loosen the mounting and adjustment bolts, then slip the drivebelt off the power steering pump pulley.
8 Remove the bolts and lift the power steering pump, together with the support bracket, from the top of the transmission.
9 Unbolt and remove the intermediate support bracket.
10 If the drivebelt is to be removed completely, remove the brake vacuum pump drivebelt.

Refitting

11 Refitting is a reversal of the removal procedure, but adjust the tension of the drivebelt(s), (refer to Chapter 1), and refill the steering system with fluid as described in Section 2.

5 Power steering pump (405 from mid-1992*) - removal and refitting

* Note: *This procedure applies to those models from mid-1992 that **DO NOT** have air conditioning and with the power steering pump located on the front lower side of the engine.*

Removal

1 From mid-1992, models with power steering are fitted with the later camshaft-driven brake vacuum pump (see Chapter 7). This fitment has resulted in the power steering pump being relocated below the alternator; one drivebelt now drives the alternator and power steering pump.
2 Drain the steering fluid by unscrewing the union nut at the steering gear valve (see Section 2).
3 Apply the handbrake, then jack up the front of the vehicle and support it on axle stands

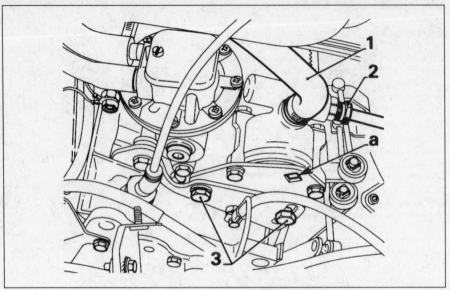

4.5 Power steering pump (early type) removal

1 Fluid supply hose	*3 Mounting and adjustment bolts*
2 Pressure pipe	*a Drivebelt tension adjustment square hole*

(see "*Jacking and vehicle support*"). Remove the front right-hand wheel.
4 Remove the right-hand front splash shield.
5 Loosen the tensioner bolts located inside the upper tensioner roller and on the bracket, then turn the adjustment bolt as necessary to move the tensioner upwards.
6 Slip the drivebelt from the pulleys and tensioner roller.
7 Loosen the clip, and disconnect the fluid supply hose from the power steering pump.
8 Unscrew the union nut, and disconnect the pressure pipe from the power steering pump.
9 Turn the pump pulley as necessary to gain access to the front mounting bolts, then unscrew and remove them.
10 Unscrew and remove the remaining mounting bolt from the rear of the power steering pump, then withdraw the pump from under the engine.

Refitting

11 Refitting is a reversal of the removal procedure. Adjust the tension of the drivebelt as described in Chapter 1, and refill the steering system with fluid as described in Section 2.

6 Power steering pump (405 from mid-1992*) - removal and refitting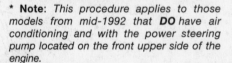

* Note: *This procedure applies to those models from mid-1992 that **DO** have air conditioning and with the power steering pump located on the front upper side of the engine.*

Removal

1 Before starting work, note that a rod is necessary to hold the automatic tension roller

in its released position (see alternator drivebelt removal in Chapter 5).
2 Drain the steering fluid by unscrewing the union nut at the steering gear valve (see Section 2).
3 Remove the drivebelt.
4 Loosen the clip, and disconnect the fluid supply hose from the power steering pump.
5 Unscrew the union nut, and disconnect the pressure pipe from the power steering pump.
6 Turn the pump pulley as necessary, so that the front mounting bolts are visible through the holes in the pulley. Unscrew and remove the front mounting bolts.
7 Unscrew and remove the rear mounting bolt, and withdraw the power steering pump from the engine.

Refitting

8 Refitting is a reversal of the removal procedure. Adjust the tension of the drivebelt as described in Chapter 1, and refill the steering system with fluid as described in Section 2.

7 Power steering gear (305 models) - removal and refitting

Removal

1 Apply the handbrake then jack up the front of the car and support on axle stands (see "*Jacking and vehicle support*"). Remove both front wheels.
2 Disconnect the battery negative lead.
3 Remove the air cleaner and ducting, as described in Chapter 4.
4 Loosen the power steering pump mounting and adjustment bolts, as applicable. Move the

pump upwards and slip the drivebelt from the pulleys.

5 Unscrew the mounting bolts and remove the pump from the bracket on the transmission. Tie or support the pump in an upright position towards the front of the engine compartment.

6 Drain the power steering system, as described in Section 2, by disconnecting the high pressure pipe.

7 Disconnect the low pressure return hose from the steering gear valve.

8 Detach the gearchange assembly from the steering gear by removing the cap and bolt and prising out the clip. Tie the assembly to one side.

9 Mark the steering column in relation to the flexible coupling, then unscrew and remove the pinchbolt. Push the column upwards as far as possible.

10 Unscrew the nuts and disconnect the track rod ends from the steering arms.

11 Unscrew and remove the mounting bolts from the subframe.

12 Unclip the fuel supply and return pipes from the underbody.

13 Rotate the steering gear, until the control valve points rearward, then turn the flexible coupling to full left hand lock. Move the steering gear to the right and release the left hand track rod from the subframe. Lower the steering gear from the car.

Refitting

14 Refitting is a reversal of removal, but tighten the nuts and bolts to the specified torque. Refill the power steering system, as described in Section 2. Adjust the drivebelt tension, referring to Chapter 1 if necessary. Check, and if necessary, adjust the front wheel alignment as described in the relevant main manual.

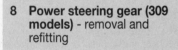

8 Power steering gear (309 models) - removal and refitting

Removal

1 Apply the handbrake then jack up the front of the car and support on axle stands (see "*Jacking and vehicle support*"). Remove both front wheels.

2 Drain the power steering system, as described in Section 2.

3 Unscrew the union nuts and disconnect the high and low pressure pipes from the steering gear valve **(see illustration)**.

4 Mark the steering column universal joint in relation to the pinion, then unscrew and remove the pinchbolt.

5 Unscrew the nuts and disconnect the track rod ends from the steering arms.

6 Release the strap and pull the left hand rubber bellows from the steering gear housing.

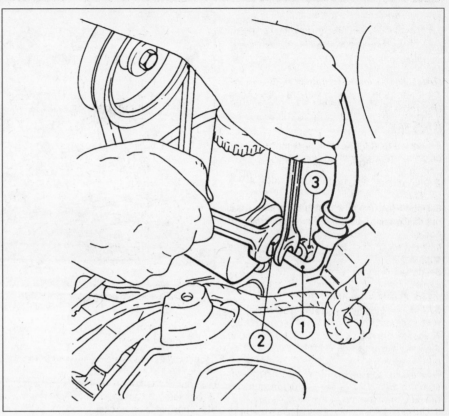

8.3 Power steering pump unions on 309 models

1 High pressure pipe   *2 High pressure pipe union*   *3 Low pressure pipe union*

7 Unscrew the left hand track rod from the rack **(see illustration)**.

8 Disconnect the gearchange control rods from the relay levers, prise out the clip and tie the assembly to one side.

9 Unscrew and remove the mounting bolts from the subframe, noting the location of the spacer tubes **(see illustration)**.

10 Release the steering gear from the column universal joint and rest it on the subframe.

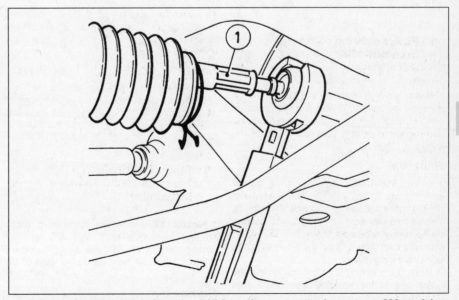

8.7 Removing the left-hand track rod (1) from the power steering gear on 309 models

11 Turn the rack fully to the left.

12 Move the steering gear to the far right, then lift the left end over the transmission and withdraw.

Refitting

13 Refitting is a reversal of removal, but tighten the nuts and bolts to the specified torque. Refill the power steering system, as described in Section 2. Adjust the drivebelt tension, referring to Chapter 1 if necessary. Check, and if necessary, adjust the front wheel alignment as described in the relevant main manual. Ensure that the low pressure hose is positioned clear of the gearchange rods.

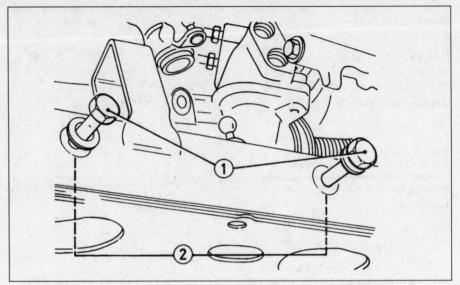

8.9 Power steering gear mounting bolts (1) and spacer tubes (2) on 309 models

Dimensions and weights

Note: *All figures and dimensions are approximate and may vary according to model. Refer to manufacturer's data for exact figures.*

Dimensions

Overall length:
205 models	3.705 m
305 models	4.262 m
309 models	4.051 m
405 models:	
Saloon	4.408 m
Estate	4.398 m
Horizon models	3.960 m

Overall width:
205 models:	
Except GRD	1.562 m
GRD	1.572 m
305 models	1.636 m
309 models	1.628 m
405 models:	
Saloon	1.714 m
Estate	1.707 m
Horizon models	1.679 m

Overall height:
205 models:	
Except Van	1.373 m
Van	1.376 m
305 models	1.410 m
309 models	1.380 m
405 models:	
Saloon	1.406 m
Estate	1.445 m
Horizon models	1.410 m

Weights

Kerb weights:
205 models:	
Except GRD	870 kg
GRD	895 kg
305 models:	
Except GRD	985 kg
GRD	1010 kg
309 models	950 kg
405 models:	
Saloon	1100 to 1260 kg
Estate	1090 to 1350 kg
Horizon models	1021 kg

Maximum trailer weight:
205 models:	
Except Van	700 kg
Van	900 kg
305 models	1051 kg
309 models	1000 kg
405 models	1200 kg
Horizon models	800 kg
Maximum roof rack load	75 kg

Conversion factors

Length (distance)

Inches (in)	x 25.4	= Millimetres (mm)	x 0.0394	= Inches (in)
Feet (ft)	x 0.305	= Metres (m)	x 3.281	= Feet (ft)
Miles	x 1.609	= Kilometres (km)	x 0.621	= Miles

Volume (capacity)

Cubic inches (cu in; in³)	x 16.387	= Cubic centimetres (cc; cm³)	x 0.061	= Cubic inches (cu in; in³)
Imperial pints (Imp pt)	x 0.568	= Litres (l)	x 1.76	= Imperial pints (Imp pt)
Imperial quarts (Imp qt)	x 1.137	= Litres (l)	x 0.88	= Imperial quarts (Imp qt)
Imperial quarts (Imp qt)	x 1.201	= US quarts (US qt)	x 0.833	= Imperial quarts (Imp qt)
US quarts (US qt)	x 0.946	= Litres (l)	x 1.057	= US quarts (US qt)
Imperial gallons (Imp gal)	x 4.546	= Litres (l)	x 0.22	= Imperial gallons (Imp gal)
Imperial gallons (Imp gal)	x 1.201	= US gallons (US gal)	x 0.833	= Imperial gallons (Imp gal)
US gallons (US gal)	x 3.785	= Litres (l)	x 0.264	= US gallons (US gal)

Mass (weight)

Ounces (oz)	x 28.35	= Grams (g)	x 0.035	= Ounces (oz)
Pounds (lb)	x 0.454	= Kilograms (kg)	x 2.205	= Pounds (lb)

Force

Ounces-force (ozf; oz)	x 0.278	= Newtons (N)	x 3.6	= Ounces-force (ozf; oz)
Pounds-force (lbf; lb)	x 4.448	= Newtons (N)	x 0.225	= Pounds-force (lbf; lb)
Newtons (N)	x 0.1	= Kilograms-force (kgf; kg)	x 9.81	= Newtons (N)

Pressure

Pounds-force per square inch (psi; lbf/in²; lb/in²)	x 0.070	= Kilograms-force per square centimetre (kgf/cm²; kg/cm²)	x 14.223	= Pounds-force per square inch (psi; lbf/in²; lb/in²)
Pounds-force per square inch (psi; lbf/in²; lb/in²)	x 0.068	= Atmospheres (atm)	x 14.696	= Pounds-force per square inch (psi; lbf/in²; lb/in²)
Pounds-force per square inch (psi; lbf/in²; lb/in²)	x 0.069	= Bars	x 14.5	= Pounds-force per square inch (psi; lbf/in²; lb/in²)
Pounds-force per square inch (psi; lbf/in²; lb/in²)	x 6.895	= Kilopascals (kPa)	x 0.145	= Pounds-force per square inch (psi; lbf/in²; lb/in²)
Kilopascals (kPa)	x 0.01	= Kilograms-force per square centimetre (kgf/cm²; kg/cm²)	x 98.1	= Kilopascals (kPa)
Millibar (mbar)	x 100	= Pascals (Pa)	x 0.01	= Millibar (mbar)
Millibar (mbar)	x 0.0145	= Pounds-force per square inch (psi; lbf/in²; lb/in²)	x 68.947	= Millibar (mbar)
Millibar (mbar)	x 0.75	= Millimetres of mercury (mmHg)	x 1.333	= Millibar (mbar)
Millibar (mbar)	x 0.401	= Inches of water (inH$_2$O)	x 2.491	= Millibar (mbar)
Millimetres of mercury (mmHg)	x 0.535	= Inches of water (inH$_2$O)	x 1.868	= Millimetres of mercury (mmHg)
Inches of water (inH$_2$O)	x 0.036	= Pounds-force per square inch (psi; lbf/in²; lb/in²)	x 27.68	= Inches of water (inH$_2$O)

Torque (moment of force)

Pounds-force inches (lbf in; lb in)	x 1.152	= Kilograms-force centimetre (kgf cm; kg cm)	x 0.868	= Pounds-force inches (lbf in; lb in)
Pounds-force inches (lbf in; lb in)	x 0.113	= Newton metres (Nm)	x 8.85	= Pounds-force inches (lbf in; lb in)
Pounds-force inches (lbf in; lb in)	x 0.083	= Pounds-force feet (lbf ft; lb ft)	x 12	= Pounds-force inches (lbf in; lb in)
Pounds-force feet (lbf ft; lb ft)	x 0.138	= Kilograms-force metres (kgf m; kg m)	x 7.233	= Pounds-force feet (lbf ft; lb ft)
Pounds-force feet (lbf ft; lb ft)	x 1.356	= Newton metres (Nm)	x 0.738	= Pounds-force feet (lbf ft; lb ft)
Newton metres (Nm)	x 0.102	= Kilograms-force metres (kgf m; kg m)	x 9.804	= Newton metres (Nm)

Power

Horsepower (hp)	x 745.7	= Watts (W)	x 0.0013	= Horsepower (hp)

Velocity (speed)

Miles per hour (miles/hr; mph)	x 1.609	= Kilometres per hour (km/hr; kph)	x 0.621	= Miles per hour (miles/hr; mph)

Fuel consumption*

Miles per gallon (mpg)	x 0.354	= Kilometres per litre (km/l)	x 2.825	= Miles per gallon (mpg)

Temperature

Degrees Fahrenheit = (°C x 1.8) + 32   Degrees Celsius (Degrees Centigrade; °C) = (°F - 32) x 0.56

It is common practice to convert from miles per gallon (mpg) to litres/100 kilometres (l/100km), where mpg x l/100 km = 282

Spare parts are available from many sources, including maker's appointed garages, accessory shops and motor factors. To be sure of obtaining the correct parts, it will sometimes be necessary to quote the vehicle identification number. If possible, it can also be useful to take the old along for positive identification. Items such as starter motors and alternators may be available through a service exchange scheme - any parts returned should always be clean.

Our advice regarding spare part sources is as follows.

Officially appointed dealers

This is the best source of parts that are peculiar to your car, that are otherwise not generally available. It is also the only place at which you should buy parts if your vehicle is still under warranty.

Accessory shops

These are often very good places to buy materials and components needed for the maintenance of your car (e.g. oil filters, spark plugs, drivebelts, oils and greases, etc.). They also sell general accessories, usually have convenient opening hours, charge lower prices and can often be found not far from home.

Motor factors

Good factors will stock all the more important components that wear out relatively quickly (e.g. clutch components, pistons, valves, exhaust systems, brake cylinders/pipes/hoses/seals/shoes and pads, etc.). Motor factors will often provide new or reconditioned components on a part exchange basis - this can save considerable amount of money.

Vehicle identification

Modifications are a continuing and unpublished process in vehicle manufacture, quite apart from major model changes. Spare parts manuals and lists are compiled upon a numerical basis, the individual vehicle numbers being essential to correct identification of the component required.

When ordering spare parts, always give as much information as possible. Quote the car model, year of manufacture and vehicle identification and/or engine numbers as appropriate (see illustrations).

The vehicle identification plate is either, riveted to the top of the front cross panel, or on the engine bulkhead and contains the following information:

a) Manufacturers name
b) EC or National acceptance number (certain countries only)
c) Vehicle identification number (VIN) - contains 17 characters
d) Gross vehicle weight
e) Kerb weight
f) Maximum front axle weight
g) Maximum rear axle weight
h) Left blank
i) Additional information (i.e. version, type, etc..)

The VIN is also stamped into the engine bulkhead cross panel, or on the right hand wing valance in the engine compartment.

The engine number and code can be found stamped on to a plate, which is riveted to the centre of the block.

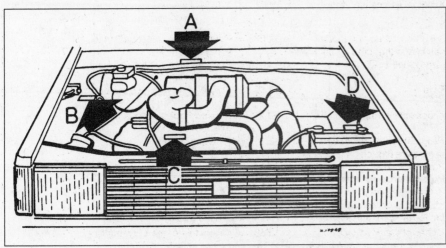

Vehicle identification plate location (Horizon models)

A Identification plate
B Serial number
C Engine number
D Paint colour

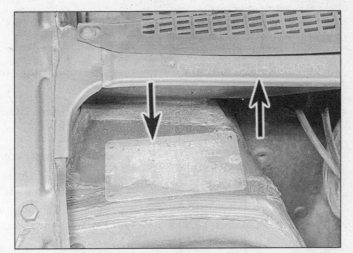

Vehicle identification plate on inner wing and body serial number stamped on scuttle panel, (205 models)

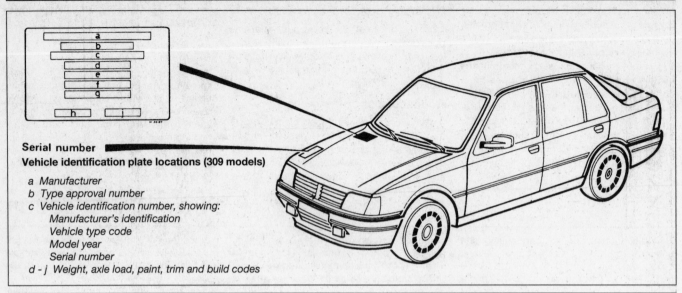

Serial number

Vehicle identification plate locations (309 models)

a Manufacturer
b Type approval number
c Vehicle identification number, showing:
　　Manufacturer's identification
　　Vehicle type code
　　Model year
　　Serial number
d - j Weight, axle load, paint, trim and build codes

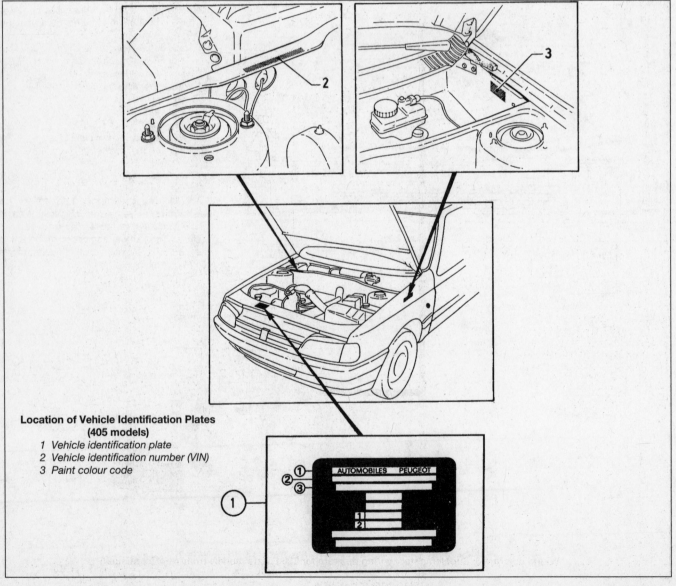

**Location of Vehicle Identification Plates
(405 models)**

1 Vehicle identification plate
2 Vehicle identification number (VIN)
3 Paint colour code

Whenever servicing, repair or overhaul work is carried out on the car or its components, observe the following procedures and instructions. This will assist in carrying out the operation efficiently and to a professional standard of workmanship.

Joint mating faces and gaskets

When separating components at their mating faces, never insert screwdrivers or similar implements into the joint between the faces in order to prise them apart. This can cause severe damage which results in oil leaks, coolant leaks, etc upon reassembly. Separation is usually achieved by tapping along the joint with a soft-faced hammer in order to break the seal. However, note that this method may not be suitable where dowels are used for component location.

Where a gasket is used between the mating faces of two components, a new one must be fitted on reassembly; fit it dry unless otherwise stated in the repair procedure. Make sure that the mating faces are clean and dry, with all traces of old gasket removed. When cleaning a joint face, use a tool which is unlikely to score or damage the face, and remove any burrs or nicks with an oilstone or fine file.

Make sure that tapped holes are cleaned with a pipe cleaner, and keep them free of jointing compound, if this is being used, unless specifically instructed otherwise.

Ensure that all orifices, channels or pipes are clear, and blow through them, preferably using compressed air.

Oil seals

Oil seals can be removed by levering them out with a wide flat-bladed screwdriver or similar implement. Alternatively, a number of self-tapping screws may be screwed into the seal, and these used as a purchase for pliers or some similar device in order to pull the seal free.

Whenever an oil seal is removed from its working location, either individually or as part of an assembly, it should be renewed.

The very fine sealing lip of the seal is easily damaged, and will not seal if the surface it contacts is not completely clean and free from scratches, nicks or grooves. If the original sealing surface of the component cannot be restored, and the manufacturer has not made provision for slight relocation of the seal relative to the sealing surface, the component should be renewed.

Protect the lips of the seal from any surface which may damage them in the course of fitting. Use tape or a conical sleeve where possible. Lubricate the seal lips with oil before fitting and, on dual-lipped seals, fill the space between the lips with grease.

Unless otherwise stated, oil seals must be fitted with their sealing lips toward the lubricant to be sealed.

Use a tubular drift or block of wood of the appropriate size to install the seal and, if the seal housing is shouldered, drive the seal down to the shoulder. If the seal housing is unshouldered, the seal should be fitted with its face flush with the housing top face (unless otherwise instructed).

Screw threads and fastenings

Seized nuts, bolts and screws are quite a common occurrence where corrosion has set in, and the use of penetrating oil or releasing fluid will often overcome this problem if the offending item is soaked for a while before attempting to release it. The use of an impact driver may also provide a means of releasing such stubborn fastening devices, when used in conjunction with the appropriate screwdriver bit or socket. If none of these methods works, it may be necessary to resort to the careful application of heat, or the use of a hacksaw or nut splitter device.

Studs are usually removed by locking two nuts together on the threaded part, and then using a spanner on the lower nut to unscrew the stud. Studs or bolts which have broken off below the surface of the component in which they are mounted can sometimes be removed using a stud extractor. Always ensure that a blind tapped hole is completely free from oil, grease, water or other fluid before installing the bolt or stud. Failure to do this could cause the housing to crack due to the hydraulic action of the bolt or stud as it is screwed in.

When tightening a castellated nut to accept a split pin, tighten the nut to the specified torque, where applicable, and then tighten further to the next split pin hole. Never slacken the nut to align the split pin hole, unless stated in the repair procedure.

When checking or retightening a nut or bolt to a specified torque setting, slacken the nut or bolt by a quarter of a turn, and then retighten to the specified setting. However, this should not be attempted where angular tightening has been used.

For some screw fastenings, notably cylinder head bolts or nuts, torque wrench settings are no longer specified for the latter stages of tightening, "angle-tightening" being called up instead. Typically, a fairly low torque wrench setting will be applied to the bolts/nuts in the correct sequence, followed by one or more stages of tightening through specified angles.

Locknuts, locktabs and washers

Any fastening which will rotate against a component or housing during tightening should always have a washer between it and the relevant component or housing.

Spring or split washers should always be renewed when they are used to lock a critical component such as a big-end bearing retaining bolt or nut. Locktabs which are folded over to retain a nut or bolt should always be renewed.

Self-locking nuts can be re-used in non-critical areas, providing resistance can be felt when the locking portion passes over the bolt or stud thread. However, it should be noted that self-locking stiffnuts tend to lose their effectiveness after long periods of use, and should then be renewed as a matter of course.

Split pins must always be replaced with new ones of the correct size for the hole.

When thread-locking compound is found on the threads of a fastener which is to be re-used, it should be cleaned off with a wire brush and solvent, and fresh compound applied on reassembly.

Special tools

Some repair procedures in this manual entail the use of special tools such as a press, two or three-legged pullers, spring compressors, etc. Wherever possible, suitable readily-available alternatives to the manufacturer's special tools are described, and are shown in use. In some instances, where no alternative is possible, it has been necessary to resort to the use of a manufacturer's tool, and this has been done for reasons of safety as well as the efficient completion of the repair operation. Unless you are highly-skilled and have a thorough understanding of the procedures described, never attempt to bypass the use of any special tool when the procedure described specifies its use. Not only is there a very great risk of personal injury, but expensive damage could be caused to the components involved.

Environmental considerations

When disposing of used engine oil, brake fluid, antifreeze, etc, give due consideration to any detrimental environmental effects. Do not, for instance, pour any of the above liquids down drains into the general sewage system, or onto the ground to soak away. Many local council refuse tips provide a facility for waste oil disposal, as do some garages. If none of these facilities are available, consult your local Environmental Health Department, or the National Rivers Authority, for further advice.

With the universal tightening-up of legislation regarding the emission of environmentally-harmful substances from motor vehicles, most vehicles have tamperproof devices fitted to the main adjustment points of the fuel system. These devices are primarily designed to prevent unqualified persons from adjusting the fuel/air mixture, with the chance of a consequent increase in toxic emissions. If such devices are found during servicing or overhaul, they should, wherever possible, be renewed or refitted in accordance with the manufacturer's requirements or current legislation.

OIL CARE
FOLLOW THE CODE
OIL BANK LINE
0800 66 33 66

Note: It is antisocial and illegal to dump oil down the drain. To find the location of your local oil recycling bank, call this number free.

Jacking and vehicle support

The jack supplied with the vehicle tool kit should only be used for changing roadwheels **(see illustration)**. The jack and wheel brace are located either in the engine compartment or in the luggage compartment, depending on the model. When carrying out any other kind of work, raise the vehicle using a hydraulic jack, and always supplement the jack with axle stands positioned under the vehicle jacking points.

When jacking up the vehicle with a trolley jack, position the jack head under one of the relevant jacking points. **Do not** jack the vehicle under the sump or any of the steering or suspension components. Supplement the jack using axle stands. The jacking points are shown in the accompanying illustrations.

Never *work under, around, or near a raised vehicle, unless it is adequately supported in at least two places.*

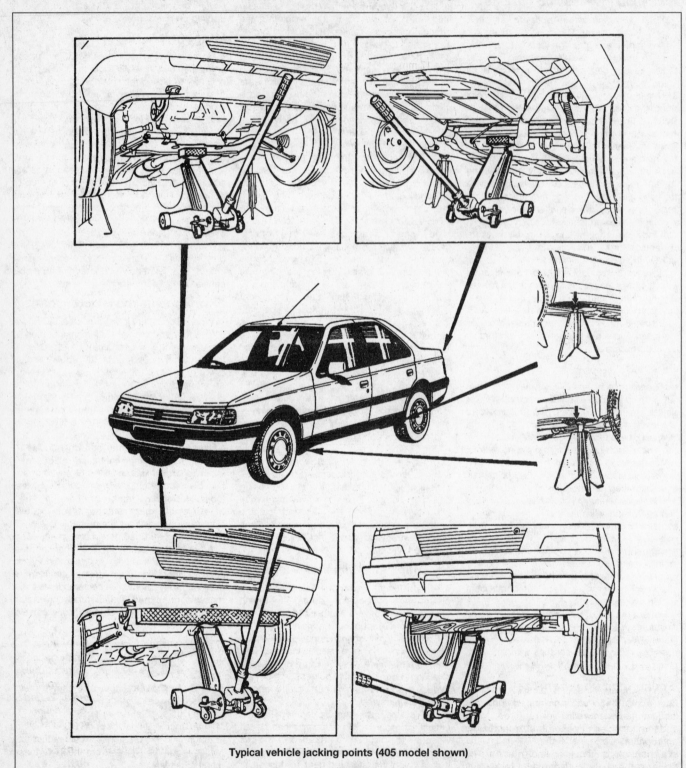

Typical vehicle jacking points (405 model shown)

Contents

1 Normal workshop tools

1 The decision as to what range of tools is necessary will depend on the work to be done, the range of vehicles which it is expected to encounter, and not least the financial resources available. The tools in the following list, with additions as necessary from the various categories of diesel-specific tools described later, should be sufficient for carrying out most routine maintenance and repair operations.

Combination spanners (see below)
Socket spanners (see below)
Ratchet, extension piece and universal joint (for use with sockets)
Torque wrench
Angle tightening indicator (see below)
Adjustable spanner
Set of sump drain plug keys
Strap or chain wrench (for fuel and oil filters)
Oil drain tray
Feeler blades
Combination pliers
Long-nosed pliers
Self-locking pliers (Mole wrench)
Screwdrivers (large and small, flat blade and cross blade)
Set of Allen keys
Set of splined and Torx keys and sockets (see below)
Ball pein hammer
Soft-faced hammer
Puller (universal type, with interchangeable jaws)
Cold chisel
Scriber
Scraper
Centre punch
Hacksaw
File
Steel rule/straight-edge
Axle stands and/or ramps
Trolley jack
Inspection light
Inspection mirror
Telescopic magnet/pick-up tool

Socket and spanner size

2 A good range of open-ended, ring and socket spanners will be required. Most modern vehicles use metric size fastenings throughout.

3 Split ring spanners (also known as flare nut spanners) are particularly useful for dealing with fuel pipe unions, on which a conventional ring or socket cannot be used because the pipe is in the way. The most common sizes are 17 mm and 19 mm on metric systems.

4 Sockets are available in various drive sizes. The half inch square drive size is most widely used and accepts most torque wrenches. Smaller drive sizes (⅜ or ¼ in) are useful for working in confined spaces, while for large high-torque fastenings (driveshaft or hub nuts, crankshaft pulley bolts) ¾ inch drive is most satisfactory.

5 The humble box spanner should not be overlooked. Box spanners are cheap and will sometimes serve as a substitute for a deep socket, though they cannot be used with a torque wrench and are easily deformed.

Angle tightening

6 For fastenings such as cylinder head bolts, many manufacturers now specify tightening in terms of angular rotation rather than an absolute torque. After an initial 'snug' torque wrench setting, subsequent tightening stages are specified as angles through which each bolt must be turned. Variations in tightening torque which could be caused by the presence or absence of dirt, oil etc. on the bolt threads thus have no effect. A further benefit is that there is no need for a high-range torque wrench.

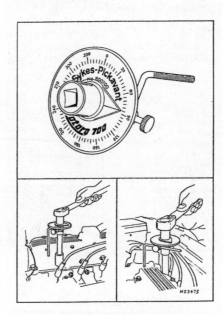

1.7 Sykes-Pickavant 800700 angle tightening gear

7 The owner-mechanic who expects to use this method of tightening only once or twice in the life of the vehicle may be content to make up a cardboard template, or mark the bolt heads with paint spots, to indicate the angle required. Greater speed and accuracy will result from using one of the many angle tightening indicators commercially available. Most of them are intended for use with ½ in drive sockets or keys (see illustration).

Splined bolt heads

8 The conventional hexagon head bolt is being replaced in many areas by the splined or 'Torx' head bolt. This type of bolt has multiple splines in place of the hexagon. A set of splined or Torx keys will be needed to deal with female splined heads. Torx bolts with male heads also exist, and for these Torx sockets will be needed. Both keys and sockets are available to accept ½ in square drives.

2 Diesel-specific tools

Basic tune-up and service

1 Besides the normal range of spanners, screwdrivers and so on, the following tools and equipment will be needed for basic tune-up and service operations :

Deep socket for removing and tightening screw-in injectors
Optical or pulse-sensitive tachometer
Electrical multi-meter, or dedicated glow plug tester
Compression or leakdown tester
Vacuum pump and/or gauge

Injector socket

2 The size most commonly required is 27mm. The socket needs to be deep in order not to foul the injector body. On some engines it also needs to be thin-walled. Suitable sockets are sold by Dieseltune, Sykes-Pickavant and Snap-On, among others.

Tachometer

3 The type of tachometer which senses ignition system HT pulses via an inductive pick-up cannot be used on diesel engines, unless a device such as the Sykes-Pickavant timing light adapter is available.

4 If an engine is fitted with a TDC sensor and a diagnostic socket, an electronic tachometer which reads the signals from the TDC sensor can be used.

5 Not all engines have TDC sensors. On those which do not, the use of an optical or pulse-sensitive tachometer is necessary **(see illustration)**.

6 The optical tachometer registers the passage of a paint mark or (more usually) a strip of reflective foil placed on the crankshaft pulley. It is not so convenient to use as the electronic or pulse-sensitive types, since it has to be held so that it can 'see' the pulley, but it has the advantage that it can be used on any engine, petrol or diesel, with or without a diagnostic socket.

7 The pulse-sensitive tachometer uses a transducer similar to that needed for a timing light. The transducer converts hydraulic or mechanical impulses in an injector pipe into electrical signals, which are displayed on the tachometer as engine speed.

8 Some dynamic timing equipment for diesel engines incorporates a means of displaying engine speed. If this equipment is available, a separate tachometer will not be required.

9 Both optical and pulse-sensitive tachometers are sold by A. M. Test Systems and Kent-Moore. Optical tachometers are sold by (inter alia) Dieseltune, and pulse-sensitive by Souriau and Bosch.

DIY alternative tachometer

10 The owner-mechanic who only wishes to check the idle speed of one engine occasionally may well feel that the purchase of a special tachometer is not justified. Assuming that mains electric light is available, the use of a stroboscopic disc is a cheap alternative. The principle will be familiar to anyone who has used such a disc to check the speed of a record-player turntable.

11 A disc must be constructed of stiff paper or card to fit onto the crankshaft pulley (or camshaft pulley, if appropriate - but remember that this rotates at half speed). The disc should be white or light-coloured, and divided using a protractor into regular segments with heavy black lines **(see Tool Tip)**. The number of segments required will depend on the desired idle speed and the frequency of the alternating current supply. For the 50 Hz supply used in the UK and most of Europe the figures are as follows:

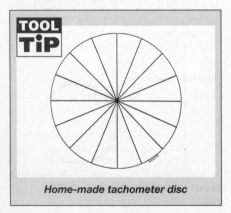

TOOL TiP

Home-made tachometer disc

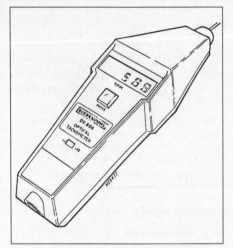

2.5 Dieseltune DX 800 optical tachometer

Speed (rpm)	No of segments	Angle per segment
706	17	21° 11'
750	16	22° 30'
800	15	24°
857	14	25° 43'
923	13	27° 42'

12 Attach the disc to the crankshaft pulley and position the car so that the disc can be viewed using only artificial light. A fluorescent tube is best. Failing this a low-wattage incandescent bulb will give better results than a high-wattage one. Run the engine at idle and observe the disc.

 Warning : Do not run the engine in a confined space without some means of extracting the exhaust fumes.

13 If the engine speed corresponds to the calculated disc speed, the disc segments will appear to be stationary. If the speed is different, the segments will appear to drift in the direction of engine rotation (too fast) or against it (too slow). The segments will also

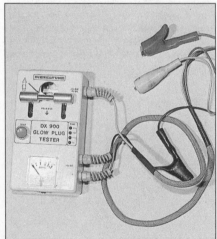

2.14 Dieseltune DX 900 glow plug tester

appear to be stationary at multiples or sub-multiples of the calculated speed - twice or half the speed, and so on - so some common sense must be used.

Electrical multi-meter or glow plug tester

14 It is possible to test glow plugs and their control circuitry with a multi-meter, or even (to a limited extent) with a 12 volt test lamp. A purpose-made glow plug tester will do the job faster and is much easier to use, but on the other hand it will not do anything else **(see illustration)**.

15 If it is decided to purchase a multi-meter, make sure that it has a high current range - ideally 0 to 100 amps - for checking glow plug current draw. Some meters require an external shunt to be fitted for this. An inductive clamp connection is preferred for high current measurement since it can be used without breaking into the circuit. Other ranges required are dc voltage (0 to 20 or 30 volts is suitable for most applications) and resistance. Some meters have a continuity buzzer in addition to a resistance scale ; the buzzer is particularly useful when working single-handed **(see illustration)**.

16 Glow plug testers are available from makers such as Beru, Dieseltune and Kent-Moore. Some incorporate a 'hot test chamber' in which the heating of individual plugs can be observed.

Compression tester

17 A tester specifically intended for diesel engines must be used **(see illustration)**. The push-in connectors used with some petrol engine compression testers cannot be used for diesel engines because of the higher pressures involved. Instead, the diesel engine compression tester screws into an injector or glow plug hole, using one of the adapters supplied with the tester.

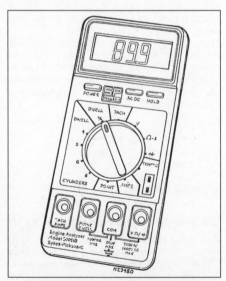

2.15 Sykes-Pickavant 300510 engine analyser/multi-meter

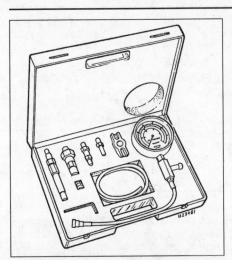

2.17 Dieseltune DX 511 compression tester

18 Most compression testers are used while cranking the engine on the starter motor. A few, such as the Dieseltune DX 511, can be used with the engine idling. This gives more reliable results, since it is hard to guarantee that cranking speed will not fall in the course of testing all four cylinders, whereas idle speed will remain constant.

19 Recording testers, which produce a pen-and-ink trace for each cylinder, are available from A. M. Test Systems and Kent-Moore. Non-recording testers are more common and are available from Dieseltune and Sykes-Pickavant as well as the makers previously mentioned.

Leak-down tester

20 The leak-down tester measures the rate at which air pressure is lost from each cylinder, and can also be used to pinpoint the source of pressure loss (valves, head gasket or bores). It depends on the availability of a supply of compressed air, typically at 5 to 10 bar (73 to 145 lbf/in²). The same tester (with different adapters) can be used on both petrol and diesel engines **(see illustration)**.

21 In use, the tester is connected to an air line and to an adapter screwed into the injector or glow plug hole, with the piston concerned at TDC on the compression stroke. Leak-down testers are offered by Dieseltune, Sykes-Pickavant and others.

2.20 Sykes-Pickavant 013800 leak-down tester

Vacuum pump and/or gauge

22 A vacuum gauge, with suitable adapters, is useful for locating blockages or air leaks in the supply side of the fuel system. A simple gauge is used with the engine running to create vacuum in the supply lines. A hand-held vacuum pump with its own gauge can be used without running the engine, and is also useful for bleeding the fuel system when a hand priming pump is not fitted **(see illustration)**.

3 Injection pump timing tools

1 If work is undertaken which disturbs the position of the fuel injection pump, certain tools will be needed to check the injection timing on reassembly. This also applies if the pump drive is disturbed - including renewal of the timing belt on some models. Checking of the timing is also a necessary part of fault diagnosis when investigating complaints such as power loss, knock and smoke.

Static timing tools

2 Static timing is still the most widely-used method of setting diesel injection pumps. It is time-consuming and sometimes messy. Precision measuring instruments are often needed for dealing with distributor pumps. Good results depend on the skill and patience of the operator.

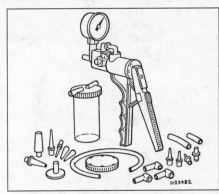

2.22 Dieseltune DX 760 'Mityvac' test kit

3 The owner-mechanic who will only be dealing with one engine should refer to the appropriate text to find out what tools will be required. The diesel tune-up specialist will typically need the following :

Dial test indicator (DTI) with magnetic stand
DTI adapters and probes for Bosch or CAV distributor pumps
Timing gear pins or pegs (when applicable)
Crankshaft or flywheel locking pins (when applicable)

Dial test indicator and magnetic stand

4 This is a useful workshop tool for many operations besides timing. It is the most accurate means of checking the protrusion or recession of swirl chambers, pistons and liners when renewing cylinder head gaskets. If major overhauls are undertaken it can also be used for measuring values such as crankshaft endfloat **(see illustration)**.

5 Two DTIs may be needed for setting the timing on some engines - one to measure the pump plunger or rotor movement and one to measure engine piston position.

DTI adapters

6 Adapters and probes for fitting the DTI to the distributor pump are of various patterns, due partly to the need to be able to use them in conditions of poor access on the vehicle **(see illustrations)**. This means that the same adapter cannot necessarily be used on the same type of pump and engine if the under-bonnet layout is different. On the bench it is often possible to use simpler equipment.

3.4 Dial test indicator and stand being used to check swirl chamber protrusion

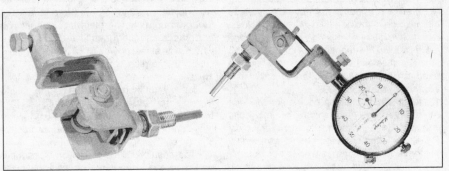

3.6a DTI and locally-made bellcrank adapter for timing a Bosch VE pump

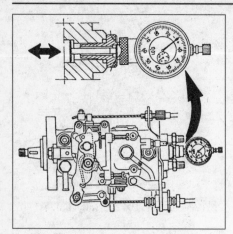

3.6b DTI and in-line adapter used for timing a Bosch VE pump

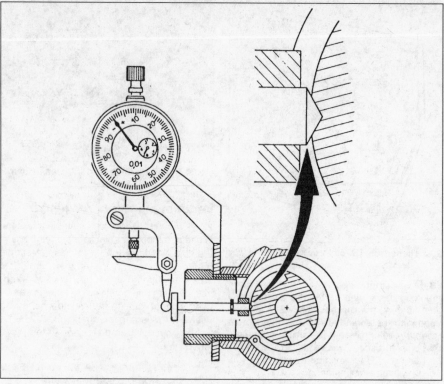

3.7 DTI and adapter used for timing Lucas/CAV pump

7 A spring-loaded probe is used on some CAV/RotoDiesel pumps to find the timing groove in the pump rotor **(see illustration)**.

Timing gear pins or pegs

8 Pins or pegs are used on some engines to lock the pump and/or the camshaft in a particular position. They are generally specific to a particular engine or manufacturer. It is sometimes possible to use suitably sized dowel rods, drill shanks or bolts instead.

Crankshaft or flywheel locking pins

9 These are used for locking the crankshaft at TDC (or at the injection point on some models).

10 The crankshaft locking pin is inserted through a hole in the side of the crankcase after removal of a plug, and enters a slot in a crankshaft counterweight or web. The flywheel pin passes through a hole in the flywheel end of the crankcase and enters a hole in the flywheel. Again, suitably sized rods or bolts can sometimes be used instead.

Dynamic timing tools

11 Dynamic timing on diesel engines has not yet become widespread, due no doubt in part to the relatively expensive equipment required. Additionally, not all vehicle manufacturers provide dynamic timing values. In principle it makes possible much faster and more accurate checking of the injection timing, just as on petrol engines. It can also be used to verify the operation of cold start advance systems.

12 Most dynamic timing equipment depends on converting mechanical or hydraulic impulses in the injection system into electrical signals. An alternative approach is adopted by one or two manufacturers who use an optical-to-electrical conversion, with a sensor which screws into a glow plug hole and 'sees' the light of combustion. The electrical signals are

used to trigger a timing light, or as part of the information fed into a diagnostic analyser.

13 Not all diesel engines have ready-made timing marks. If the engine has a TDC sensor (or provision for fitting one) and the timing equipment can read the sensor output, this is not a problem. Some engines have neither timing marks nor TDC sensors. In such cases there is no choice but to establish TDC accurately and make marks on the flywheel or crankshaft pulley.

Timing lights

14 The simplest dynamic timing equipment uses a transducer to convert the pressure pulse in the injector pipe into an electrical signal which triggers a timing light. Such transducers are of two types - in-line and clamp-on **(see illustration)**.

15 The in-line transducer is connected into No 1 injector pipe using adapters to suit the fuel pipe unions. The electrical connection from the transducer goes to the timing light, which will also require a 12 volt or mains supply to energise its tube.

16 The clamp-on transducer is used in a similar way but instead of actually tapping into the injector pipe it clamps onto it. The transducer must be of the right size for the pipe concerned and any dirt, rust or protective coating on the pipe must be removed.

17 The position of the clamp-on transducer on the pipe is important. The injection pulse takes a finite amount of time to travel from one end of the pipe to the other. If the

transducer is in the wrong place, a false result will be obtained. Place the transducer as directed by the equipment or engine manufacturer.

18 The timing light itself may be an existing inductive type light normally used on petrol engines, if the transducer output is suitable. Other types of transducer can only be used with their own timing light.

Diagnostic analysers

19 Diagnostic engine analysers (Crypton, AVL, Souriau etc.) will display timing and speed information with the aid of diesel adapters or interface units. These will normally be specific to the equipment concerned; consult the manufacturers for details.

20 The output from the Sykes-Pickavant diesel adapter can be used to drive the inductive HT pick-up on a diagnostic anaiyser.

3.14 Clamping a timing light transducer onto an injector pipe

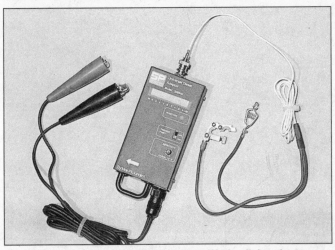

3.22a Sykes-Pickavant 300540 diesel timing light adapter

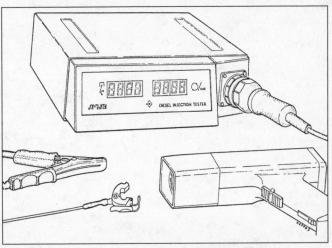

3.22b AVL Diesel Injection Tester 873

Injection testers

21 Injection testers are halfway between simple timing light/tachometer combinations and full-blown diagnostic analysers. They interpret the transducer output to provide a 'start-of-injection' signal, enabling comparison to be made between all the injectors on an engine, so that defective injectors can be identified.

22 The diesel adapter sold by Sykes-Pickavant for use with a conventional inductive timing light has an injection testing facility **(see illustration)**. More sophisticated equipment, such as the AVL Diesel Injection Tester 873 **(see illustration)**, accepts an input from the engine's TDC sensor (if fitted) as well, giving a digital read-out of injection timing without the need for a stroboscope.

4 Injector testing equipment

⚠ *Warning : Never expose the hands, face or any other part of the body to injector spray. The high working pressure can penetrate the skin, with potentially fatal results. When possible use injector test oil rather than fuel for testing. Take precautions to avoid inhaling the vaporised fuel or injector test fluid. Remember that even diesel fuel is inflammable when vaporised.*

1 Some kind of injector tester will be needed if it is wished to identify defective injectors, or to test them after cleaning or prolonged storage. Various makes and models are available, but the essential components of all of them are a high pressure hand-operated pump and a pressure gauge.

2 For safety reasons, injector test or calibration fluid should be used for bench testing rather than diesel fuel or paraffin. Use the fluid specified by the maker of the test equipment if possible.

3 One of the simplest testers currently available is Dieseltune's DX 710 **(see illustrations)**. This has the advantage that (access permitting) it can be used to test opening pressure and back leakage without removing the injectors from the engine. Its small reservoir makes it of limited use for bench testing, but good results can be obtained with practice.

4 Another method of testing injectors on the engine is to connect a pressure gauge into the line between the injection pump and the

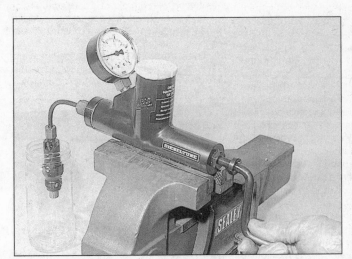

4.3a Dieseltune DX 710 tester in use on the bench. . .

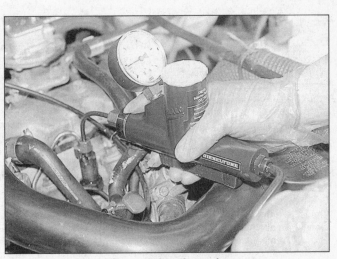

4.3b . . . and on the engine

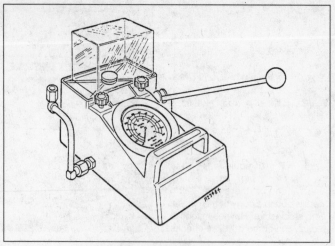

4.5 Dieseltune 111 injector tester

injector. This test can also detect faults caused by the injection pump high pressure piston or delivery valve.

5 The workshop which tests or calibrates injectors regularly will need a bench-mounted tester. These testers have a lever-operated pump, and a larger fluid reservoir than the hand-held tester. The best models also incorporate a transparent chamber for safe viewing of the injector spray pattern and perhaps a test fluid recirculation system **(see illustration)**.

6 Some means of extracting the vapour produced when testing, such as a hood connected to the workshop's fume extraction system, is desirable. Although injector test fluid is relatively non-toxic, its vapour is not particularly pleasant to inhale.

5 Injection pump testing and calibration equipment

The equipment needed for testing and calibration of injection pumps is beyond the scope of this book. Any such work should be entrusted to the pump manufacturer's agent - though the opportunity is taken to say yet again that the injection pump is often blamed for faults when in fact the trouble lies elsewhere.

6 Smoke testing equipment

1 Smoke emission testing is part of the MOT test for cars and light commercial vehicles.

2 Smoke testing equipment falls into two categories - indirect and direct reading. With the indirect systems, a sample of exhaust gas is passed over a filter paper and the change in opacity of the paper is measured using a separate machine. With the direct systems, an optically sensitive probe measures the opacity of the exhaust gas and an immediate read-out is available.

3 The smoke sampling kit from Bosch is an example of the indirect reading system and is used in conjunction with a photoelectric measuring unit. Dieseltune's Smokemeter is an example of the direct reading machine **(see illustrations)**.

4 As far as the DIY mechanic is concerned, the purchase of smoke testing equipment is unlikely to be an economic proposition. If accurate smoke testing is necessary, take the vehicle to an MOT testing station or a Diesel injection specialist.

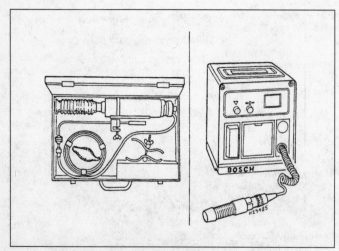

6.3a Bosch smoke sampling kit (left) and measuring unit

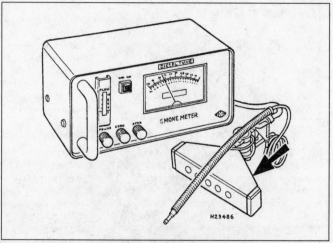

6.3b Dieseltune Smokemeter

This is a guide to getting your vehicle through the MOT test. Obviously it will not be possible to examine the vehicle to the same standard as the professional MOT tester. However, working through the following checks will enable you to identify any problem areas before submitting the vehicle for the test.

Where a testable component is in borderline condition, the tester has discretion in deciding whether to pass or fail it. The basis of such discretion is whether the tester would be happy for a close relative or friend to use the vehicle with the component in that condition. If the vehicle presented is clean and evidently well cared for, the tester may be more inclined to pass a borderline component than if the vehicle is scruffy and apparently neglected.

It has only been possible to summarise the test requirements here, based on the regulations in force at the time of printing. Test standards are becoming increasingly stringent, although there are some exemptions for older vehicles. For full details obtain a copy of the Haynes publication Pass the MOT! (available from stockists of Haynes manuals).

An assistant will be needed to help carry out some of these checks.

The checks have been sub-divided into four categories, as follows:

1 Checks carried out **FROM THE DRIVER'S SEAT**

2 Checks carried out **WITH THE VEHICLE ON THE GROUND**

3 Checks carried out **WITH THE VEHICLE RAISED AND THE WHEELS FREE TO TURN**

4 Checks carried out on **YOUR VEHICLE'S EXHAUST EMISSION SYSTEM**

---

1 Checks carried out **FROM THE DRIVER'S SEAT**

Handbrake

☐ Test the operation of the handbrake. Excessive travel (too many clicks) indicates incorrect brake or cable adjustment.

☐ Check that the handbrake cannot be released by tapping the lever sideways. Check the security of the lever mountings.

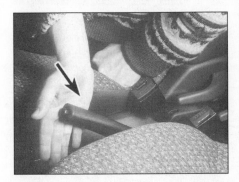

Footbrake

☐ Depress the brake pedal and check that it does not creep down to the floor, indicating a master cylinder fault. Release the pedal, wait a few seconds, then depress it again. If the pedal travels nearly to the floor before firm resistance is felt, brake adjustment or repair is necessary. If the pedal feels spongy, there is air in the hydraulic system which must be removed by bleeding.

☐ Check that the brake pedal is secure and in good condition. Check also for signs of fluid leaks on the pedal, floor or carpets, which would indicate failed seals in the brake master cylinder.

☐ Check the servo unit (when applicable) by operating the brake pedal several times, then keeping the pedal depressed and starting the engine. As the engine starts, the pedal will move down slightly. If not, the vacuum hose or the servo itself may be faulty.

Steering wheel and column

☐ Examine the steering wheel for fractures or looseness of the hub, spokes or rim.

☐ Move the steering wheel from side to side and then up and down. Check that the steering wheel is not loose on the column, indicating wear or a loose retaining nut. Continue moving the steering wheel as before, but also turn it slightly from left to right.

☐ Check that the steering wheel is not loose on the column, and that there is no abnormal

movement of the steering wheel, indicating wear in the column support bearings or couplings.

Windscreen and mirrors

☐ The windscreen must be free of cracks or other significant damage within the driver's field of view. (Small stone chips are acceptable.) Rear view mirrors must be secure, intact, and capable of being adjusted.

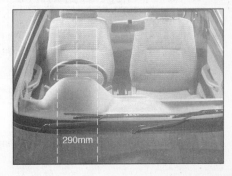

290mm

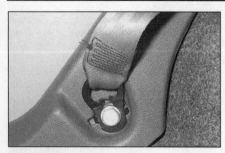

Seat belts and seats

Note: *The following checks are applicable to all seat belts, front and rear.*

☐ Examine the webbing of all the belts (including rear belts if fitted) for cuts, serious fraying or deterioration. Fasten and unfasten each belt to check the buckles. If applicable, check the retracting mechanism. Check the security of all seat belt mountings accessible from inside the vehicle.
☐ The front seats themselves must be securely attached and the backrests must lock in the upright position.

Doors

☐ Both front doors must be able to be opened and closed from outside and inside, and must latch securely when closed.

2 Checks carried out WITH THE VEHICLE ON THE GROUND

Vehicle identification

☐ Number plates must be in good condition, secure and legible, with letters and numbers correctly spaced – spacing at (A) should be twice that at (B).

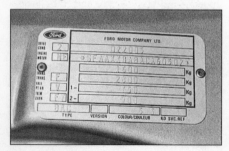

☐ The VIN plate and/or homologation plate must be legible.

Electrical equipment

☐ Switch on the ignition and check the operation of the horn.
☐ Check the windscreen washers and wipers, examining the wiper blades; renew damaged or perished blades. Also check the operation of the stop-lights.

☐ Check the operation of the sidelights and number plate lights. The lenses and reflectors must be secure, clean and undamaged.
☐ Check the operation and alignment of the headlights. The headlight reflectors must not be tarnished and the lenses must be undamaged.
☐ Switch on the ignition and check the operation of the direction indicators (including the instrument panel tell-tale) and the hazard warning lights. Operation of the sidelights and stop-lights must not affect the indicators - if it does, the cause is usually a bad earth at the rear light cluster.
☐ Check the operation of the rear foglight(s), including the warning light on the instrument panel or in the switch.

Footbrake

☐ Examine the master cylinder, brake pipes and servo unit for leaks, loose mountings, corrosion or other damage.

☐ The fluid reservoir must be secure and the fluid level must be between the upper (**A**) and lower (**B**) markings.

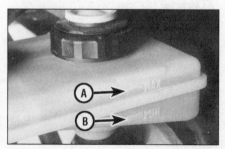

☐ Inspect both front brake flexible hoses for cracks or deterioration of the rubber. Turn the steering from lock to lock, and ensure that the hoses do not contact the wheel, tyre, or any part of the steering or suspension mechanism. With the brake pedal firmly depressed, check the hoses for bulges or leaks under pressure.

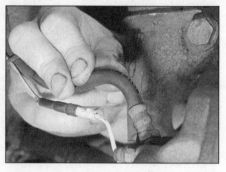

Steering and suspension

☐ Have your assistant turn the steering wheel from side to side slightly, up to the point where the steering gear just begins to transmit this movement to the roadwheels. Check for excessive free play between the steering wheel and the steering gear, indicating wear or insecurity of the steering column joints, the column-to-steering gear coupling, or the steering gear itself.
☐ Have your assistant turn the steering wheel more vigorously in each direction, so that the roadwheels just begin to turn. As this is done, examine all the steering joints, linkages, fittings and attachments. Renew any component that shows signs of wear or damage. On vehicles with power steering, check the security and condition of the steering pump, drivebelt and hoses.
☐ Check that the vehicle is standing level, and at approximately the correct ride height.

Shock absorbers

☐ Depress each corner of the vehicle in turn, then release it. The vehicle should rise and then settle in its normal position. If the vehicle continues to rise and fall, the shock absorber is defective. A shock absorber which has seized will also cause the vehicle to fail.

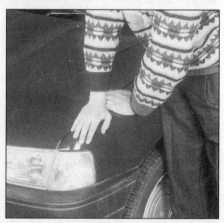

Exhaust system

☐ Start the engine. With your assistant holding a rag over the tailpipe, check the entire system for leaks. Repair or renew leaking sections.

3 Checks carried out **WITH THE VEHICLE RAISED AND THE WHEELS FREE TO TURN**

Jack up the front and rear of the vehicle, and securely support it on axle stands. Position the stands clear of the suspension assemblies. Ensure that the wheels are clear of the ground and that the steering can be turned from lock to lock.

Steering mechanism

☐ Have your assistant turn the steering from lock to lock. Check that the steering turns smoothly, and that no part of the steering mechanism, including a wheel or tyre, fouls any brake hose or pipe or any part of the body structure.
☐ Examine the steering rack rubber gaiters for damage or insecurity of the retaining clips. If power steering is fitted, check for signs of damage or leakage of the fluid hoses, pipes or connections. Also check for excessive stiffness or binding of the steering, a missing split pin or locking device, or severe corrosion of the body structure within 30 cm of any steering component attachment point.

Front and rear suspension and wheel bearings

☐ Starting at the front right-hand side, grasp the roadwheel at the 3 o'clock and 9 o'clock positions and shake it vigorously. Check for free play or insecurity at the wheel bearings, suspension balljoints, or suspension mountings, pivots and attachments.
☐ Now grasp the wheel at the 12 o'clock and 6 o'clock positions and repeat the previous inspection. Spin the wheel, and check for roughness or tightness of the front wheel bearing.

☐ If excess free play is suspected at a component pivot point, this can be confirmed by using a large screwdriver or similar tool and levering between the mounting and the component attachment. This will confirm whether the wear is in the pivot bush, its retaining bolt, or in the mounting itself (the bolt holes can often become elongated).

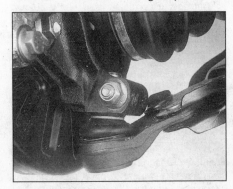

☐ Carry out all the above checks at the other front wheel, and then at both rear wheels.

Springs and shock absorbers

☐ Examine the suspension struts (when applicable) for serious fluid leakage, corrosion, or damage to the casing. Also check the security of the mounting points.
☐ If coil springs are fitted, check that the spring ends locate in their seats, and that the spring is not corroded, cracked or broken.
☐ If leaf springs are fitted, check that all leaves are intact, that the axle is securely attached to each spring, and that there is no deterioration of the spring eye mountings, bushes, and shackles.

☐ The same general checks apply to vehicles fitted with other suspension types, such as torsion bars, hydraulic displacer units, etc. Ensure that all mountings and attachments are secure, that there are no signs of excessive wear, corrosion or damage, and (on hydraulic types) that there are no fluid leaks or damaged pipes.
☐ Inspect the shock absorbers for signs of serious fluid leakage. Check for wear of the mounting bushes or attachments, or damage to the body of the unit.

Driveshafts (fwd vehicles only)

☐ Rotate each front wheel in turn and inspect the constant velocity joint gaiters for splits or damage. Also check that each driveshaft is straight and undamaged.

Braking system

☐ If possible without dismantling, check brake pad wear and disc condition. Ensure that the friction lining material has not worn excessively, (A) and that the discs are not fractured, pitted, scored or badly worn (B).

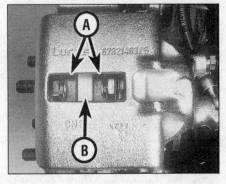

☐ Examine all the rigid brake pipes underneath the vehicle, and the flexible hose(s) at the rear. Look for corrosion, chafing or insecurity of the pipes, and for signs of bulging under pressure, chafing, splits or deterioration of the flexible hoses.
☐ Look for signs of fluid leaks at the brake calipers or on the brake backplates. Repair or renew leaking components.
☐ Slowly spin each wheel, while your assistant depresses and releases the footbrake. Ensure that each brake is operating and does not bind when the pedal is released.

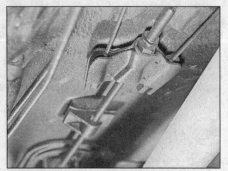

☐ Examine the handbrake mechanism, checking for frayed or broken cables, excessive corrosion, or wear or insecurity of the linkage. Check that the mechanism works on each relevant wheel, and releases fully, without binding.

☐ It is not possible to test brake efficiency without special equipment, but a road test can be carried out later to check that the vehicle pulls up in a straight line.

Fuel and exhaust systems

☐ Inspect the fuel tank (including the filler cap), fuel pipes, hoses and unions. All components must be secure and free from leaks.

☐ Examine the exhaust system over its entire length, checking for any damaged, broken or missing mountings, security of the retaining clamps and rust or corrosion.

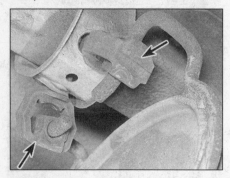

Wheels and tyres

☐ Examine the sidewalls and tread area of each tyre in turn. Check for cuts, tears, lumps, bulges, separation of the tread, and exposure of the ply or cord due to wear or damage. Check that the tyre bead is correctly seated on the wheel rim, that the valve is sound and

properly seated, and that the wheel is not distorted or damaged.

☐ Check that the tyres are of the correct size for the vehicle, that they are of the same size and type on each axle, and that the pressures are correct.

☐ Check the tyre tread depth. The legal minimum at the time of writing is 1.6 mm over at least three-quarters of the tread width. Abnormal tread wear may indicate incorrect front wheel alignment.

Body corrosion

☐ Check the condition of the entire vehicle structure for signs of corrosion in load-bearing areas. (These include chassis box sections, side sills, cross-members, pillars, and all suspension, steering, braking system and seat belt mountings and anchorages.) Any corrosion which has seriously reduced the thickness of a load-bearing area is likely to cause the vehicle to fail. In this case professional repairs are likely to be needed.

☐ Damage or corrosion which causes sharp or otherwise dangerous edges to be exposed will also cause the vehicle to fail.

4 Checks carried out on YOUR VEHICLE'S EXHAUST EMISSION SYSTEM

Petrol models

☐ Have the engine at normal operating temperature, and make sure that it is in good tune (ignition system in good order, air filter element clean, etc).

☐ Before any measurements are carried out, raise the engine speed to around 2500 rpm, and hold it at this speed for 20 seconds. Allow

the engine speed to return to idle, and watch for smoke emissions from the exhaust tailpipe. If the idle speed is obviously much too high, or if dense blue or clearly-visible black smoke comes from the tailpipe for more than 5 seconds, the vehicle will fail. As a rule of thumb, blue smoke signifies oil being burnt (engine wear) while black smoke signifies unburnt fuel (dirty air cleaner element, or other carburettor or fuel system fault).

☐ An exhaust gas analyser capable of measuring carbon monoxide (CO) and hydrocarbons (HC) is now needed. If such an instrument cannot be hired or borrowed, a local garage may agree to perform the check for a small fee.

CO emissions (mixture)

☐ At the time of writing, the maximum CO level at idle is 3.5% for vehicles first used after August 1986 and 4.5% for older vehicles. From January 1996 a much tighter limit (around 0.5%) applies to catalyst-equipped vehicles first used from August 1992. If the CO level cannot be reduced far enough to pass the test (and the fuel and ignition systems are otherwise in good condition) then the carburettor is badly worn, or there is some problem in the fuel injection system or catalytic converter (as applicable).

HC emissions

☐ With the CO emissions within limits, HC emissions must be no more than 1200 ppm (parts per million). If the vehicle fails this test at idle, it can be re-tested at around 2000 rpm; if the HC level is then 1200 ppm or less, this counts as a pass.

☐ Excessive HC emissions can be caused by oil being burnt, but they are more likely to be due to unburnt fuel.

Diesel models

☐ The only emission test applicable to Diesel engines is the measuring of exhaust smoke density. The test involves accelerating the engine several times to its maximum unloaded speed.

Note: *It is of the utmost importance that the engine timing belt is in good condition before the test is carried out.*

☐ Excessive smoke can be caused by a dirty air cleaner element. Otherwise, professional advice may be needed to find the cause.

Note: *For further diagnosis, refer to the relevant main manual.*

Engine

- ☐ Engine will not turn over when starter switch is operated
- ☐ Engine turns normally, but will not start
- ☐ Starter motor turns engine slowly
- ☐ Engine idles unevenly
- ☐ Poor compression
- ☐ Lack of power
- ☐ Excessive oil consumption

- ☐ Unusual noises
- ☐ Excessive smoke in exhaust
- ☐ Engine overheats
- ☐ Low engine oil pressure

Fuel and exhaust systems

- ☐ Erratic idling
- ☐ Lack of power
- ☐ Excessive fuel consumption
- ☐ Excessive knocking

Introduction

The vehicle owner who does his or her own maintenance according to the recommended schedules should not have to use this section of the manual very often. Modern component reliability is such that, provided those items subject to wear or deterioration are inspected or renewed at the specified intervals, sudden failure is comparatively rare. Faults do not usually just happen as a result of sudden failure, but develop over a period of time. Major mechanical failures in particular are usually preceded by characteristic symptoms over hundreds or even thousands of miles. Those components which do occasionally fail without warning are often small and easily carried in the vehicle.

With any fault finding, the first step is to decide where to begin investigations. Sometimes this is obvious, but on other occasions a little detective work will be necessary. The owner who makes half a dozen haphazard adjustments or replacements may be successful in curing a fault (or its symptoms), but he will be none the wiser if the fault recurs and he may well have spent more time and money than was necessary. A calm and logical approach will be found to be more satisfactory in the long run. Always take into account any warning signs or abnormalities that may have been noticed in the period preceding the fault - power loss, high or low gauge readings, unusual noises or smells, etc. - and remember that failure of components such as fuses may only be pointers to some underlying fault.

The pages that follow provide an easy reference guide to the more common problems that may occur during the operation of the vehicle. These problems and their possible causes are grouped under headings denoting various components or systems, such as Engine, Fuel system, etc.. The Chapter that deals with the problem is also shown in brackets. Whatever the fault, certain basic principles apply. These are as follows:

Verify the fault. This is simply a matter of being sure that you know what the symptoms are before starting work. This is particularly important if you are investigating a fault for someone else who may not have described it very accurately.

Do not overlook the obvious. For example, if the vehicle will not start, is there fuel in the tank? (Do not take anyone else's word on this particular point, and do not trust the fuel gauge either!) If an electrical fault is indicated, look for loose or broken wires before digging out the test gear.

Cure the disease, not the symptom. Substituting a flat battery with a fully charged one will get you off the hard shoulder, but if the underlying cause is not attended to, the new battery will go the same way.

Do not take anything for granted. Particularly, do not forget that a "new" component may itself be defective (especially if it's been rattling round in the boot for months), and do not leave components out of a fault diagnosis sequence just because they are new or recently fitted. When you do finally diagnose a difficult fault, you will probably realise that all the evidence was there from the start.

Engine

Engine will not turn over when starter switch is operated

- ☐ Flat battery (Chapter 1)
- ☐ Battery connections corroded or loose (Chapter 1)
- ☐ Starter solenoid connections loose (Chapter 5)
- ☐ Engine/transmission earth cable loose or broken (Chapter 5)
- ☐ Starter motor defective (Chapter 5)
- ☐ Major mechanical failure (seizure), (Chapter 2)

Engine turns normally, but will not start

- ☐ Incorrect starting procedure (owners handbook)
- ☐ Fuel tank empty (owners handbook)
- ☐ Wax in fuel (very cold conditions only)
- ☐ Fuel filter blocked (Chapter 1)
- ☐ Injection pump timing incorrect (Chapter 4)
- ☐ Fast idle cable broken or thermostatic sensor faulty (Chapter 4)
- ☐ Injection pump stop solenoid faulty or wire disconnected (Chapter 4)
- ☐ Other fuel system or preheater fault (Chapter 4)
- ☐ Timing belt broken (Chapter 2)
- ☐ Poor compression (see below), (Chapter 2)

Starter motor turns engine slowly

- ☐ Partially discharged battery (recharge or use jump leads), (Chapter 1)
- ☐ Battery terminals loose or corroded (Chapter 1)
- ☐ Battery earth to body defective (Chapter 1)
- ☐ Engine earth strap loose (Chapter 1)
- ☐ Starter motor (or solenoid) wiring loose (Chapter 5)
- ☐ Starter motor internal fault (Chapter 5)

Engine idles unevenly

- ☐ Fuel system fault (Chapter 4)
- ☐ Incorrect valve clearance (Chapter 2)
- ☐ Burnt out valves (Chapter 2)
- ☐ Blown head gasket (Chapter 2)

Poor compression

- ☐ Burnt out valves (Chapter 2)
- ☐ Valve clearances too small (Chapter 2)
- ☐ Blown head gasket (Chapter 2)
- ☐ Worn piston rings/cylinder bores (Chapter 2)
- ☐ Cylinder head or block cracked (Chapter 2)

Engine (continued)

Lack of power

- [ ] Poor compression (see above) (Chapter 2)
- [ ] Injection pump timing incorrect (Chapter 4)
- [ ] Worn or dirty injectors (Chapter 4)
- [ ] Air cleaner clogged (Chapter 4)

Excessive oil consumption

- [ ] Oil leaks from crankshaft or camshaft oil seals (Chapter 2)
- [ ] Worn piston rings/cylinder bores (smoky exhaust is an indication) (Chapter 2)
- [ ] External leakage (Chapter 2)

Unusual noises

Whistling or wheezing

- [ ] Leaking vacuum hose (main manual)
- [ ] Leaking manifold gasket (Chapter 4)
- [ ] Blowing head gasket (Chapter 2)

Tapping or rattling

- [ ] Incorrect valve clearances (Chapter 2)
- [ ] Worn valve gear (Chapter 2)
- [ ] Worn oil pump chain (Chapter 2)
- [ ] Broken piston ring (ticking noise) (Chapter 2)

Knocking or thumping

- [ ] Unintentional mechanical contact (e.g. fan blades) (Chapter 2)
- [ ] Worn drivebelt (Chapter 1)
- [ ] Worn timing belt (Chapter 2)
- [ ] Peripheral component fault (alternator, water pump etc.) (as applicable)
- [ ] Fuel injector(s) leaking or sticking (Chapter 4)
- [ ] Injection pump fault (Chapter 4)
- [ ] Worn big-end bearings (regular heavy knocking, perhaps less under load) (Chapter 2)
- [ ] Worn main bearings (rumbling and knocking, perhaps worsening under load) (Chapter 2)
- [ ] Piston slap (most noticeable when cold, not to be confused with diesel knock) (Chapter 2)

Excessive smoke in exhaust

- [ ] Oil being burnt (blue smoke) (Chapter 2)
- [ ] Fuel system fault (Chapter 4)

Engine overheats

Note: *Do not add cold water to an overheated engine or damage may result.*

- [ ] Coolant loss due to internal or external leakage (Chapter 3)
- [ ] Thermostat defective (Chapter 3)
- [ ] Low oil level (Chapter 1)
- [ ] Brakes binding (Chapter 1)
- [ ] Radiator clogged externally or internally (Chapter 3)
- [ ] Electric cooling fan not operating correctly (main manual)
- [ ] Engine waterways clogged (Chapter 2)

Low engine oil pressure

Note: *Low oil pressure in a high-mileage engine at tickover is not necessarily a cause for concern. Sudden pressure loss at speed is far more significant. In any event check the gauge or warning light sender before condemning the engine.*

- [ ] Oil level low or incorrect grade (Chapter 1)
- [ ] Defective gauge or sender unit (main manual)
- [ ] Wire to sender unit earthed (main manual)
- [ ] Engine overheating (Chapter 2 or 3)
- [ ] Oil filter clogged or bypass valve defective (Chapter 1)
- [ ] Oil pressure relief valve defective (Chapter 2)
- [ ] Oil pick-up strainer clogged (Chapter 2)
- [ ] Oil pump worn or mountings loose (Chapter 2)
- [ ] Worn main or big-end bearings (Chapter 2)

Fuel injection system

Note: *Faults in the fuel injection system can produce noises suggesting bearing failure. To locate such a fault slacken each injector union in turn with the engine running. The noise will disappear when the union on the faulty injector is slackened, however, to prove conclusively that the injector is faulty, fit it to another cylinder and carry out the test again. Air or other contaminants in the fuel can also cause knocking noises.*

Erratic idling

- [ ] Idle speed adjustment incorrect (Chapter 1)
- [ ] Injection pump defective (Chapter 4)
- [ ] Injector(s) defective (Chapter 4)

Lack of power

- [ ] Fuel filter blocked (Chapter 1)
- [ ] Fuel tank vent blocked (vacuum will be heard when releasing filler cap) (main manual)
- [ ] Air cleaner blocked (Chapter 4)
- [ ] Air or water in fuel (Chapter 1)
- [ ] Injection pump timing incorrect (Chapter 4)
- [ ] Injector(s) defective (Chapter 4)

Excessive fuel consumption

- [ ] Fuel leakage (Chapter 4)
- [ ] Air cleaner blocked (Chapter 4)
- [ ] Injector(s) defective (Chapter 4)
- [ ] Injection pump timing incorrect (Chapter 4)

Excessive knocking

- [ ] Injector(s) defective (sticking), (Chapter 4)
- [ ] Injection pump timing incorrect (Chapter 4)
- [ ] Excessive carbon deposit (Chapter 2)

A

ABS (Anti-lock brake system) A system, usually electronically controlled, that senses incipient wheel lockup during braking and relieves hydraulic pressure at wheels that are about to skid.

Air bag An inflatable bag hidden in the steering wheel (driver's side) or the dash or glovebox (passenger side). In a head-on collision, the bags inflate, preventing the driver and front passenger from being thrown forward into the steering wheel or windscreen.

Air cleaner A metal or plastic housing, containing a filter element, which removes dust and dirt from the air being drawn into the engine.

Air filter element The actual filter in an air cleaner system, usually manufactured from pleated paper and requiring renewal at regular intervals.

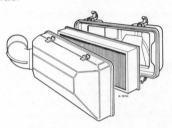

Air filter

Allen key A hexagonal wrench which fits into a recessed hexagonal hole.

Alligator clip A long-nosed spring-loaded metal clip with meshing teeth. Used to make temporary electrical connections.

Alternator A component in the electrical system which converts mechanical energy from a drivebelt into electrical energy to charge the battery and to operate the starting system, ignition system and electrical accessories.

Ampere (amp) A unit of measurement for the flow of electric current. One amp is the amount of current produced by one volt acting through a resistance of one ohm.

Anaerobic sealer A substance used to prevent bolts and screws from loosening. Anaerobic means that it does not require oxygen for activation. The Loctite brand is widely used.

Antifreeze A substance (usually ethylene glycol) mixed with water, and added to a vehicle's cooling system, to prevent freezing of the coolant in winter. Antifreeze also contains chemicals to inhibit corrosion and the formation of rust and other deposits that would tend to clog the radiator and coolant passages and reduce cooling efficiency.

Anti-seize compound A coating that reduces the risk of seizing on fasteners that are subjected to high temperatures, such as exhaust manifold bolts and nuts.

Asbestos A natural fibrous mineral with great heat resistance, commonly used in the composition of brake friction materials.

Asbestos is a health hazard and the dust created by brake systems should never be inhaled or ingested.

Axle A shaft on which a wheel revolves, or which revolves with a wheel. Also, a solid beam that connects the two wheels at one end of the vehicle. An axle which also transmits power to the wheels is known as a live axle.

Axleshaft A single rotating shaft, on either side of the differential, which delivers power from the final drive assembly to the drive wheels. Also called a driveshaft or a halfshaft.

B

Ball bearing An anti-friction bearing consisting of a hardened inner and outer race with hardened steel balls between two races.

Bearing The curved surface on a shaft or in a bore, or the part assembled into either, that permits relative motion between them with minimum wear and friction.

Bearing

Big-end bearing The bearing in the end of the connecting rod that's attached to the crankshaft.

Bleed nipple A valve on a brake wheel cylinder, caliper or other hydraulic component that is opened to purge the hydraulic system of air. Also called a bleed screw.

Brake bleeding Procedure for removing air from lines of a hydraulic brake system.

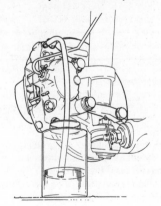

Brake bleeding

Brake disc The component of a disc brake that rotates with the wheels.

Brake drum The component of a drum brake that rotates with the wheels.

Brake linings The friction material which contacts the brake disc or drum to retard the vehicle's speed. The linings are bonded or riveted to the brake pads or shoes.

Brake pads The replaceable friction pads that pinch the brake disc when the brakes are applied. Brake pads consist of a friction material bonded or riveted to a rigid backing plate.

Brake shoe The crescent-shaped carrier to which the brake linings are mounted and which forces the lining against the rotating drum during braking.

Braking systems For more information on braking systems, consult the *Haynes Automotive Brake Manual*.

Breaker bar A long socket wrench handle providing greater leverage.

Bulkhead The insulated partition between the engine and the passenger compartment.

C

Caliper The non-rotating part of a disc-brake assembly that straddles the disc and carries the brake pads. The caliper also contains the hydraulic components that cause the pads to pinch the disc when the brakes are applied. A caliper is also a measuring tool that can be set to measure inside or outside dimensions of an object.

Camshaft A rotating shaft on which a series of cam lobes operate the valve mechanisms. The camshaft may be driven by gears, by sprockets and chain or by sprockets and a belt.

Canister A container in an evaporative emission control system; contains activated charcoal granules to trap vapours from the fuel system.

Canister

Carburettor A device which mixes fuel with air in the proper proportions to provide a desired power output from a spark ignition internal combustion engine.

Castellated Resembling the parapets along the top of a castle wall. For example, a castellated balljoint stud nut.

Castor In wheel alignment, the backward or forward tilt of the steering axis. Castor is positive when the steering axis is inclined rearward at the top.

Catalytic converter A silencer-like device in the exhaust system which converts certain pollutants in the exhaust gases into less harmful substances.

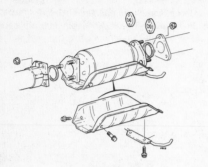

Catalytic converter

Circlip A ring-shaped clip used to prevent endwise movement of cylindrical parts and shafts. An internal circlip is installed in a groove in a housing; an external circlip fits into a groove on the outside of a cylindrical piece such as a shaft.

Clearance The amount of space between two parts. For example, between a piston and a cylinder, between a bearing and a journal, etc.

Coil spring A spiral of elastic steel found in various sizes throughout a vehicle, for example as a springing medium in the suspension and in the valve train.

Compression Reduction in volume, and increase in pressure and temperature, of a gas, caused by squeezing it into a smaller space.

Compression ratio The relationship between cylinder volume when the piston is at top dead centre and cylinder volume when the piston is at bottom dead centre.

Constant velocity (CV) joint A type of universal joint that cancels out vibrations caused by driving power being transmitted through an angle.

Core plug A disc or cup-shaped metal device inserted in a hole in a casting through which core was removed when the casting was formed. Also known as a freeze plug or expansion plug.

Crankcase The lower part of the engine block in which the crankshaft rotates.

Crankshaft The main rotating member, or shaft, running the length of the crankcase, with offset "throws" to which the connecting rods are attached.

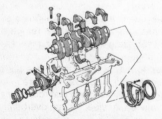

Crankshaft assembly

Crocodile clip See Alligator clip

D

Diagnostic code Code numbers obtained by accessing the diagnostic mode of an engine management computer. This code can be used to determine the area in the system where a malfunction may be located.

Disc brake A brake design incorporating a rotating disc onto which brake pads are squeezed. The resulting friction converts the energy of a moving vehicle into heat.

Double-overhead cam (DOHC) An engine that uses two overhead camshafts, usually one for the intake valves and one for the exhaust valves.

Drivebelt(s) The belt(s) used to drive accessories such as the alternator, water pump, power steering pump, air conditioning compressor, etc. off the crankshaft pulley.

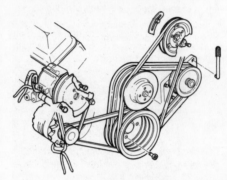

Accessory drivebelts

Driveshaft Any shaft used to transmit motion. Commonly used when referring to the axleshafts on a front wheel drive vehicle.

Drum brake A type of brake using a drum-shaped metal cylinder attached to the inner surface of the wheel. When the brake pedal is pressed, curved brake shoes with friction linings press against the inside of the drum to slow or stop the vehicle.

E

EGR valve A valve used to introduce exhaust gases into the intake air stream.

Electronic control unit (ECU) A computer which controls (for instance) ignition and fuel injection systems, or an anti-lock braking system. For more information refer to the *Haynes Automotive Electrical and Electronic Systems Manual*.

Electronic Fuel Injection (EFI) A computer controlled fuel system that distributes fuel through an injector located in each intake port of the engine.

Emergency brake A braking system, independent of the main hydraulic system, that can be used to slow or stop the vehicle if the primary brakes fail, or to hold the vehicle stationary even though the brake pedal isn't depressed. It usually consists of a hand lever that actuates either front or rear brakes mechanically through a series of cables and linkages. Also known as a handbrake or parking brake.

Endfloat The amount of lengthwise movement between two parts. As applied to a crankshaft, the distance that the crankshaft can move forward and back in the cylinder block.

Engine management system (EMS) A computer controlled system which manages the fuel injection and the ignition systems in an integrated fashion.

Exhaust manifold A part with several passages through which exhaust gases leave the engine combustion chambers and enter the exhaust pipe.

F

Fan clutch A viscous (fluid) drive coupling device which permits variable engine fan speeds in relation to engine speeds.

Feeler blade A thin strip or blade of hardened steel, ground to an exact thickness, used to check or measure clearances between parts.

Feeler blade

Firing order The order in which the engine cylinders fire, or deliver their power strokes, beginning with the number one cylinder.

Flywheel A heavy spinning wheel in which energy is absorbed and stored by means of momentum. On cars, the flywheel is attached to the crankshaft to smooth out firing impulses.

Free play The amount of travel before any action takes place. The "looseness" in a linkage, or an assembly of parts, between the initial application of force and actual movement. For example, the distance the brake pedal moves before the pistons in the master cylinder are actuated.

Fuse An electrical device which protects a circuit against accidental overload. The typical fuse contains a soft piece of metal which is calibrated to melt at a predetermined current flow (expressed as amps) and break the circuit.

Fusible link A circuit protection device consisting of a conductor surrounded by heat-resistant insulation. The conductor is smaller than the wire it protects, so it acts as the weakest link in the circuit. Unlike a blown fuse, a failed fusible link must frequently be cut from the wire for replacement.

G

Gap The distance the spark must travel in jumping from the centre electrode to the side electrode in a spark plug. Also refers to the spacing between the points in a contact breaker assembly in a conventional points-type ignition, or to the distance between the reluctor or rotor and the pickup coil in an electronic ignition.

Adjusting spark plug gap

Gasket Any thin, soft material - usually cork, cardboard, asbestos or soft metal - installed between two metal surfaces to ensure a good seal. For instance, the cylinder head gasket seals the joint between the block and the cylinder head.

Gasket

Gauge An instrument panel display used to monitor engine conditions. A gauge with a movable pointer on a dial or a fixed scale is an analogue gauge. A gauge with a numerical readout is called a digital gauge.

H

Halfshaft A rotating shaft that transmits power from the final drive unit to a drive wheel, usually when referring to a live rear axle.

Harmonic balancer A device designed to reduce torsion or twisting vibration in the crankshaft. May be incorporated in the crankshaft pulley. Also known as a vibration damper.

Hone An abrasive tool for correcting small irregularities or differences in diameter in an engine cylinder, brake cylinder, etc.

Hydraulic tappet A tappet that utilises hydraulic pressure from the engine's lubrication system to maintain zero clearance (constant contact with both camshaft and valve stem). Automatically adjusts to variation in valve stem length. Hydraulic tappets also reduce valve noise.

I

Ignition timing The moment at which the spark plug fires, usually expressed in the number of crankshaft degrees before the piston reaches the top of its stroke.

Inlet manifold A tube or housing with passages through which flows the air-fuel mixture (carburettor vehicles and vehicles with throttle body injection) or air only (port fuel-injected vehicles) to the port openings in the cylinder head.

J

Jump start Starting the engine of a vehicle with a discharged or weak battery by attaching jump leads from the weak battery to a charged or helper battery.

L

Load Sensing Proportioning Valve (LSPV) A brake hydraulic system control valve that works like a proportioning valve, but also takes into consideration the amount of weight carried by the rear axle.

Locknut A nut used to lock an adjustment nut, or other threaded component, in place. For example, a locknut is employed to keep the adjusting nut on the rocker arm in position.

Lockwasher A form of washer designed to prevent an attaching nut from working loose.

M

MacPherson strut A type of front suspension system devised by Earle MacPherson at Ford of England. In its original form, a simple lateral link with the anti-roll bar creates the lower control arm. A long strut - an integral coil spring and shock absorber - is mounted between the body and the steering knuckle. Many modern so-called MacPherson strut systems use a conventional lower A-arm and don't rely on the anti-roll bar for location.

Multimeter An electrical test instrument with the capability to measure voltage, current and resistance.

N

NOx Oxides of Nitrogen. A common toxic pollutant emitted by petrol and diesel engines at higher temperatures.

O

Ohm The unit of electrical resistance. One volt applied to a resistance of one ohm will produce a current of one amp.

Ohmmeter An instrument for measuring electrical resistance.

O-ring A type of sealing ring made of a special rubber-like material; in use, the O-ring is compressed into a groove to provide the sealing action.

Overhead cam (ohc) engine An engine with the camshaft(s) located on top of the cylinder head(s).

Overhead valve (ohv) engine An engine with the valves located in the cylinder head, but with the camshaft located in the engine block.

Oxygen sensor A device installed in the engine exhaust manifold, which senses the oxygen content in the exhaust and converts this information into an electric current. Also called a Lambda sensor.

P

Phillips screw A type of screw head having a cross instead of a slot for a corresponding type of screwdriver.

Plastigage A thin strip of plastic thread, available in different sizes, used for measuring clearances. For example, a strip of Plastigage is laid across a bearing journal. The parts are assembled and dismantled; the width of the crushed strip indicates the clearance between journal and bearing.

Plastigage

Propeller shaft The long hollow tube with universal joints at both ends that carries power from the transmission to the differential on front-engined rear wheel drive vehicles.

Proportioning valve A hydraulic control valve which limits the amount of pressure to the rear brakes during panic stops to prevent wheel lock-up.

R

Rack-and-pinion steering A steering system with a pinion gear on the end of the steering shaft that mates with a rack (think of a geared wheel opened up and laid flat). When the steering wheel is turned, the pinion turns, moving the rack to the left or right. This movement is transmitted through the track rods to the steering arms at the wheels.

Radiator A liquid-to-air heat transfer device designed to reduce the temperature of the coolant in an internal combustion engine cooling system.

Refrigerant Any substance used as a heat transfer agent in an air-conditioning system. R-12 has been the principle refrigerant for many years; recently, however, manufacturers have begun using R-134a, a non-CFC substance that is considered less harmful to the ozone in the upper atmosphere.

Rocker arm A lever arm that rocks on a shaft or pivots on a stud. In an overhead valve engine, the rocker arm converts the upward movement of the pushrod into a downward movement to open a valve.

Rotor In a distributor, the rotating device inside the cap that connects the centre electrode and the outer terminals as it turns, distributing the high voltage from the coil secondary winding to the proper spark plug. Also, that part of an alternator which rotates inside the stator. Also, the rotating assembly of a turbocharger, including the compressor wheel, shaft and turbine wheel.

Runout The amount of wobble (in-and-out movement) of a gear or wheel as it's rotated. The amount a shaft rotates "out-of-true." The out-of-round condition of a rotating part.

S

Sealant A liquid or paste used to prevent leakage at a joint. Sometimes used in conjunction with a gasket.

Sealed beam lamp An older headlight design which integrates the reflector, lens and filaments into a hermetically-sealed one-piece unit. When a filament burns out or the lens cracks, the entire unit is simply replaced.

Serpentine drivebelt A single, long, wide accessory drivebelt that's used on some newer vehicles to drive all the accessories, instead of a series of smaller, shorter belts. Serpentine drivebelts are usually tensioned by an automatic tensioner.

Serpentine drivebelt

Shim Thin spacer, commonly used to adjust the clearance or relative positions between two parts. For example, shims inserted into or under bucket tappets control valve clearances. Clearance is adjusted by changing the thickness of the shim.

Slide hammer A special puller that screws into or hooks onto a component such as a shaft or bearing; a heavy sliding handle on the shaft bottoms against the end of the shaft to knock the component free.

Sprocket A tooth or projection on the periphery of a wheel, shaped to engage with a chain or drivebelt. Commonly used to refer to the sprocket wheel itself.

Starter inhibitor switch On vehicles with an automatic transmission, a switch that prevents starting if the vehicle is not in Neutral or Park.

Strut See MacPherson strut.

T

Tappet A cylindrical component which transmits motion from the cam to the valve stem, either directly or via a pushrod and rocker arm. Also called a cam follower.

Thermostat A heat-controlled valve that regulates the flow of coolant between the cylinder block and the radiator, so maintaining optimum engine operating temperature. A thermostat is also used in some air cleaners in which the temperature is regulated.

Thrust bearing The bearing in the clutch assembly that is moved in to the release levers by clutch pedal action to disengage the clutch. Also referred to as a release bearing.

Timing belt A toothed belt which drives the camshaft. Serious engine damage may result if it breaks in service.

Timing chain A chain which drives the camshaft.

Toe-in The amount the front wheels are closer together at the front than at the rear. On rear wheel drive vehicles, a slight amount of toe-in is usually specified to keep the front wheels running parallel on the road by offsetting other forces that tend to spread the wheels apart.

Toe-out The amount the front wheels are closer together at the rear than at the front. On front wheel drive vehicles, a slight amount of toe-out is usually specified.

Tools For full information on choosing and using tools, refer to the *Haynes Automotive Tools Manual*.

Tracer A stripe of a second colour applied to a wire insulator to distinguish that wire from another one with the same colour insulator.

Tune-up A process of accurate and careful adjustments and parts replacement to obtain the best possible engine performance.

Turbocharger A centrifugal device, driven by exhaust gases, that pressurises the intake air. Normally used to increase the power output from a given engine displacement, but can also be used primarily to reduce exhaust emissions (as on VW's "Umwelt" Diesel engine).

U

Universal joint or U-joint A double-pivoted connection for transmitting power from a driving to a driven shaft through an angle. A U-joint consists of two Y-shaped yokes and a cross-shaped member called the spider.

V

Valve A device through which the flow of liquid, gas, vacuum, or loose material in bulk may be started, stopped, or regulated by a movable part that opens, shuts, or partially obstructs one or more ports or passageways. A valve is also the movable part of such a device.

Valve clearance The clearance between the valve tip (the end of the valve stem) and the rocker arm or tappet. The valve clearance is measured when the valve is closed.

Vernier caliper A precision measuring instrument that measures inside and outside dimensions. Not quite as accurate as a micrometer, but more convenient.

Viscosity The thickness of a liquid or its resistance to flow.

Volt A unit for expressing electrical "pressure" in a circuit. One volt that will produce a current of one ampere through a resistance of one ohm.

W

Welding Various processes used to join metal items by heating the areas to be joined to a molten state and fusing them together. For more information refer to the *Haynes Automotive Welding Manual*.

Wiring diagram A drawing portraying the components and wires in a vehicle's electrical system, using standardised symbols. For more information refer to the *Haynes Automotive Electrical and Electronic Systems Manual*.

Note: References throughout this index are in the from - "Chapter number" • "page number"

Haynes Manuals – The Complete List

Title	Book No.
ALFA ROMEO	
Alfa Romeo Alfasud/Sprint (74 - 88) up to F	0292
Alfa Romeo Alfetta (73 - 87) up to E	0531
ALFA ROMEO	
Audi 80 (72 - Feb 79) up to T	0207
Audi 80, 90 (79 - Oct 86) up to D & Coupe (81 - Nov 88) up to F	0605
Audi 80, 90 (Oct 86 - 90) D to H & Coupe (Nov 88 - 90) F to H	1491
Audi 100 (Oct 82 - 90) up to H & 200 (Feb 84 - Oct 89) A to G	0907
Audi 100 & A6 Petrol & Diesel (May 91 - May 97) H to P	3504
Audi A4 (95 - Feb 00) M to V	3575
AUSTIN	
Austin/MG/Rover Maestro 1.3 & 1.6 (83 - 95) up to M	0922
Austin/MG Metro (80 - May 90) up to G	0718
Austin/Rover Montego 1.3 & 1.6 (84 - 94) A to L	1066
Austin/MG/Rover Montego 2.0 (84 - 95) A to M	1067
Mini (59 - 69) up to H	0527
Mini (69 - Oct 96) up to P	0646
Austin/Rover 2.0 litre Diesel Engine (86 - 93) C to L	1857
BEDFORD	
Bedford CF (69 - 87) up to E	0163
Bedford/Vauxhall Rascal & Suzuki Supercarry (86 - Oct 94) C to M	3015
BMW	
BMW 316, 320 & 320i (4-cyl) (75 - Feb 83) up to Y	0276
BMW 320, 320i, 323i & 325i (6-cyl) (Oct 77 - Sept 87) up to E	0815
BMW 3-Series (Apr 91 - 96) H to N	3210
BMW 3- & 5-Series (sohc) (81 - 91) up to J	1948
BMW 520i & 525e (Oct 81 - June 88) up to E	1560
BMW 525, 528 & 528i (73 - Sept 81) up to X	0632
CITROEN	
Citroën 2CV, Ami & Dyane (67 - 90) up to H	0196
Citroën AX Petrol & Diesel (87 - 97) D to P	3014
Citroën BX (83 - 94) A to L	0908
Citroën C15 Van Petrol & Diesel (89 - Oct 98) F to S	3509
Citroën CX (75 - 88) up to F	0528
Citroën Saxo Petrol & Diesel (96 - 98) N to S	3506
Citroën Visa (79 - 88) up to F	0620
Citroën Xantia Petrol & Diesel (93 - 98) K to S	3082
Citroën XM Petrol & Diesel (89 - 98) G to R	3451
Citroën ZX Diesel (91 - 93) J to L	1922
Citroën ZX Petrol (91 - 94) H to M	1881
Citroën 1.7 & 1.9 litre Diesel Engine (84 - 96) A to N	1379
COLT	
Colt/Mitsubishi 1200, 1250 & 1400 (79 - May 84) up to A	0600
FIAT	
Fiat 500 (57 - 73) up to M	0090
Fiat Cinquecento (93 - 98) K to R	3501
Fiat Panda (81 - 95) up to M	0793
Fiat Punto Petrol & Diesel (94 - Oct 99) L to V	3251
Fiat Regata (84 - 88) A to F	1167

Title	Book No.
Fiat Tipo (88 - 91) E to J	1625
Fiat Uno (83 - 95) up to M	0923
Fiat X1/9 (74 - 89) up to G	0273
FORD	
Ford Capri II (& III) 1.6 & 2.0 (74 - 87) up to E	0283
Ford Capri II (& III) 2.8 & 3.0 (74 - 87) up to E	1309
Ford Cortina Mk IV (& V) 1.6 & 2.0 (76 - 83) up to A	0343
Ford Escort (75 - Aug 80) up to V	0280
Ford Escort (Sept 80 - Sept 90) up to H	0686
Ford Escort & Orion (Sept 90 - 97) H to P	1737
Ford Escort Mk II Mexico, RS 1600 & RS 2000 (75 - 80) up to W	0735
Ford Fiesta (76 - Aug 83) up to Y	0334
Ford Fiesta (Aug 83 - Feb 89) A to F	1030
Ford Fiesta (Feb 89 - Oct 95) F to N	1595
Ford Fiesta Petrol & Diesel (Oct 95 - 97) N to R	3397
Ford Granada (Sept 77 - Feb 85) up to B	0481
Ford Granada & Scorpio (Mar 85 - 94) B to M	1245
Ford Ka (96 - 99) P to T	3570
Ford Mondeo Petrol (93 - 99) K to T	1923
Ford Mondeo Diesel (93 - 96) L to N	3465
Ford Orion (83 - Sept 90) up to H	1009
Ford Sierra 4 cyl. (82 - 93) up to K	0903
Ford Sierra V6 (82 - 91) up to J	0904
Ford Transit Petrol (Mk 2) (78 - Jan 86) up to C	0719
Ford Transit Petrol (Mk 3) (Feb 86 - 89) C to G	1468
Ford Transit Diesel (Feb 86 - 99) C to T	3019
Ford 1.6 & 1.8 litre Diesel Engine (84 - 96) A to N	1172
Ford 2.1, 2.3 & 2.5 litre Diesel Engine (77 - 90) up to H	1606
FREIGHT ROVER	
Freight Rover Sherpa (74 - 87) up to E	0463
HILLMAN	
Hillman Avenger (70 - 82) up to Y	0037
HONDA	
Honda Accord (76 - Feb 84) up to A	0351
Honda Civic (Feb 84 - Oct 87) A to E	1226
Honda Civic (Nov 91 - 96) J to N	3199
HYUNDAI	
Hyundai Pony (85 - 94) C to M	3398
JAGUAR	
Jaguar E Type (61 - 72) up to L	0140
Jaguar MkI & II, 240 & 340 (55 - 69) up to H	0098
Jaguar XJ6, XJ & Sovereign; Daimler Sovereign (68 - Oct 86) up to D	0242
Jaguar XJ6 & Sovereign (Oct 86 - Sept 94) D to M	3261
Jaguar XJ12, XJS & Sovereign; Daimler Double Six (72 - 88) up to F	0478
JEEP	
Jeep Cherokee Petrol (93 - 96) K to N	1943
LADA	
Lada 1200, 1300, 1500 & 1600 (74 - 91) up to J	0413
Lada Samara (87 - 91) D to J	1610
LAND ROVER	
Land Rover 90, 110 & Defender Diesel (83 - 95) up to N	3017
Land Rover Discovery Diesel (89 - 95) G to N	3016
Land Rover Series IIA & III Diesel (58 - 85) up to C	0529

Title	Book No.
Land Rover Series II, IIA & III Petrol (58 - 85) up to C	0314
MAZDA	
Mazda 323 (Mar 81 - Oct 89) up to G	1608
Mazda 323 (Oct 89 - 98) G to R	3455
Mazda 626 (May 83 - Sept 87) up to E	0929
Mazda B-1600, B-1800 & B-2000 Pick-up (72 - 88) up to F	0267
MERCEDES BENZ	
Mercedes-Benz 190, 190E & 190D Petrol & Diesel (83 - 93) A to L	3450
Mercedes-Benz 200, 240, 300 Diesel (Oct 76 - 85) up to C	1114
Mercedes-Benz 250 & 280 (68 - 72) up to L	0346
Mercedes-Benz 250 & 280 (123 Series) (Oct 76 - 84) up to B	0677
Mercedes-Benz 124 Series (85 - Aug 93) C to K	3253
MG	
MGB (62 - 80) up to W	0111
MG Midget & AH Sprite (58 - 80) up to W	0265
MITSUBISHI	
Mitsubishi Shogun & L200 Pick-Ups (83 - 94) up to M	1944
MORRIS	
Morris Ital 1.3 (80 - 84) up to B	0705
Morris Minor 1000 (56 - 71) up to K	0024
NISSAN	
Nissan Bluebird (May 84 - Mar 86) A to C	1223
Nissan Bluebird (Mar 86 - 90) C to H	1473
Nissan Cherry (Sept 82 - 86) up to D	1031
Nissan Micra (83 - Jan 93) up to K	0931
Nissan Micra (93 - 99) K to T	3254
Nissan Primera (90 - Aug 99) H to T	1851
Nissan Stanza (82 - 86) up to D	0824
Nissan Sunny (May 82 - Oct 86) up to D	0895
Nissan Sunny (Oct 86 - Mar 91) D to H	1378
Nissan Sunny (Apr 91 - 95) H to N	3219
OPEL	
Opel Ascona & Manta (B Series) (Sept 75 - 88) up to F	0316
Opel Ascona (81 - 88) *(Not available in UK see Vauxhall Cavalier 0812)*	3215
Opel Astra (Oct 91 - Feb 98) *(Not available in UK see Vauxhall Astra 1832)*	3156
Opel Calibra (90 - 98) *(See Vauxhall/Opel Calibra Book No. 3502)*	
Opel Corsa (83 - Mar 93) *(Not available in UK see Vauxhall Nova 0909)*	3160
Opel Corsa (Mar 93 - 97) *(Not available in UK see Vauxhall Corsa 1985)*	3159
Opel Frontera Petrol & Diesel (91 - 98) *(See Vauxhall/Opel Frontera Book No. 3454)*	
Opel Kadett (Nov 79 - Oct 84)	0634
Opel Kadett (Oct 84 - Oct 91) *(Not available in UK see Vauxhall Astra & Belmont 1136)*	3196
Opel Omega & Senator (86 - 94) *(Not available in UK see Vauxhall Carlton & Senator 1469)*	3157
Opel Omega (94 - 99) *(See Vauxhall/Opel Omega Book No. 3510)*	
Opel Rekord (Feb 78 - Oct 86) up to D	0543

Title	Book No	Title	Book No	Title	Book No.
Opel Vectra (Oct 88 - Oct 95)		**SEAT**		Volkswagen Golf & Jetta Mk 1 1.1 & 1.3 (74 - 84) up	
(Not available in UK see Vauxhall Cavalier 1570) **3158**		Seat Ibiza & Cordoba Petrol & Diesel		to A	0716
Opel Vectra Petrol & Diesel (95 - 98)		(Oct 93 - Oct 99) L to V	3571	Volkswagen Golf, Jetta & Scirocco Mk 1 1.5,1.6 & 1.8	
(Not available in UK see Vauxhall Vectra 3396) **3523**		Seat Ibiza & Malaga (85 - 92) B to K	1609	(74 - 84) up to A	0726
PEUGEOT		**SKODA**		Volkswagen Golf & Jetta Mk 1 Diesel (78 - 84) up to A	0451
Peugeot 106 Petrol & Diesel (91 - 98) J to S	1882	Skoda Estelle (77 - 89) up to G	0604	Volkswagen Golf & Jetta Mk 2 (Mar 84 - Feb 92) A to J	1081
Peugeot 205 (83 - 95) A to N	0932	Skoda Favorit (89 - 96) F to N	1801	Volkswagen Golf & Vento Petrol & Diesel	
Peugeot 305 (78 - 89) up to G	0538	Skoda Felicia Petrol & Diesel (95 - 99) M to T	3505	(Feb 92 - 96) J to N	3097
Peugeot 306 Petrol & Diesel (93 - 99) K to T	3073	**SUBARU**		Volkswagen LT vans & light trucks (76 - 87) up to E	0637
Peugeot 309 (86 - 93) C to K	1266	Subaru 1600 & 1800 (Nov 79 - 90) up to H	0995	Volkswagen Passat & Santana	
Peugeot 405 Petrol (88 - 96) E to N	1559	**SUZUKI**		(Sept 81 - May 88) up to E	0814
Peugeot 405 Diesel (88 - 96) E to N	3198	Suzuki SJ Series, Samurai & Vitara (4-cyl)		Volkswagen Passat Petrol & Diesel	
Peugeot 406 Petrol & Diesel (96 - 97) N to R	3394	(82 - 97) up to P	1942	(May 88 - 96) E to P	3498
Peugeot 505 (79 - 89) up to G	0762	Suzuki Supercarry (86 - Oct 94) C to M	3015	Volkswagen Polo & Derby (76 - Jan 82) up to X	0335
Peugeot 1.7/1.8 & 1.9 litre Diesel Engine		**TALBOT**		Volkswagen Polo (82 - Oct 90) up to H	0813
(82 - 96) up to N	0950	Talbot Alpine, Solara, Minx & Rapier (75 - 86) up to D	0337	Volkswagen Polo (Nov 90 - Aug 94) H to L	3245
Peugeot 2.0, 2.1, 2.3 & 2.5 litre Diesel Engines		Talbot Horizon (78 - 86) up to D	0473	Volkswagen Polo Hatchback Petrol & Diesel	
(74 - 90) up to H	1607	Talbot Samba (82 - 86) up to D	0823	(94 - 99) M to S	3500
PORSCHE		**TOYOTA**		Volkswagen Scirocco (82 - 90) up to H	1224
Porsche 911 (65 - 85) up to C	0264	Toyota Carina E (May 92 - 97) J to P	3256	Volkswagen Transporter 1600 (68 - 79) up to V	0082
Porsche 924 & 924 Turbo (76 - 85) up to C	0397	Toyota Corolla (Sept 83 - Sept 87) A to E	1024	Volkswagen Transporter 1700, 1800 & 2000	
PROTON		Toyota Corolla (80 - 85) up to C	0683	(72 - 79) up to V	0226
Proton (89 - 97) F to P	3255	Toyota Corolla (Sept 87 - Aug 92) E to K	1683	Volkswagen Transporter (air-cooled) (79 - 82) up to Y	0638
RANGE ROVER		Toyota Corolla (Aug 92 - 97) K to P	3259	Volkswagen Transporter (water-cooled)	
Range Rover V8 (70 - Oct 92) up to K	0606	Toyota Hi-Ace & Hi-Lux (69 - Oct 83) up to A	0304	(82 - 90) up to H	3452
RELIANT		**TRIUMPH**		**VOLVO**	
Reliant Robin & Kitten (73 - 83) up to A	0436	Triumph Acclaim (81 - 84) up to B	0792	Volvo 142, 144 & 145 (66 - 74) up to N	0129
RENAULT		Triumph GT6 & Vitesse (62 - 74) up to N	0112	Volvo 240 Series (74 - 93) up to K	0270
Renault 5 (Feb 85 - 96) B to N	1219	Triumph Spitfire (62 - 81) up to X	0113	Volvo 262, 264 & 260/265 (75 - 85) up to C	0400
Renault 9 & 11 (82 - 89) up to F	0822	Triumph Stag (70 - 78) up to T	0441	Volvo 340, 343, 345 & 360 (76 - 91) up to J	0715
Renault 18 (79 - 86) up to D	0598	Triumph TR7 (75 - 82) up to Y	0322	Volvo 440, 460 & 480 (87 - 97) D to P	1691
Renault 19 Petrol (89 - 94) F to M	1646	**VAUXHALL**		Volvo 740 & 760 (82 - 91) up to J	1258
Renault 19 Diesel (89 - 95) F to N	1946	Vauxhall Astra (80 - Oct 84) up to B	0635	Volvo 850 (92 - 96) J to P	3260
Renault 21 (86 - 94) C to M	1397	Vauxhall Astra & Belmont		Volvo 940 (90 - 96) H to N	3249
Renault 25 (84 - 92) B to K	1228	(Oct 84 - Oct 91) B to J	1136	Volvo S40 & V40 (96 - 99) N to V	3569
Renault Clio Petrol (91 - May 98) H to R	1853	Vauxhall Astra (Oct 91 - Feb 98) J to R	1832	Volvo S70, V70 & C70 (96 - 99) P to V	3573
Renault Clio Diesel (91 - June 96) H to N	3031	Vauxhall/Opel Calibra (90 - 98) G to S	3502	**YUGO/ZASTAVA**	
Renault Espace Petrol & Diesel (85 - 96) C to N	3197	Vauxhall Carlton (Oct 78 - Oct 86) up to D	0480	Yugo/Zastava (81 - 90) up to H	1453
Renault Fuego (80 - 86) up to C	0764	Vauxhall Carlton & Senator (Nov 86 - 94) D to L	1469	**AUTOMOTIVE TECHBOOKS**	
Renault Laguna Petrol & Diesel		Vauxhall Cavalier 1600, 1900 & 2000		Automotive Brake Manual	3050
(94 - 96) L to P	3252	(75 - July 81) up to W	0315	Automotive Carburettor Manual	3288
Renault Mégane & Scénic Petrol & Diesel		Vauxhall Cavalier (81 - Oct 88) up to F	0812	Automotive Diagnostic Fault Codes Manual	3472
(96 - 98) N to R	3395	Vauxhall Cavalier (Oct 88 - 95) F to N	1570	Automotive Diesel Engine Service Guide	3286
ROVER		Vauxhall Chevette (75 - 84) up to B	0285	Automotive Disc Brake Manual	3542
Rover 213 & 216 (84 - 89) A to G	1116	Vauxhall Corsa (Mar 93 - 97) K to R	1985	Automotive Electrical and Electronic Systems Manual	3049
Rover 214 & 414 (89 - 96) G to N	1689	Vauxhall/Opel Frontera Petrol & Diesel		Automotive Engine Management and Fuel Injection	
Rover 216 & 416 (89 - 96) G to N	1830	(91 - Sept 98) J to S	3454	Systems Manual	3344
Rover 211, 214, 216, 218 & 220 Petrol & Diesel		Vauxhall Nova (83 - 93) up to K	0909	Automotive Gearbox Overhaul Manual	3473
(Dec 95 - 98) N to R	3399	Vauxhall/Opel Omega (94 - 99) L to T	3510	Automotive Service Summaries Manual	3475
Rover 414, 416 & 420 Petrol & Diesel		Vauxhall Vectra Petrol & Diesel (95 - 98) N to R	3396	Automotive Timing Belts Manual – Austin/Rover	3549
(May 95 - 98) M to R	3453	Vauxhall/Opel 1.5, 1.6 & 1.7 litre		Automotive Timing Belts Manual - Ford	3474
Rover 618, 620 & 623 (93 - 97) K to P	3257	Diesel Engine (82 - 96) up to N	1222	Automotive Timing Belts Manual – Peugeot/Citroën	3568
Rover 820, 825 & 827 (86 - 95) D to N	1380	**VOLKSWAGEN**		Automotive Timing Belts Manual – Vauxhall/Opel	3577
Rover 3500 (76 - 87) up to E	0365	Volkswagen Beetle 1200 (54 - 77) up to S	0036	Automotive Welding Manual	3053
Rover Metro, 111 & 114 (May 90 - 96) G to N	1711	Volkswagen Beetle 1300 & 1500 (65 - 75) up to P	0039	In-Car Entertainment Manual (3rd Edition)	3363
SAAB		Volkswagen Beetle 1302 & 1302S (70 - 72)		**OTHER TITLES**	
Saab 90, 99 & 900 (79 - Oct 93) up to L	0765	up to L	0110	Haynes Diesel Engine Systems & Data Book (91 -00)	3548
Saab 900 (Oct 93 - 98) L to R	3512	Volkswagen Beetle 1303, 1303S & GT		Haynes Petrol Models Data Book (94 - 00)	3718
Saab 9000 (4-cyl) (85 - 95) C to N	1686	(72 - 75) up to P	0159		

CL09.04/00

Preserving Our Motoring Heritage

> The Model J Duesenberg Derham Tourster. Only eight of these magnificent cars were ever built – this is the only example to be found outside the United States of America

Almost every car you've ever loved, loathed or desired is gathered under one roof at the Haynes Motor Museum. Over 300 immaculately presented cars and motorbikes represent every aspect of our motoring heritage, from elegant reminders of bygone days, such as the superb Model J Duesenberg to curiosities like the bug-eyed BMW Isetta. There are also many old friends and flames. Perhaps you remember the 1959 Ford Popular that you did your courting in? The magnificent 'Red Collection' is a spectacle of classic sports cars including AC, Alfa Romeo, Austin Healey, Ferrari, Lamborghini, Maserati, MG, Riley, Porsche and Triumph.

A Perfect Day Out

Each and every vehicle at the Haynes Motor Museum has played its part in the history and culture of Motoring. Today, they make a wonderful spectacle and a great day out for all the family. Bring the kids, bring Mum and Dad, but above all bring your camera to capture those golden memories for ever. You will also find an impressive array of motoring memorabilia, a comfortable 70 seat video cinema and one of the most extensive transport book shops in Britain. The Pit Stop Cafe serves everything from a cup of tea to wholesome, home-made meals or, if you prefer, you can enjoy the large picnic area nestled in the beautiful rural surroundings of Somerset.

> John Haynes O.B.E., Founder and Chairman of the museum at the wheel of a Haynes Light 12.

> Graham Hill's Lola Cosworth Formula 1 car next to a 1934 Riley Sports.

The Museum is situated on the A359 Yeovil to Frome road at Sparkford, just off the A303 in Somerset. It is about 40 miles south of Bristol, and 25 minutes drive from the M5 intersection at Taunton.

Open 9.30am - 5.30pm (10.00am - 4.00pm Winter) 7 days a week, *except Christmas Day, Boxing Day and New Years Day*

Special rates available for schools, coach parties and outings   Charitable Trust No. 292048